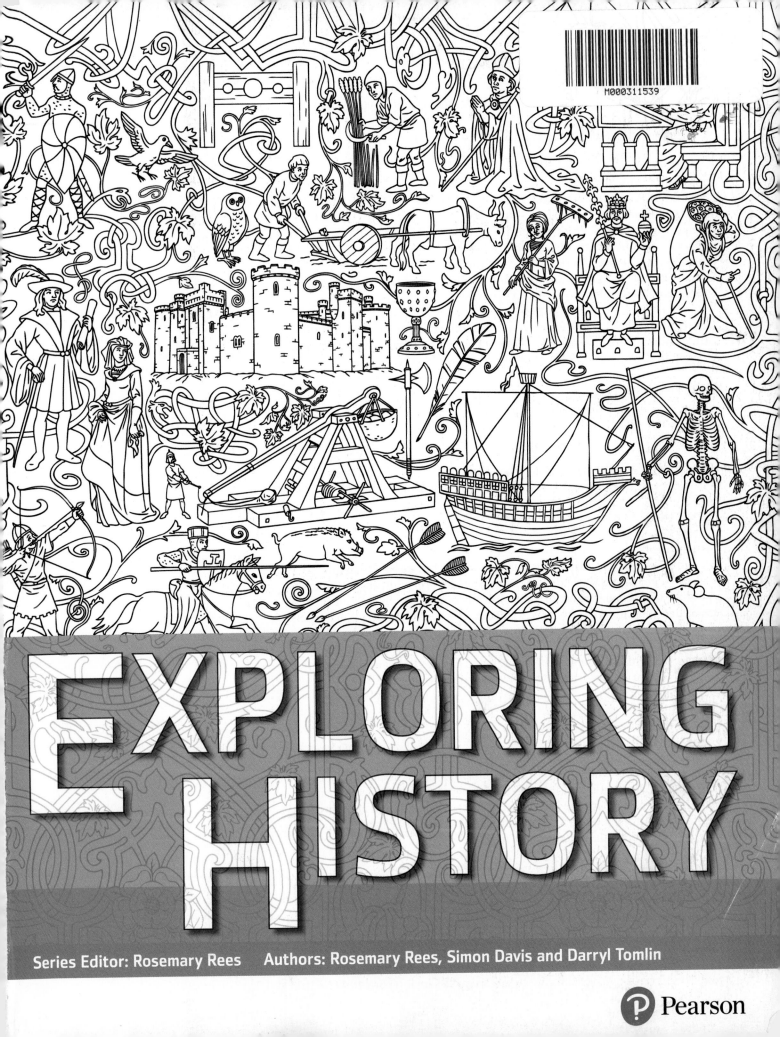

# EXPLORING HISTORY

Series Editor: Rosemary Rees   Authors: Rosemary Rees, Simon Davis and Darryl Tomlin

Pearson

Published by Pearson Education Limited, 80 Strand, London WC2R 0RL.

www.pearsonschoolsandfecolleges.co.uk

Text © Pearson Education Limited 2017
Series editor: Rosemary Rees
Designed by Poppy Marks, Pearson Education Limited
Typeset by Kamae Design, Oxford
Original illustrations © Pearson Education Limited 2017
Illustrated by KJA Artists Illustration Agency
Cover design by Poppy Marks, Pearson Education Limited
Picture research by Jane Smith jane@janesmithmedia.co.uk
Cover photo/illustration © 381Mike@kja-artists

The rights of Simon Davis, Rosemary Rees and Darryl Tomlin to be identified as
authors of this work have been asserted by them in accordance with the Copyright,
Designs and Patents Act 1988.

First published 2017

20 19 18
10 9 8 7 6 5 4 3

**British Library Cataloguing in Publication Data**
A catalogue record for this book is available from the British Library

ISBN 9781292218694

Printed in Italy by Lego S.p.A.

**Websites**
Pearson Education Limited is not responsible for the content of any external
internet sites. It is essential for tutors to preview each website before using it in
class so as to ensure that the URL is still accurate, relevant and appropriate. We
suggest that tutors bookmark useful websites and consider enabling students to
access them through the school/college intranet.

**Note from the publisher**
Pearson has robust editorial processes, including answer and fact checks, to
ensure the accuracy of the content in this publication, and every effort is made
to ensure this publication is free of errors. We are, however, only human, and
occasionally errors do occur. Pearson is not liable for any misunderstandings
that arise as a result of errors in this publication, but it is our priority to
ensure that the content is accurate. If you spot an error, please do contact us at
resourcescorrections@pearson.com so we can make sure it is corrected.

# Contents

# How to use this book

This book is the first in a series of three designed to help you study history at Key Stage 3.

Book 1, *Monarchs, Monks & Migrants*, looks at the medieval period of history, also known as the Middle Ages, and focuses on the 11th to the 15th century (see the Medieval timeline on pages 12–13).

The content has been carefully chosen to cover important background knowledge relevant to the Edexcel GCSE (9–1) History units. The book has depth, breadth and thematic topics to prepare you for the types of history you'll study at GCSE.

## Features

As well as exciting history, the book is full of useful features to help you improve.

### Enquiry questions

Every few weeks, you'll start looking at a new enquiry question. This will help you focus your learning within each chapter on a few key questions.

At the end of each enquiry, you'll find an activity that will help you to return to the enquiry question and reflect on what you have discovered.

### Learning objectives

At the start of each section, you'll be set some learning objectives. These tell you what you should know and understand by the end of the section. You might cover the objectives in one or two lessons.

### What do you think?

These questions give you the opportunity to show what you already know and think about what more you would like to discover about the topic.

**What do you think?**

Why do you think the king would want to control the Church?

### Key terms

Where you see a word followed by an asterisk, like this: Shield wall*, you'll find a Key term box nearby that explains what the word means.

All the key terms are listed alphabetically in the Glossary on pages 200–202.

**Key term**

Shield wall*: Barrier created by soldiers standing shoulder to shoulder, holding their shields in front of them so that they formed a wall.

### Your turn!

Every few pages you'll find a box containing activities designed to help check and embed knowledge and get you to think carefully about what you have studied. The activities may start with some simple questions, but they get more challenging as you work through them!

### Checkpoints

These help you to check and reflect on your learning at the end of a section, reinforcing the knowledge and understanding you have gained and ensuring you are familiar with the basic ideas and skills.

## Sources and interpretations

So you can really understand and explore this period of history, the book contains a lot of pictures and texts from the Middle Ages, showing what people at the time said, thought or created. These are known as **sources** – you'll need to interrogate these to discover the past.

**Source B:** Part of the Bayeux Tapestry, which was made in about 1070. It shows Harold Godwinson making a promise to Duke William.

Also included are extracts from the work of historians, and other reflections of the past like poems, plays and film, which show how modern people have interpreted historical events. These are known as **interpretations**.

You'll need to examine both sources and interpretations during your work on the history of the medieval period.

**Interpretation 3:** This interpretation was written by Richard Humble in his book *The Fall of Saxon England*, published in 1975.

Harold was defeated for three main reasons: William's grip on the battle and his skill at changing his tactics; the lack of discipline of the Saxon fyrd; and the relentless Norman arrow-fire.

## Did you know?

These features contain interesting additional information that adds depth to your knowledge. Some are useful, some are just fun!

**Did you know?**

The Domesday Book was first called the Book of Winchester because that is the town where it was kept. After about 100 years it was nicknamed the Domesday Book because people thought that by counting everything, it marked the end of the world, or 'dooms day', when God would judge the world and everything in it.

## What have you learned?

In the middle and at the end of each chapter you'll find pages designed to help you reflect on the chapter as a whole and think about what you have studied in a more analytical way.

There is also a **quick quiz** at the end of each chapter, ideal for checking your knowledge of the whole chapter. The answers are supplied at the end of the book.

## Writing Historically

Alongside the 'What have you learned?' sections are pages to help you improve your writing skills. These include simple techniques you can use to help you write better, clearer and more focused answers to historical questions. Many of these pages embed skills you'll need for GCSE.

## Pearson Progression Scale

The Pearson Progression Scale has been used to determine the difficulty of content as students progress through the course and to provide coherent differentiation. Where questions are aimed at a particular Step on the Pearson Progression Scale, we have added a small icon to indicate the Step. This gives an idea of how hard the question is – the higher the Step, the harder the question:

5ᵗʰ **2** Sources A and B are both written by monks. Give one reason why monks are a useful source of information from this time period.

6ᵗʰ **3** Read Sources A and B. What evidence is there that the authors of these sources may have thought the world was ending? Explain in a paragraph.

We have used another icon to indicate where skills relevant to GCSE are being developed. This example indicates that the content is moving students towards being able to answer GCSE-style inference questions:

Inference questions

# Historical anachronisms

An anachronism is something, or someone, that is out of their correct historical time. So, for example, a picture of a Roman soldier with a rifle would be an anachronism, and so would a medieval nun using a word processor to write up her chronicle. These would both be easy to spot. However, it's more difficult when the objects are closer in time to the period in which they appear.

Look at this modern drawing of a medieval market. How many anachronisms can you find? (Hint: there are 14. For answers see page 203.)

# What is chronology?

In this section you will:

- learn the key terms that historians use to describe and order time
- understand the key ages and periods into which history is divided.

**What do you think?**

Why do you think it is important to put events in the correct order?

Look at the long-range timeline below.

## Primary school history

## A brief history of human communication

|  |  | |
|---|---|---|
| **4500 BC–1900 BC**<br>Ancient Sumer<br><br>**3300 BC–1700 BC**<br>The Indus Valley civilisation | **Bronze Age**<br>(3000 BC–<br>1500 BC) | |
| **2686 BC–525 BC**<br>Ancient Egypt<br><br>**1600 BC–1100 BC**<br>Shang Dynasty of<br>Ancient China<br><br>**750 BC–100 BC**<br>Ancient Greece | **Iron Age**<br>(1500 BC–<br>27 BC) | |
| | **Roman<br>Empire**<br>(27 BC–<br>AD 476) | |
| | **Medieval<br>period**<br>(AD 476–<br>AD 1500) | |
| | **Early<br>Modern<br>period**<br>(AD 1500–<br>AD 1750) | |
| | **Modern<br>period**<br>(AD 1750–<br>Present) | |

**3000 BC**
Picture-based writing, known as cuneiform, first used.

**1440s**
Printing press built by Gutenberg to print books.

**1844**
Electric telegraph, which sends messages in Morse code, invented.

**1876**
Alexander Graham Bell invents the telephone.

**1983**
First national mobile phone network launched in the UK.

**1989**
Development of the World Wide Web begins.

## Ordering time

A huge number of events happened in the past. To write about them, historians* need to organise them. One of the ways they do this is to place events in chronological* order. The table below shows some of the terms historians use as part of this process.

| Term | Definition |
| --- | --- |
| BC | Before Christ. Used to indicate the year counting backwards from the birth of Jesus Christ. For example, 500 BC is 500 years before Christ was born. It is also known as Before the Common Era (BCE). |
| AD | Anno Domini (Latin, meaning 'in the year of the Lord'). Used to indicate the year counting forwards from the birth of Christ. For example, AD 500 is 500 years after Christ was born. It is also known as the Common Era (CE). |
| Period | A label used by historians to identify the time between two dates in history. For example, the Tudor, Victorian or medieval periods. |
| Era/Age | Similar to a time period, but usually with a larger date range. Examples include the Stone, Bronze and Iron Ages. |

### Key terms

**Historian*:** A person who studies the events of the past, usually by working with written sources, objects and paintings left behind.

**Chronological*:** Organised in the order in which they occurred.

## Importance of chronology

Look at the history of communication in the timeline. Imagine that a historian thought the internet was invented before the electric telegraph. They would struggle to explain why Samuel Morse invented a way of sending a few beeps over a long-distance wire when he could just have sent an e-mail or had a video chat.

Ignoring chronology would also cause historians to write incorrect explanations. If they thought mobile phones existed in the medieval period, they would think messages travelled between individuals much faster than they did. They might think a monarch was lazy if a distant city was attacked and they did not react immediately. In reality, they were probably unaware of the attack for a few days.

The last reason chronology is important is that the past happened in time order. If a historian mixed up that order, it would turn history into fiction.

### Your turn!

1 Write down one history topic you studied at primary school. The timeline might help you here.

2 Underneath the topic write down answers to the following questions.
   a) Did it happen in the BC or AD part of the timeline?
   b) Did it take place over one year, a decade (10 years), a century (100 years) or a millennium (1000 years)?
   c) Which time period or age did it take place in?

3 Write a short explanation of why it is important to know when an event took place. Use your chosen history topic as an example.

# What is History?

History is a lot more than 'learning about things that happened in the past'. In this section you will learn:

- what the academic subject of History is
- how History books like this one are created
- what interpretations are and how they are created.

Why interpretations differ

## The past

Events such as the Battle of Hastings happened in the past. These never change, as we can't travel back in time to cause any changes in them – at least not yet!

## Evidence

Time always moves forward and each time period generates evidence.

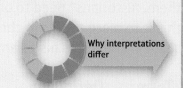

Written records

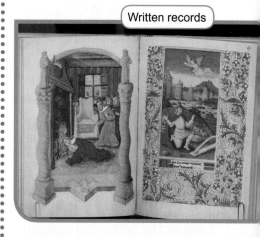

Paintings – not just on canvas but also on the walls of buildings like churches

Coins

1 Draw a flow chart to show how history is created. Include the following headings: 'Events in the past', 'Evidence', 'Interpretation'. Add notes to explain each stage.

2 You have been asked to promote the subject of History to Year 6 students who have never studied it before. Using the information on this page, design a poster for your school's open evening, to answer the question 'What is History?'

Buildings

Photos and film – these didn't appear until the 19th century so we don't have photographs from medieval times!

Human remains

## Interpreting the past

Although we can't travel in time, historians can use the evidence that the past has generated to try and understand what the past was like. This enables historians to create their interpretation of the past, for example by writing a textbook like this one. One of the fascinating things about History is that there are so many different interpretations of the past. Here are some of the reasons why.

The evidence clearly suggests people in the Dark Ages were superstitious and uncivilised.

Historians can come to different conclusions after looking at evidence

I disagree. The evidence I've looked at suggests that they were far more civilised that we originally thought.

We've been too focused on the lives of the rich and powerful for too long. My new book is about the lives of ordinary people instead.

New evidence comes to light which changes our understanding

Times change and the way we interpret the past changes too

This brings us to you. As you read this book, remember that you are interpreting the past too. Make sure to ask plenty of questions and try to come up with your own ideas. Who knows – maybe one day you will be responsible for the next big breakthrough in history!

# Medieval Timeline

**Medieval Monarchs**

Edward the Confessor: 1042–1066

Harold Godwinson: 1066 (Jan to Oct)

William I: 1066–1087

William II: 1087–1100

Henry I: 1100–1135

Stephen: 1135–1154

Henry II: 1154–1189

Richard I: 1189–1199

John I: 1199–1216

Henry III: 1216–1272

**AD 1000**      **AD 1100**      **AD 1200**

**Medieval Events**

1135–1153
The Anarchy, when Matilda and Stephen contested the crown

1187
Fall of Jerusalem to Saladin

1215
Magna Carta is signed

1095–1099
The First Crusade

1170
Murder of Thomas Becket

1066
The Battle of Hastings

Feudal system established

1086
Domesday Book completed

Early 13th century
The wheelbarrow is invented

1069–1070
The harrying of the North

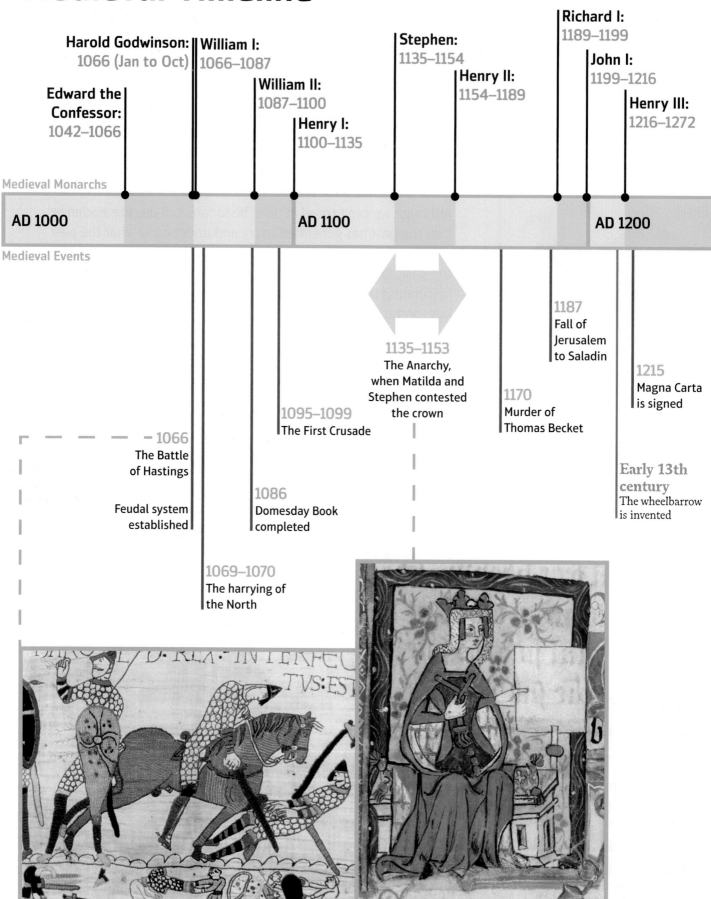

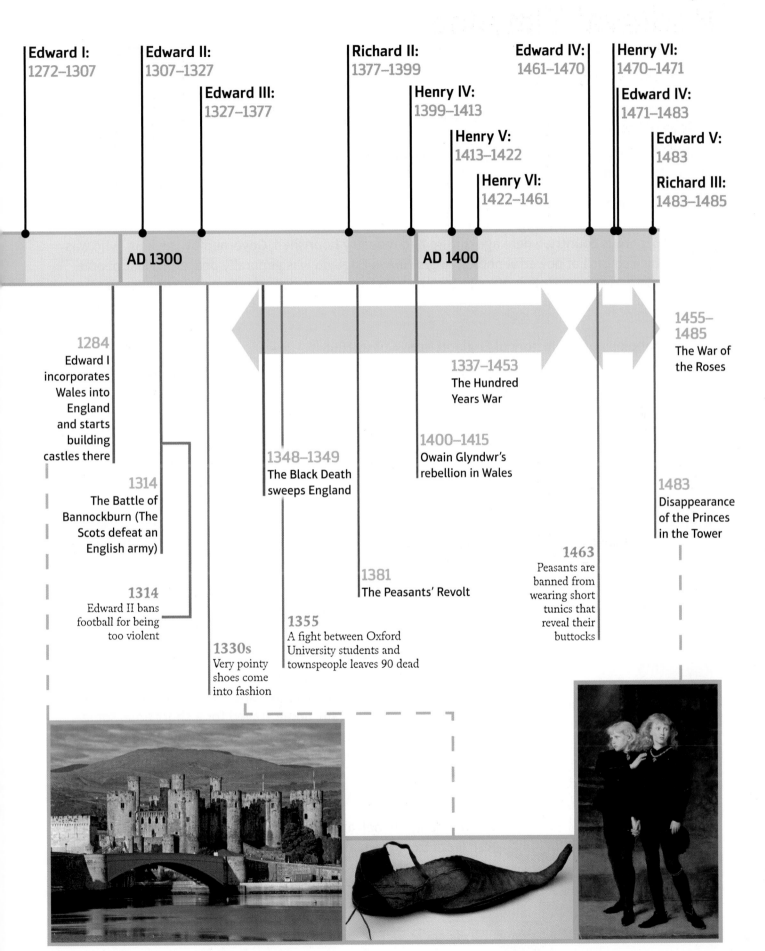

**Edward I:**
1272–1307

**Edward II:**
1307–1327

**Edward III:**
1327–1377

**Richard II:**
1377–1399

**Henry IV:**
1399–1413

**Henry V:**
1413–1422

**Henry VI:**
1422–1461

**Edward IV:**
1461–1470

**Henry VI:**
1470–1471

**Edward IV:**
1471–1483

**Edward V:**
1483

**Richard III:**
1483–1485

AD 1300

AD 1400

**1284**
Edward I incorporates Wales into England and starts building castles there

**1314**
The Battle of Bannockburn (The Scots defeat an English army)

**1314**
Edward II bans football for being too violent

**1330s**
Very pointy shoes come into fashion

**1348–1349**
The Black Death sweeps England

**1355**
A fight between Oxford University students and townspeople leaves 90 dead

**1381**
The Peasants' Revolt

**1337–1453**
The Hundred Years War

**1400–1415**
Owain Glyndwr's rebellion in Wales

**1463**
Peasants are banned from wearing short tunics that reveal their buttocks

**1455–1485**
The War of the Roses

**1483**
Disappearance of the Princes in the Tower

13

# What was England like before the Battle of Hastings?

England before the Battle of Hastings was a land of huge forests, great open fields, villages and small towns. It had been part of the Roman Empire since AD 43, but in 410 the Roman army left, along with most of the Roman people who had settled in Britain. Rome itself was being threatened by tribes from northern Europe and the army was needed to defend the city. The same tribes raided, invaded and settled in England, a country that the Romans had left almost defenceless.

In 1042, England was finally peacefully united under one king: King Edward the Confessor. About 1.5 million people, mainly Anglo-Saxons*, lived in England and most of them worked on the land. It was a prosperous country, where agriculture and industry flourished. Governed by the king, who was advised by a council of powerful nobles, Anglo-Saxon England was generally peaceful. Most people understood and accepted their place in society: who they had to obey, and who had to obey them.

This section of the book will look at:

- the chronology of the history of England from 410 to 1066

- the ways in which people lived and were governed in Anglo-Saxon England from 1042 to 1066

- some of the ways that archaeologists and historians have found out about Anglo-Saxon England.

# Welcome to Anglo-Saxon England

## Learning objectives

- Know about the chronology of English history from 410 to 1066.
- Understand the importance of the work of archaeologists and historians in finding out about Anglo-Saxon England.

## What do you think?

What do you think life in England was like before 1066?

## Key terms

**Anglo-Saxon\*:** The name 'Anglo-Saxon' comes from the Angles and the Saxons, two of the north European tribes that invaded and lived in Britain from the fifth century onwards.

'Look to your own defences.' With these chilling words from their emperor in AD 410, the Roman army left Britain. In the centuries that followed, Scots and Picts, Jutes and Vikings, Angles and Saxons raided and invaded Britain. Some stayed for a short time, some for longer, and some didn't stay for any more time than it took to grab whatever their raiding parties could lay their hands on. Most of them fought each other. What sort of country, and what sort of people, emerged from these chaotic years?

We are going to look at some items from this period to see what we can learn from them about the people who made them and used them. But first we need to get the raiders and invaders, and the important things they did, in the right order, which is shown in the Timeline opposite.

## What can we learn from archaeologists and historians about Anglo-Saxon England?

Historians living in England before 1066 were usually monks. They were among the few people who could both read and write. They took a keen interest in what was happening around them and what had happened in the past. Monks often had a very firm point of view.

**Source A:** Written by a monk, the Venerable Bede, in his *Ecclesiastical History of the English People* in 731. Here he is describing the arrival of the Saxons in around AD 440.

They came from three very powerful Germanic tribes, the Saxons, Angles and Jutes. From the Saxon country, that is, the district now known as Old Saxony, came the east Saxons, the South Saxons and the West Saxons. It was not long before such hordes of these alien people crowded into the island that the natives who had invited them began to live in terror. These heathen conquerors devastated the surrounding cities and countryside and established a stranglehold over nearly all the doomed island.

**Source B:** A necklace found in the grave of a Saxon woman. It is made from gold, glass and garnets, which are semi-precious stones. Archaeologists date it from around AD 600.

### Timeline

Invaders of Britain, 410–1042

**410:** Roman army leaves Britain

**440s:** Saxon raids begin

**477–95:** Saxons settle in Sussex and Wessex

**597:** Augustine's Christian mission arrives in Kent

**620s:** Sutton Hoo burial

**793–95:** Vikings raid Lindisfarne, Jarrow and Iona

**865:** Viking 'Great Army' arrives

**871:** Alfred becomes king of Wessex

**878:** Alfred defeats the Vikings at Edington

### Your turn!

1 In which centuries did these events occur:
   a the Saxon raids began
   b the Vikings raided Lindisfarne
   c Alfred became king of Wessex?

2 Work with a partner. Write down everything you can find out from Source A about the Saxon invasions.

3 The author of Source A was a monk. Do you think this would have influenced the way he wrote about the invasions? Discuss this in your class. Try to reach a decision together.

4 Look carefully at Source B. What does it tell you about Anglo-Saxon society at that time? Write two or three sentences about this. For example, you might think about craft skills or the importance in society of some women.

# The Sutton Hoo burial

In 1939, archaeologists* excavated a grassy mound at Sutton Hoo in Suffolk. They discovered a huge Anglo-Saxon ship that had been dragged inland and laid in a trench. By comparing it to ship burials in Scandinavia, archaeologists knew the ship had been used as a burial place. The wooden ship had rotted away, but what remained included gold and silver bowls and brooches, spoons and swords, coins and all kinds of treasure. These had been put there in the belief that the dead person could use them in his next life. Archaeologists and historians worked out that this was probably the burial place of Raedwald, king of East Anglia, who died in about AD 625.

## Key term

**Archaeologist*:** A person who studies people in the past, usually by excavating (digging) for the remains they have left behind.

**Source C:** Archaeologists excavating the Sutton Hoo ship. The wood had rotted away but the outline of the ship's timbers, as well as the rivets that held them together, can still be seen in the sand.

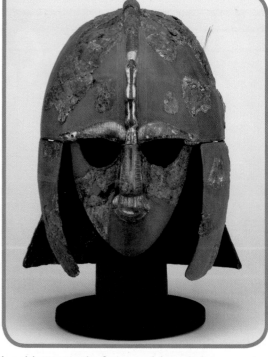

**Source D:** Two of the objects found in the Sutton Hoo ship. The buckle is made from gold and the complicated designs involve animals and birds. The iron helmet has a beautifully decorated face mask. It shows scenes of war, such as a warrior on a horse trampling an enemy.

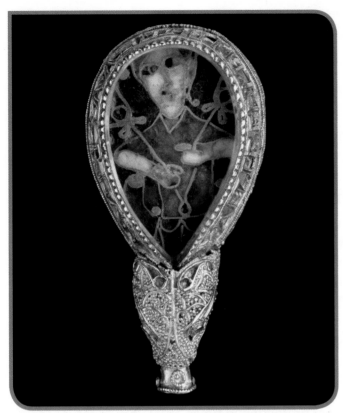

**Source E:** Archaeologists believe that this was the handle of a pointer stick, used for following words when reading a book. It is made from gold, rock crystal and enamel. It was found in 1693 near Athelney in Somerset, which was the stronghold of King Alfred. Around the edge is written 'Alfred had me made'. Because it belonged to King Alfred, it is called 'the Alfred jewel'.

**Source F:** From the entry in the *Anglo-Saxon Chronicle** for the year 793. It describes the Viking attack on the Holy Island of Lindisfarne, off the coast of Northumbria.

This year came dreadful warnings over the land of the Northumbrians, terrifying the people most woefully. Immense sheets of light rushed through the air, and whirlwinds, and fiery dragons flying across the skies. These tremendous signs were followed by a great famine; and not long after came the dreadful invasions of heathen men. They made terrible havoc in the church of God in Holy Island by rape and slaughter.

## Key term

***Anglo-Saxon Chronicle*:** This book was started by monks towards the end of the ninth century and updated by them until about 1154. It detailed the history of the Anglo-Saxons.

## Checkpoint

1 In which century did Augustine's Christian mission land in Kent?

2 In which decade of the ninth century did Alfred become king of Wessex?

3 Who was the Venerable Bede and why is he important?

4 What did archaeologists find at Sutton Hoo?

5 What is the *Anglo-Saxon Chronicle*?

## Your turn!

3rd 1 Look carefully at Sources D–F. Write down three things that they tell us about the Anglo-Saxons.

3rd 2 Share the three things you have found out in question 1 with others in your class. Make a class list of everything you have all found out from these sources.

4th 3 What don't Sources D–F tell you about the Anglo-Saxons? Make another class list of questions you would like to be answered.

4th 4 Choose one thing from the list you wrote in question 3 and write two to three sentences saying how you would find out about it.

# What did the Anglo-Saxons do all day?

### Did you know?

In 1065, Anglo-Saxon villagers used vegetable dyes to make their clothes brightly coloured. They hadn't invented buttons and they used moss or grass as toilet paper.

### Key term

**Hide*:** The amount needed to support a family.

## Working on the land

Most Anglo-Saxons lived in villages and worked on the land. There were ceorls, who were free men, and thralls, who were slaves. Each ceorl worked at least one hide* of land in the great open fields that surrounded the villages. They grew barley, rye and wheat, along with peas, beans and flax. Barley was used in brewing beer, rye and wheat in bread-making, and flax was spun and woven into cloth. Sheep, pigs, hens and cows provided wool, meat, eggs and milk, while honey from bees was used for sweetening.

Most villages had a lord, usually a thegn (see page 20) who the villagers looked to for protection in times of trouble. In return for this protection, the village ceorls and thralls worked the lord's land for him and gave him 'food rent' – eggs, meat, peas or milk – whatever it was that they produced.

**Source A:** In about AD 1000, an unknown monk produced a chronology. This was a calendar with one page for each month. At the bottom of each page the monk drew a picture of the work villagers did in that month. These are two of those pictures.

## Working in towns

Some villages grew into towns, and in AD 1000 about 10 per cent of the population of England lived in a town. Towns grew from markets where people from the surrounding countryside came to buy and sell; some towns specialised in, for example, leather-work or weaving or soap-making. Towns on the coast became busy ports. Ships would carry goods to other ports on the coast of England, or across the seas to Europe. By the 11th century, England was a prosperous country – a rich prize for any invader.

**Your turn!**

 **1** Look at Source A.
  **a** What work is being done in these pictures?
  **b** Why do you think a monk bothered to draw pictures of people working on the land?

**2 a** Can you solve the riddles in Source B?
  **b** Write your own Saxon riddle and see if anyone in your class can solve it.
  **c** Put together a class riddle book.

**3 a** Look at the map in Figure 1.1. With a partner, discuss why people would want to invade England. Put these reasons on a spider diagram with a centre labelled 'Pull factors'.
  **b** Write a paragraph to explain why, by the 11th century, England was attractive to invaders.

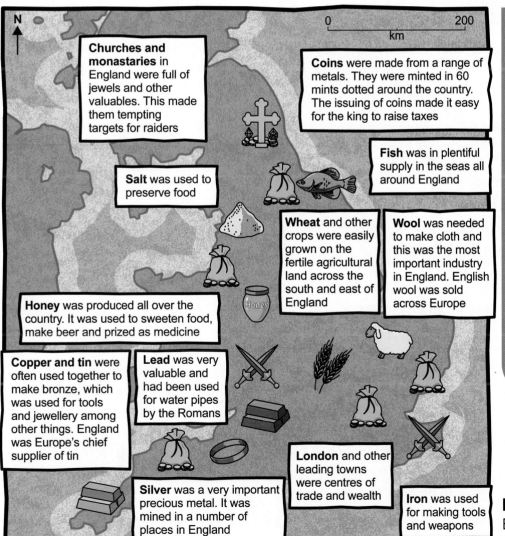

**Churches and monastaries** in England were full of jewels and other valuables. This made them tempting targets for raiders

**Coins** were made from a range of metals. They were minted in 60 mints dotted around the country. The issuing of coins made it easy for the king to raise taxes

**Fish** was in plentiful supply in the seas all around England

**Salt** was used to preserve food

**Wheat** and other crops were easily grown on the fertile agricultural land across the south and east of England

**Wool** was needed to make cloth and this was the most important industry in England. English wool was sold across Europe

**Honey** was produced all over the country. It was used to sweeten food, make beer and prized as medicine

**Copper and tin** were often used together to make bronze, which was used for tools and jewellery among other things. England was Europe's chief supplier of tin

**Lead** was very valuable and had been used for water pipes by the Romans

**London** and other leading towns were centres of trade and wealth

**Iron** was used for making tools and weapons

**Silver** was a very important precious metal. It was mined in a number of places in England

0    200
km

**Source B:** Anglo-Saxons were fond of jokes and riddles. Here are two of them.

Multi-coloured, I flee the sky and the deep earth. There is no place for me on the ground, I make the world grow green with my tears. What am I?

I grow tall and am hairy underneath. Sometimes a beautiful girl grips me, rips off my head and puts me in a pan of water. I make her cry. What am I?

(Answers on page 203.)

**Figure 1.1:** Map showing England's prosperity in the 11th century.

**Source C:** Anglo-Saxon painting of a Witan.

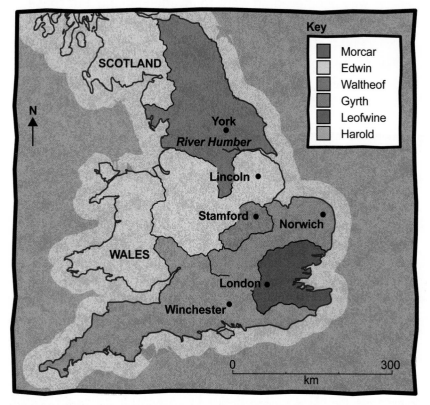

**Figure 1.2:** Map showing the six earldoms of England in 1065, the earls who ran them and the largest towns.

## Running the country

In 1043, Edward the Confessor was crowned king of England. He ruled England with the help of the Witan.

### Witans

The Witan was an assembly of 'wise men'. Edward could invite whoever he wanted to come to a Witan. However, it made good sense to invite the most powerful men in the kingdom. These were the earls, who helped Edward run large areas of England (see the map in Figure 1.2) in return for promising him military help if he needed it. To involve the earls meant they would be likely to support any decisions he made and there would be no rebellions. As well as earls, Edward sometimes invited thegns, bishops and abbots to come to a Witan. Witans did not always meet in the same place and did not always consist of the same people. It all depended on where Edward was and on what problem he was asking for their advice. Witans only gave advice: Edward could still do exactly what he wanted.

### Justice

Anglo-Saxon justice was based on the family. If anyone was wronged, their family was expected to seek revenge. Everyone had a life-price, called a 'wergild'. Thegns were worth more than ceorls, who were worth more than thralls. If a person was murdered, the murderer's family had to pay the murdered person's wergild in full. For lesser crimes like injuring someone, proportions of wergild had to be handed over.

Saxons held regular open-air meetings, called folk-moots, which dealt with people who broke the law.

## Reconstructing the past

Anglo-Saxon houses that were lived in by ordinary people have not survived, and there are no drawings or paintings to tell us what they looked like. So how can we find out?

**Interpretation 1:** A reconstruction of 11th-century Anglo-Saxon houses in Norwich, Norfolk.

### Your turn!

1 In two to three sentences, explain why it was a good idea for the king to invite the most powerful nobles in the kingdom to advise him.

2 Look at Interpretation 1. Working with a partner, decide what evidence the artist who drew the reconstruction would have needed to make sure the drawing was as accurate as possible.

### Checkpoint

1 Where did most Anglo-Saxons work?

2 Who was king of England from 1043 to 1066?

3 What were Witans?

4 Name two men who were earls in 1065.

5 Name two things that made Anglo-Saxon people feel secure in 1065.

6 What was wergild and why was it important?

# What was England like before the Battle of Hastings?

- Work in groups of five. On a large piece of paper, draw a triangle like the one in the diagram on the right. Write labels or draw pictures to show ceorls, earls, monarch, thegns and thralls in the correct sections on the triangle, with the most powerful at the top and the least powerful at the bottom.

- Divide the five roles on the triangle between members of your group. Write your job description on a slip of paper, and add a note saying what you expect from the person in the role below yours. If your role is the one at the bottom of the triangle, write your job description and then what you have to do for the role above you. Stick these slips of paper in the correct places on the triangle.

# Why was England a battlefield in 1066?

1066 was a dreadful year for Anglo-Saxon England. In January, King Edward the Confessor died. Three noblemen – Harold Godwinson, Harald Hardrada and William of Normandy – all thought they should be king, and they fought each other for the throne. The country was torn apart. This section of the book will look at:

- what made a good medieval monarch

- the claims of the three challengers for the throne of England

- the Battle of Stamford Bridge and its impact on Harold Godwinson's army

- the Battle of Hastings and the reasons for the victory of William of Normandy.

## What do you think?

What do you think might lead to people rebelling against their monarch?

# What made a good medieval monarch?

## Learning objectives

- Know about the qualities that were essential to be a good monarch.
- Understand the claims of the three men who wanted to occupy the throne of England.

Keep law and order

Defend the country

Successfully lead the army

Spend taxes wisely

Work with the Church

Take the advice of the nobles

Marry and have healthy sons

Have a claim to the throne that people accept

Gain the respect of the people

**Figure 1.3:** Qualities needed by a medieval monarch.

In the Middle Ages, the monarch was the most important person in the country. They had an enormous amount of power. But being a monarch could be a dangerous occupation.

## Your turn!

1. Play the Snakes and Ladders game in Figure 1.4. Did you reach the end and enjoy a long and happy reign? Write a paragraph to explain what happened during your reign.

2. Look at these words: cruel, brave, strong, greedy, clever, artistic, handsome, cowardly, mean, weak. Choose three of them and put them in a sentence that describes what a medieval king should be. Then choose another three and put them in a sentence that describes what a medieval king shouldn't be.

3. Look at the two sentences you wrote in answer to question 2. For one of those sentences explain why you chose the words you did.

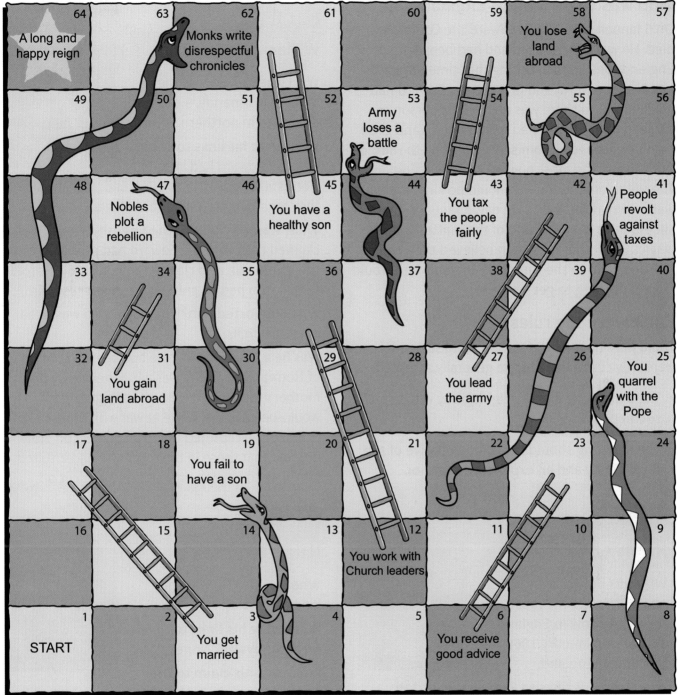

**Figure 1.4:** Snakes and Ladders: did you have a long and happy reign?

## Did you know?

Eighteen kings reigned in England between 1066 and 1485. Two died from severe diarrhoea, two died in battle and four were murdered – one, some believe, by having a red hot poker pushed up his bottom!

## Who was to be king of England?

On 5 January 1066, King Edward the Confessor died. He was 62 years old and had been king of England for 24 years. During that time England had been peaceful and prosperous. Edward had no children, so there was no obvious person to succeed him. Edward had many times – and even on his deathbed – promised the throne to Harold Godwinson, the most powerful noble in England. The Witan agreed Harold should be king, and he was crowned the following day, 6 January. That should have been the end of the matter, but it wasn't. Two other men each believed they had a rightful claim to the throne of England, and would stop at nothing to get it.

## What were the rules?

There were no rules as to who should succeed. There were only customs that were generally accepted.

- The dying king had the right to say who should succeed him.

- The new king should be a blood relative of the royal family and an experienced warrior.

### Fact file

### Harold Godwinson

**Who was he?** He was the earl of Wessex, the most powerful noble in England and, after 6 January 1066, the king of England.

**What were his links to English royalty?** His sister was married to King Edward.

**What was his claim to the English throne?** King Edward had promised him the throne, and the Witan had agreed he should be king. He had governed England well when Edward was ill.

**Who supported him?** The Witan.

**Was he a good warrior?** He was brave and respected, but experienced only in Britain where he cruelly put down a revolt in Wales.

### Fact file

### William of Normandy

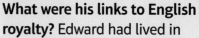

**Who was he?** He was the duke of Normandy, a powerful dukedom in northern France.

**What were his links to English royalty?** Edward had lived in Normandy from 1016 to 1041, and William said they regarded each other as brothers.

**What was his claim to the English throne?** He claimed that, in 1051, Edward had promised him the throne. He also claimed that, in 1064, Harold Godwinson had promised to support his claim.

**Who supported him?** The pope, who was head of the Church.

**Was he a good warrior?** He had been in control of Normandy since he was a boy, helped by his mother's family, and was used to fighting off would-be invaders. While at war with other dukes in France he captured the town of Alençon. He ordered that those in the town who had insulted him were to have their hands and feet cut off.

### Fact file

### Harald Hardrada

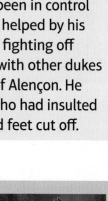

**Who was he?** He was the king of Norway.

**What were his links to English royalty?** None.

**What was his claim to the English throne?** He claimed that Harthacnut, who ruled England from 1040 to 1042, had promised King Magnus of Norway that his descendants would have the throne of England.

**Who supported him?** Tostig, Harold Godwinson's brother, who was a powerful English noble.

**Was he a good warrior?** He was the most feared warrior in the whole of Europe. He was brave and cruel. He was experienced in fighting alongside Norwegian and foreign leaders.

**Source A:** Written by a Norman monk called William of Jumieges in his book *The Deeds of the Norman Dukes*. He wrote the book in 1070 after King William asked him to write an account of the Norman Conquest.

In 1051 Edward, king of the English, having no heir, sent Robert, Archbishop of Canterbury, to William of Normandy to appoint him as the next King of England. But he also, at a later date, sent to him Harold, so that Harold could swear loyalty to William.

**Source B:** Part of the Bayeux Tapestry, which was made in about 1070. It shows Harold Godwinson making a promise to Duke William.

## Did you know?

The Bayeux Tapestry isn't really a tapestry at all, but an embroidery. It was commissioned by Bishop Odo of Bayeux, William's half-brother, and was probably stitched in about 1070 by women working in Kent, England. It tells the story of the Norman Conquest from the Norman point of view. There is nothing similar that tells the story from the Anglo-Saxon viewpoint.

## Your turn!

 **1 a** Read Source A. What had Edward done to promise the throne to Duke William?
   **b** Read Source A and look at Source B. Write two or three sentences to describe the ways in which they tell the same story.
   **c** Sources A and B were both produced by Normans. Does this mean we can't trust what they tell us? Write a paragraph to explain your answer.

**2** You have read about the three challengers for the throne, and you are going to decide whose claim you think was the best. Give the answer to each question on their Fact files a score out of ten. Add up the scores to find out who you think has the best claim.

**3** Now write a paragraph to explain why your 'winner' from question 3 has the best claim to the throne of England.

**4** Harold Godwinson, Harald Hardrada and William of Normandy all needed to recruit men into their armies. Design a poster that could have been used by one of them to attract men to his army.

## Checkpoint

**1** What qualities did a medieval monarch need in order to be successful?

**2** In what ways could being a medieval monarch be dangerous?

**3** Who were the three challengers for the throne of England?

**4** Whose claim was the strongest, and why?

# Invasion in the North

**Did you know?**

Tostig, Harold Godwinson's brother, was once earl of Northumbria. In 1065, the people there rebelled against him, accusing him of murder. Harold took the side of the rebels and forced Tostig to leave England. This is why Tostig supported Harald Hardrada.

Harold Godwinson had been crowned in January 1066 but he knew his position as king of England was not secure. He expected to have to fight Harald Hardrada and William of Normandy if he was to hold on to his throne. He knew they would invade England – but he didn't know when and he didn't know which attack would come first. So Harold divided his army in half. One half guarded the south coast in case of an invasion from Normandy; the other half waited in the North in case of an invasion from Norway. Nine months passed and nothing happened. In September 1066, Harold was forced to send his armies home. He could not afford for them to stand around doing nothing, and they were needed at home to gather in the harvest. It was then that his enemies struck – the Vikings had landed.

## The Vikings have landed!

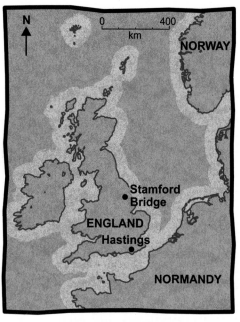

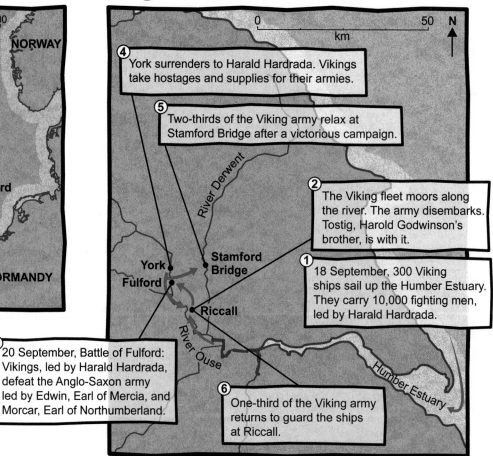

4. York surrenders to Harald Hardrada. Vikings take hostages and supplies for their armies.

5. Two-thirds of the Viking army relax at Stamford Bridge after a victorious campaign.

2. The Viking fleet moors along the river. The army disembarks. Tostig, Harold Godwinson's brother, is with it.

1. 18 September, 300 Viking ships sail up the Humber Estuary. They carry 10,000 fighting men, led by Harald Hardrada.

3. 20 September, Battle of Fulford: Vikings, led by Harald Hardrada, defeat the Anglo-Saxon army led by Edwin, Earl of Mercia, and Morcar, Earl of Northumberland.

6. One-third of the Viking army returns to guard the ships at Riccall.

**Figure 1.5:** Harald Hardrada's invasion, September 1066.

# The Battle of Stamford Bridge, 25 September 1066

Harold was in London when news reached him of the Viking invasion. He immediately marched north, gathering troops as he went. Harald Hardrada and the Vikings were at Stamford Bridge. The Vikings were relaxing in the sun; most had taken their armour off and they certainly were not expecting an Anglo-Saxon army to appear from the south.

Harold and the Anglo-Saxons covered the 185 miles from London in four days. Arriving at Stamford Bridge, they had to cross a narrow wooden bridge to reach the Viking army on the other side of the river. The *Anglo-Saxon Chronicle* (written by English monks) says that one Viking, armed with an axe, held up the entire army for long enough to give the Vikings time to get their armour on and form a shield wall* to face the Anglo-Saxon attack. The battle raged for hours and gradually the Viking shield wall broke. Hardrada and Tostig were both killed, along with hundreds of their men. Reinforcements from Riccall arrived too late. The Vikings that remained fled for Riccall and their ships. There were so few Vikings left that, of the 300 ships that brought them to England, only 24 ships were needed to take them back to Norway. It was a great victory for Harold and the Anglo-Saxon army.

While Harold and the Anglo-Saxons were celebrating in York, word came that Duke William of Normandy had landed on the south coast of England.

**Source A:** From the *Anglo-Saxon Chronicle*. The monks are writing about the end of the Battle of Stamford Bridge.

… the English fiercely attacked [the Vikings] from behind until some of them… drowned, and some [were] also burnt… so that there were few survivors, and the English [were in command] of the place of slaughter. [Our] king then gave safe-conduct to Olaf, the son of the king of the [Norwegians], and to their bishop, and to the Earl of Orkney, and to all those who were left on the ships. And they then went up to our king, and swore oaths that they would always keep peace and friendship in this land, and [our] king let them go with 24 ships.

## Your turn!

1 Imagine you are one of Harold's advisers in January 1066. You are expecting invasions from Norway and France. What do you advise Harold to do? Discuss this in your class.

2 Make a timeline of events from the day the Vikings landed until they were relaxing at Stamford Bridge. For each event, decide whether the Vikings were lucky or skilful.

3 Identify the three main reasons why the Vikings lost the Battle of Stamford Bridge and put them in order of importance.

## Key term

**Shield wall*:** Barrier created by soldiers standing shoulder to shoulder, holding their shields in front of them so that they formed a wall.

## Who will win: Anglo-Saxons or Normans?

The celebrations in York, following Harold's victory at Stamford Bridge, stopped abruptly because of the news that William and his Norman army had landed on the south coast of England. Harold and the Anglo-Saxon army had defeated the Viking invasion in the North; they were determined to defeat the Norman invasion in the South, too.

## Harold's Anglo-Saxon army

Harold's army consisted of housecarls and the fyrd. These were very different groups of fighting men.

### Fact file

### Anglo-Saxon housecarls

**Who were they?**
Professional soldiers, highly trained, well paid and fiercely loyal to Harold.

**How were they armed?**
Their main weapon was a battle axe. The handle was a metre long and the axe head was made from sharpened iron. One swing of the axe could cut the head off a horse or split a man's head in half. Sometimes they used a double-edged sword. They carried shields, and wore short coats of chain mail and pointed iron helmets.

**What were their tactics?** In defence, they formed a shield wall. In attack, they swung their axes. They fought on foot.

### Fact file

### Anglo-Saxon fyrd

**Who were they?** Working men who were called up to help the king in time of danger. Led by the king's thegns, they were trained as fighters.

**How were they armed?**
The thegns had swords and spears and some were archers; the ordinary working men used their own farming tools like axes, pitchforks and scythes.

**What were their tactics?** The fyrd fought on foot and engaged the enemy in hand-to-hand fighting.

Harold could usually depend on having over 2000 housecarls to fight for him. However, over half had been killed at Stamford Bridge. Harold and his remaining housecarls, exhausted from battling with the Vikings, marched south to meet the invading Normans. Men joined the fyrd as the housecarls marched south. Even so, when they reached London, Harold's army was only up to half the strength it could have been if Harold had waited for more Saxons to join him.

Gyrth, Harold's brother, had a plan. He would lead the army against William so that Harold wouldn't risk being killed. Meanwhile, the crops and villages in the surrounding countryside would be burned. The Normans would have nothing to live on as winter closed in, and would be forced to return to France. Those that stayed behind would be wiped out by the Anglo-Saxons. But would Harold agree?

## William's Norman army

William's Norman army was very different from Harold's Anglo-Saxon one.

### Fact file

### Norman knights

**Who were they?** William's best soldiers, highly trained, well paid and loyal to William.

**How were they armed?** They had spears, swords and heavy iron clubs covered in spikes.

**What were their tactics?** They charged at the enemy, riding on strong war horses, cutting down the enemy's foot soldiers.

### Fact file

### Norman archers

**Who were they?** Trained and well-paid members of the army.

**How were they armed?** They had bows and arrows but very little armour.

**What were their tactics?** They could fire up to six arrows a minute, killing a man from 180 metres away.

### Fact file

### Norman foot soldiers

**Who were they?** The main part of William's army.

**How were they armed?** They had swords and shields.

**What were their tactics?** They went in for the kill after the knights and archers had done their work.

### Your turn!

1 **a** Write down one strength and one weakness of Harold's Anglo-Saxon army.

   **b** Write down one strength and one weakness of William's Norman army.

2 Which army do you think would prefer:
   **a** to make a surprise attack
   **b** a pre-arranged battle
   **c** a series of battles over a few days?
   Write two to three sentences to explain each of your choices.

### Checkpoint

1 List three reasons why Harold and the Anglo-Saxons managed to defeat Harald Hardrada and the Vikings.

2 What was the fyrd and what weapons did they use?

3 How did thegns fight?

4 What was a shield wall?

5 What weapons did William's army have that Harold's army did not?

6 Who do you think had the strongest army, William or Harold?

# The Battle of Hastings, 14 October 1066

## Learning objectives

- Learn what happened at the Battle of Hastings and why King Harold lost.
- Understand that there are different accounts of the battle, and the reasons for these differences.
- Understand that historians have different interpretations of the reasons why Harold lost.

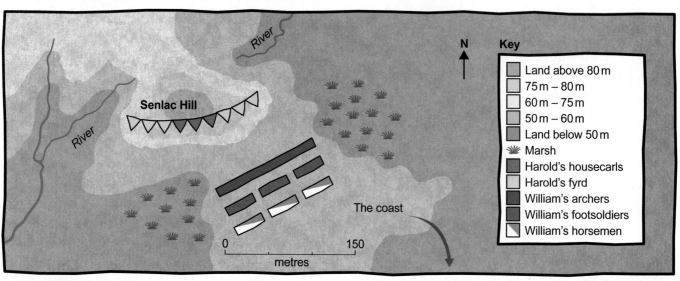

**Figure 1.6:** The positions of the two armies at the start of the Battle of Hastings.

At nine o'clock on the morning of 14 October 1066, two armies faced each other. The Anglo-Saxon army, led by Harold Godwinson, king of England, was defending its country against foreign invaders. Duke William of Normandy and his army were fighting for the throne of England that William believed was rightfully his. With the throne would come the rich rewards of England.

**Source A:** Part of the Bayeux Tapestry, showing the Normans trying to break through the Anglo-Saxon shield wall.

## Early tactics

Harold positioned his army on Senlac Hill. He was planning to wear the Normans out by forcing them to fight uphill and then, when the Normans were exhausted, to send in the housecarls and the fyrd to slaughter them.

The Normans attacked, trying to gain ground, but this was difficult as they were fighting uphill. Anglo-Saxon battle axes cut through the Normans' armour. The noise – the shouting and screaming of the men, the bellowing of the horses and the clash of weapons – would have been tremendous. The Anglo-Saxon shield wall held firm.

## Change of tactics

A rumour went round that William was dead. Immediately he took his helmet off and stood up in his stirrups so everyone could see him.

Then William used an old trick. Norman soldiers attacked up Senlac Hill, but then pretended to run away. Some of the fyrd chased them.

Once the fyrd were off the hill and no longer behind a shield wall the Normans turned round and massacred them. Leofwine and Gyrth, Harold's brothers, were killed.

Some of the fyrd took fright and ran away. The remaining housecarls formed a tight shield wall around Harold but it was too late. Harold was killed along with all the housecarls.

**Source B:** Part of the Bayeux Tapestry, showing the death of King Harold. The Latin words 'Harold rex interfectus est' mean 'King Harold has been killed'. But which person is King Harold?

## The death of King Harold: a puzzle

There is no doubt that King Harold was killed at the Battle of Hastings, along with his brothers and all of his housecarls. There is, however, a mystery as to how exactly Harold met his death. The problem is that all the sources say something a bit different to one another. We need to ask whether or not the sources are reliable – how far can they be trusted to tell us the truth about the death of King Harold? One problem is that there is no surviving Saxon account of how Harold died. We have to depend on the Norman accounts.

- **The Bayeux Tapestry** is the earliest source, but it was made on the orders of a Norman, Odo, to record the Norman victory. He was present at the battle.

- **Guy of Amiens** was a French ally of William. He was not present at the battle.

- **William of Malmesbury** was an English monk. He believed it was important to use original source material. Historians believe he wrote his account after seeing the Bayeux Tapestry.

- **William of Poitiers** was a Norman who served under Duke William as a soldier, although he wasn't involved in the Battle of Hastings. He would have spoken to soldiers who had been involved.

**Source C:** Written by Guy of Amiens, a French ally of William, in 1068.

The first knight pierced Harold's shield with his sword that then penetrated his chest, drenching the ground with his blood. With his sword, the second knight cut off Harold's head below the protection of his helmet, and the third pierced the innards of his belly. The fourth knight hacked off his leg at the thigh. Struck down, Harold's dead body lay on the ground

**Source D:** Written by William of Malmesbury, an English monk and historian, in about 1125.

Harold fell from having his brain pierced by an arrow and gave himself up to death. One of William's soldiers gashed his thigh with a sword as he lay on the ground. For this shameful and cowardly action he was condemned by William and expelled from the army.

**Source E:** Written by William of Poitiers, a Norman soldier, in 1071.

Victory won, the duke [William] returned to the field of battle. He was met with a scene of carnage, which he regarded with pity. Far and wide the ground was covered with the best of English nobility and youth. Harold's two brothers were found lying beside him.

## After the battle

Hundreds of bodies were left on the battlefield, some half alive and moaning in agony, others clearly dead. William needed to be sure that Harold was dead. If Harold escaped the battlefield he could rally the Saxons and fight back. However, most of the Saxon bodies were so mutilated that it was impossible to tell who they were. Faces had been slashed, arms and legs cut off and many Saxons stripped naked.

Saxon women, wives, sisters and mothers came to the battlefield to identify their loved ones and take them home for proper burial. This was what usually happened after any battle. There is a legend that Edith Swanneck, the woman by whom Harold had had six children, came looking for him. She found his crushed body and knew it was Harold by a special mark that only she knew about.

William of Poitiers records that Countess Gytha, Harold's mother, went to William and begged him for her son's body so that she could give Harold a Christian burial. William refused. He refused again even when Gytha offered him Harold's weight in gold. William was probably afraid that Harold's grave would become a place of pilgrimage for the English, and the focus of rebellions against the Normans. Instead, William gave Harold's body to a trusted Norman and ordered it to be buried in an unmarked grave beside the sea. 'Buried', as one storyteller says, 'beside the shore he failed to defend.'

**Interpretation 1:** Edith Swanneck finding Harold's body.

### Your turn!

1  a  Draw a table headed 'Why Harold lost the Battle of Hastings', with three columns headed 'Luck', 'Good decisions by William' and 'Poor decisions by Harold'. Work with a partner and, starting with Harold leaving York and ending with his death, complete the table.

  b  Write a paragraph explaining why Harold lost the Battle of Hastings.

2  Look at Source B. Read Source C and use it to help you find Harold on the Bayeux Tapestry. Now use Source D to find Harold on the Bayeux Tapestry. Did you find the same person?

3  Read Source E. William of Poitiers doesn't mention Harold's death by an arrow in his eye at all. Write down two reasons why you think this was.

4  Write a paragraph to explain how Harold died. Remember to use evidence to back up your ideas. It is all right to say it's impossible to say exactly how he was killed, provided you say why.

**Interpretation 2:** Jason Askew is an artist who specialises in painting historical scenes. This is his interpretation of the Battle of Hastings, painted in around 1990.

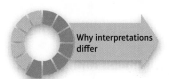
Why interpretations differ

## How do we know about the past?

Present-day historians and historical artists interpret the past. They show us and tell us what they think happened during events long before they were born. The best historians and historical artists take great care in using as many sources as they can find in order to be sure their interpretation is accurate.

## The problem with the Battle of Hastings

The problem with the Battle of Hastings is that only one person who fought there left any record of what it was like. This was Bishop Odo of Normandy. He commissioned the Bayeux Tapestry, but no one knows whether he gave the embroiderers detailed instructions, nor whether he checked it for accuracy once it was finished. No one knows when it was made; experts in the history of embroidery say that it was made in about 1070, four years after the battle. That is all the information we have. There are no Anglo-Saxon records.

Modern historians collect all the evidence they can that relates to the event about which they are writing. In the case of the Battle of Hastings, the obvious starting point is the Bayeux Tapestry. Then they would look at later accounts (like Sources C and D on page 32) until they can build up a picture of what actually happened. As you have seen, some sources provide conflicting accounts. Historians need to decide which sources are likely to give an accurate account of what happened. It is then that historians need to prioritise their source material: they need to put it in order of importance. Not all historians will have the same order of importance.

**Interpretation 3:** This interpretation was written by Richard Humble in his book *The Fall of Saxon England*, published in 1975.

```
Harold was defeated
for three main
reasons: William's
grip on the battle
and his skill
at changing his
tactics; the lack of
discipline of the
Saxon fyrd; and the
relentless Norman
arrow-fire.
```

**Interpretation 4:** This interpretation was written by Ian W. Walker in his book *Harold: The Last Anglo-Saxon King*, published in 1997.

```
All Harold needed to do was stand his ground
and force William into submission. He almost
succeeded in this, failing just before
nightfall. The evidence suggests that it was
King Harold's fall to a chance arrow which
finally broke English resistance and left the
field to the Normans.
```

**Interpretation 5:** This interpretation was written by Frank Barlow in his book *The Godwins*, published in 2002.

Harold can possibly be blamed for risking all on a battle. William, after three weeks' wait on the south coast, must have been at his wits' end over what to do. What happened, it would seem, is that Harold, flushed with victory in the north, thought that he could deal as successfully with William. And he very nearly did.

## Your turn!

**1** Look carefully at Interpretation 2. In your class, discuss which sources of information the artist would have needed to consult in order to make sure his painting was accurate. How much would have been left to his imagination?

**2** Read Interpretations 3, 4 and 5. What reasons do they give for William's victory?

**3** Write a paragraph to say which interpretation you agree with most, and why.

## Checkpoint

**1** Where was Harold, and his army, positioned at the start of the Battle of Hastings?

**2** Where was William, and his army, positioned at the start of the Battle of Hastings?

**3** What tactics were used (a) by Harold and (b) by William?

**4** What was the key change of tactic by William that won him the battle?

**5** Why were there different ideas in the 11th and 12th centuries about how Harold was killed?

**6** How do historical artists make sure their paintings are as accurate as possible?

**7** Give one reason why historians reach different conclusions about what happened in the past.

# Why was England a battlefield in 1066?

- The Bayeux Tapestry tells the story of William's claim to the throne of England, the preparations for the Norman invasion and the Battle of Hastings. As a group, plan, design and draw a frieze that tells the story of the defeat of Harald Hardrada. You will need to copy the pattern of the Bayeux Tapestry: include sections on the claim of Harold Godwinson, the march north, the Battle of Fulford, the Battle of Stamford Bridge and what happened afterwards.

- There is no surviving Saxon evidence about the Battle of Hastings. All Harold's thegns were killed and the fyrd couldn't read or write. Imaging you are a young Saxon who watched everything. Write your account of the battle – and remember you are a Saxon.

In this section, you have learned:

- that a single event, like the Battle of Hastings, can have many causes.

The study of history is all about asking questions. Historians ask 'How?', 'Where?', 'When?', 'Who?', 'What?' and, most important, 'Why?' As soon as you think you have the answer to 'Why?', you need to follow that with 'Why then, and not at any other time?' When you ask why something happened, you are thinking about causation. You are working out what caused something, like the Battle of Hastings, to happen. Just as importantly, you will go on to ask and answer the question 'Why then, and not in 1065 or 1067?'

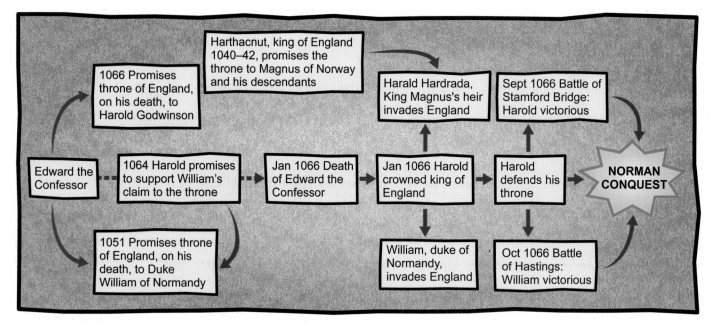

**Figure 1.7:** Why did the Norman Conquest happen?

## Your turn!

1 The flow chart in Figure 1.7 shows that the Norman Conquest had several causes.
   a Using the flow chart, decide which causes you think were so important that the Norman Conquest wouldn't have happened without them.
   b Which causes were so unimportant that, if they hadn't happened, the Norman Conquest would have happened anyway?
   c Draw up two lists, one of important causes and one of unimportant causes, and then discuss them in your class. Produce two lists with which you all agree.

2 Write a paragraph in answer to the question 'Why did the Norman Conquest happen in 1066?'

Causation questions

# Writing historically

You are going to write an answer to the question 'Why did Harold, king of England, lose the Battle of Hastings?' Don't just write down everything you know! First, you must structure your answer so that is has a beginning, a middle and an end, as shown below.

## Introduction

This is where you show you understand the question, and grab the attention of the reader.

You could, for example, begin with:

> 'In October 1066, Harold, king of England, suffered a violent and bloody death at the hands of the Norman invaders. There were many reasons why the Saxon king lost his throne.'

## Paragraphs

You now need to develop your answer in a logical way, giving reasons why Harold lost the battle. Use one paragraph for each reason.

1   You could begin each paragraph with 'One reason was…', 'A second reason was…'. This makes it clear each time you are talking about a new reason.

2   Remember to support what you are saying with factual evidence, otherwise people will not believe you! For example, don't just say 'Harold's troops were tired', but add that they were tired because they had just marched hundreds of kilometres.

3   Remember, too, to use connective words such as 'therefore', 'however' and 'because' to show how your ideas link together.

An example of a strong paragraph could look something like this:

> 'One reason that Harold lost the Battle of Hastings was that his troops were tired and depleted. This was because they had fought the Battle of Stamford Bridge only two weeks before. Some of Harold's troops had died in the battle, and the rest had had to march south very quickly to face the Normans. Therefore the Saxon army was not at full strength at Hastings.'

## Conclusion

This is where you sum up your ideas and say which reason was the most important. In other words, you provide a direct answer to the question. Your paragraphs should have already provided the evidence for your conclusion.

You could begin your conclusion with:

> 'The most important reason why Harold lost the battle of Hastings was…'.

Now go ahead and write an answer to the question 'Why did Harold, king of England, lose the Battle of Hastings?' Use all the advice above.

# How did William take control of England?

William had won the Battle of Hastings, but one battle was not enough to give him control of the whole of England. The Anglo-Saxons were not going to give in that easily. However, within just 21 years Norman power reached every corner of England. William was firmly in control and his throne was safe. This section of the book will look at:

- the way in which castles and terror were used by the Normans to establish control of England

- the way in which the feudal system and the Domesday Book helped to maintain control

- the extent to which the Norman Conquest changed the lives of the Anglo-Saxons.

# Taking control using terror

### Learning objectives

- Learn how William used terror to frighten the Saxons.
- Understand why the Normans used castles to control the Saxons.

### What do you think?

Are there problems with establishing control by force?

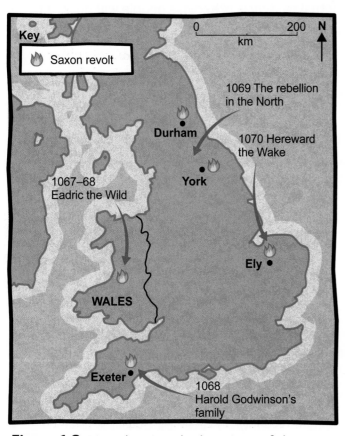

**Figure 1.8:** Map showing the locations of the most important Saxon revolts.

William knew he had to act quickly. He had killed the king of England at the Battle of Hastings, but that did not give him control of the whole country. William marched on London, burning villages and destroying crops as he went. This sent a powerful message to the Saxon people. The Normans would not tolerate any opposition. Faced with this level of destruction, the Saxon earls reluctantly agreed to accept William as their king.

On Christmas Day 1066, William was crowned in Westminster Abbey. As the coronation ceremony was taking place, Saxons and Normans were fighting in the streets. This was not a good beginning to William's reign.

### Did you know?

Today we hear about terror and terrorist acts where extremists try to frighten the civilian population and spread fear. The Normans used terror, too, to frighten the English people into obeying them.

## The harrying of the North

Revolts broke out across the country and were cruelly put down by the Norman army.

The most serious revolt happened in the North of England in 1069. Trouble began when the Saxons massacred William's trusted friend, Earl Robert, and 900 of William's soldiers when they were sent to rule Durham. The earls Morcar and Edwin turned against William. Helped by a small force of Vikings sent by the king of Denmark, they seized York and threatened to set up a separate kingdom in northern England. William responded in the only way he knew: he marched north with specially selected soldiers. They massacred men, women and children, burned their villages, destroyed their crops and slaughtered their animals. Those who survived faced famine and disease. The Vikings, bribed by William and seeing the Saxons defeated and destroyed, sailed away, never to return.

**Source A:** Part of the Bayeux Tapestry showing the Normans burning a Saxon house, and a woman and child escaping.

**Source B:** Written by an English monk, Orderic Vitalis, in *The Ecclesiastical History*, between 1123 and 1141. Orderic said that this was William's deathbed confession. William died in 1087 and Orderic wasn't there at the time. He relied on what people had told him.

I fell upon the English in the northern shires like a hungry lion. I ordered their houses and corn, with all their tools and belongings, to be burned. I ordered large herds of cattle and beasts of burden to be butchered wherever they were found. By so doing, alas, I became the barbarous murderer of many thousands, both young and old, of that fine race of people.

### Your turn!

1   Look at the map in Figure 1.8 showing Saxon revolts against Norman rule. Imagine William has asked for your advice. Write a short paragraph saying what you would advise him to do, and why. Should he, for example, send in troops to put down the revolt, build a castle or burn all the countryside in the area of the revolt so that the people starve?

2   In what ways do Sources A and B agree?

3   Choose one of the sources and explain how a historian could use it as evidence of the way William treated the Saxons in the North of England.

4   What can you learn from Source B about William? Why would a historian have to be careful using this source as evidence of William's character?

5   Source C describes a terrible situation. What questions would a historian have to ask before using it as evidence of the harrying of the North?

### Did you know?

Historians call William's destruction of northern England 'the harrying of the North'. 'Harrying' means to repeatedly attack someone or something over a period of time.

**Source C:** Written by a monk, Simeon of Durham, in the 1100s.

There was such hunger that men ate human flesh, and the flesh of horses and dogs and cats. Others sold themselves into slavery so they could live out their miserable lives. It was horrible to look into the ruined farmyards and houses and see the rotting human corpses, for there were none to bury them ... There was no village inhabited between York and Durham.

# Control by castles

Castles were vital to William's takeover of England. Wherever his army took control, they built castles. They built castles to:

- keep Normans safe in hostile areas and have a base from which to launch attacks

- control the surrounding countryside, making sure there were no rebellions

- remind people of the power of the Normans.

The first castles were made from wood. This was later replaced by stone. A castle might be built on a 'motte', which was a simple mound or hill. If there wasn't a suitable hill, then earth was dug to make a mound. If the Normans decided to build a castle in a town, then houses were pulled down to clear a big enough space. A 'bailey' was a cleared space which gave a good view of the surrounding area. It prevented people sneaking up in a surprise attack and gave defenders a clear area from which to shoot. It was also a safe place where Normans could live and work.

The Normans made the English carry out all the hard work involved in building the castles. A castle was usually the highest building in an entire area. There were no castles like these in England before the Norman Conquest, and this gave castles an air of sinister mystery and importance.

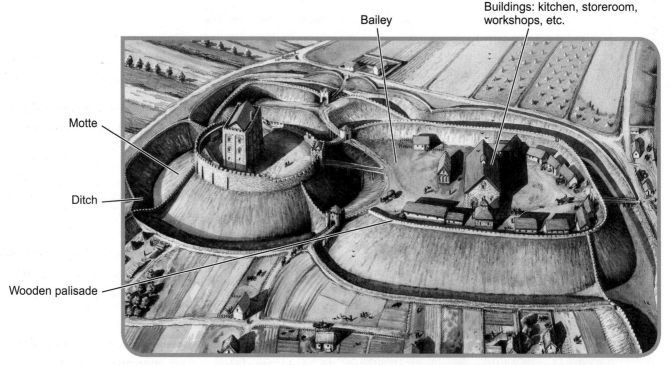

**Interpretation 1:** A modern artist, Sue Walker White, drew this picture in 2002 to show what early Norman castles would have looked like.

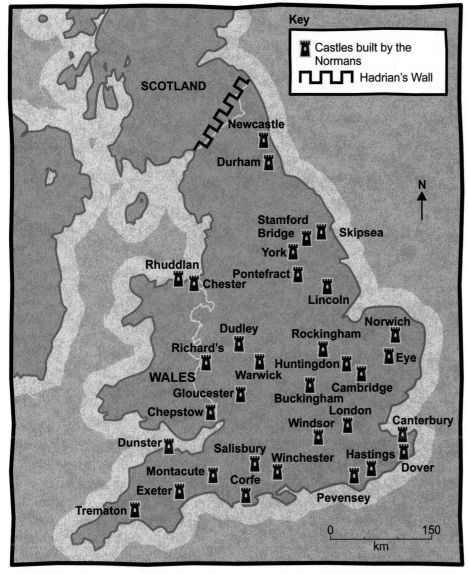

**Figure 1.9:** Map to show the extent of Norman control over England by 1070.

## Checkpoint

1 What was the 'harrying of the North'?

2 Why did William order the harrying of the North?

3 What impact did the harrying of the North have on the people who lived there?

4 Give two things historians need to check when using sources to write about the past.

5 Give two ways in which the Normans used castles to control the English people.

## Your turn!

 1 There were no rebellions in England after 1070. Does this mean that William's castle-building programme was a success? Use the map in Figure 1.9 and discuss this in your class.

2 You are one of a band of English people who don't want to co-operate with the Normans. Use Interpretation 1 and work with a partner to plan your attack on a Norman castle. Think about where the castle's weak points are and how you could get to them without Norman soldiers pouring out of the castle and wiping you out.

# Taking control peacefully

## Learning objectives

- Know how the feudal system and the Domesday survey helped William keep control of England.
- Understand how much change the Normans brought to England after 1066.

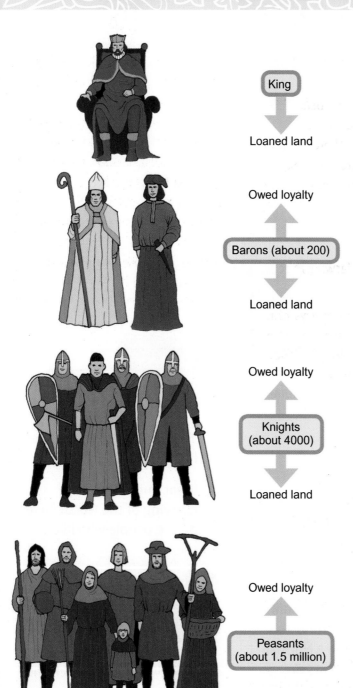

King

Loaned land

Owed loyalty

Barons (about 200)

Loaned land

Owed loyalty

Knights (about 4000)

Loaned land

Owed loyalty

Peasants (about 1.5 million)

**Figure 1.10:** The feudal system.

William realised that he could not hold England by sheer force forever. He needed a plan. He needed help to run England. He had to reward the powerful Normans who had supported him while at the same time making sure they stayed loyal.

## The feudal system

William developed the feudal system. He started by saying that all the land in England belonged to him. However, he would lend it to trusted followers in exchange for their loyalty. The feudal system meant that William had a constant supply of money and loyalty, and still owned the land.

## The Domesday survey

In order for the feudal system to work properly, William had to have an accurate record of the state of his land. He had to know exactly who owned what and how much it was worth, so that he could tax them correctly. He also wanted to know how much tax had been paid during Edward the Confessor's reign. This was so that he could show people he was continuing to follow what was customary in Edward's time. In 1085, William sent royal commissioners over all the country to collect this evidence. People, animals and land were all counted so that William could see how rich or poor his subjects were.

**Source A:** An entry in the *Anglo-Saxon Chronicle* for the year 1085.

The king had great deliberations and very deep speech with his counsellors about this land, how it was occupied and by what men. He then sent his men over all England into each shire to find out how many hides of land there were, what and how much each man was holding in England, in land, in livestock, and how much money it was worth. So very closely did he let it be searched out that there was not a single hide of land, not an ox, a cow, a pig was left out, and all the documents were brought to him afterwards.

**Source B:** A description of the city of York, from the Domesday Book.

In the city of York, before 1066 there were 6 shires and one belonging to the archbishop. One of these has now been laid waste for the castles. In 5 shires there were 1418 inhabited dwellings. There are now 391 inhabited. 400 dwellings are not inhabited; the better ones pay 1 penny and the others less; and 540 dwellings so empty that they pay nothing at all. The Frenchmen hold 145 dwellings.

**Source C:** A description of the village of Coleshill, Warwickshire, from the Domesday Book.

Richard holds Coleshill from William, son of Ansculf and it pays him £1 in rent. The lord in King Edward's time was Wulwin and the value to him was £1. There are 9 households and land for six ploughs. There is one lord's plough team* and 2 men's plough teams. There is a wood that is half a mile long.

**Your turn!**

 1 Look back at the triangle showing Saxon roles that you drew in answer to the first enquiry question on page 21. Put it beside the diagram of the feudal system in Figure 1.10. Make a list of the differences you can find, and another list of what stayed the same.

2 Read Source A. List the information it gives us about how the Domesday survey was carried out.

3 Read Sources B and C. Which area changed the most? Discuss with a partner why there was this difference.

4 Explain how the feudal system and the Domesday survey worked together to help William control England.

Change questions

## What did the Norman Conquest change?

Imagine you are Wigberht, a Saxon shepherd looking after a large flock of sheep. The spring lambs are fattening up nicely and you are wondering what price they will fetch at market. Suddenly you look up and gaze in puzzlement at the horizon. A cluster of what look like black dots has appeared at sea. As they grow closer, you see to your horror that they are ships. You don't know it, but your life is about to change forever. Or is it?

**Figure 1.11:** A Saxon shepherd with his sheep.

**Wigberht:** I don't know what all the fuss is about. My life has been pretty good under the Normans. I have carried on working as a shepherd, my village has a new lord who looks after us and if anything goes wrong we have the protection of the castle.

**Eldrida:** I'm not so sure. I don't like being bossed about by Normans. They aren't our people and they've just taken over. To make matters worse, my daughter is going to call her son Robert. What's wrong with good old Saxon names?

**Alfric:** It was terrible when the Normans came. They forced me and my family to spend weeks digging in the mud to make a gigantic mound. Then they put a building on top so they could control all of us. This was slavery!

**Meghan:** Times are hard. The land we've been given to work is stony and won't grow much, yet the lord is demanding more corn from us than in the old days. To make matters worse, my husband can't sneak off into the forest to catch rabbits.

**Figure 1.12:** Different Saxon experiences.

The Norman Conquest changed many things in England. Some of the changes were huge and affected a large number of people; some were small and affected only a few people. Some changes may seem big, but had little impact on the lives of ordinary people.

- The **landscape** changed: huge castles dominated much of the countryside. The landscape in the North of England was devastated: burnt fields and destroyed villages were all that could be seen.

- **Land ownership** changed: by 1087, only two of the great landowners were English; all the rest were Normans. The new landowners created luxury areas like deer parks and planted vineyards.

- The **Church** changed: by 1090, only one out of the 16 bishops was English; the rest were Norman. By 1200, all the wooden Saxon churches had been replaced by stone ones.

- **Language** changed: new words came into the language. People began using first names like Robert, William and Richard. Words like 'beef' and 'pork' were used to describe meat from cows and pigs.

- Two **new laws** were introduced by William:

  ○ **Forest Laws** protected William's hunting. There were vast forests in England. After the Norman Conquest some were named 'royal' forests. Ordinary people were not allowed to kill or capture any animals in royal forests and there were severe punishments for poaching.

  ○ A **Murdrum fine** was imposed on any area where a Norman had been killed and his murderer had not been caught.

Apart from these new laws, William kept the old Saxon legal system, even though it was different from the one he was used to. But he made sure the legal system was run by the Normans, not the English. William had won England by conquest and controlled the country partly by force and partly by making peaceful changes. He needed to show the English people that he was the true heir to Edward the Confessor, with as much continuity as change in the way he ran the country.

## Your turn!

**1** Work in groups of four. You are to take the parts of Wigberht, Eldrida, Alfric and Meghan. Develop the discussion they have started by bringing in more points about change and continuity under Norman rule. Write up the scene and act it to the rest of your class.

**2** In 1187, 90 per cent of the people in England lived in villages and farmed the land. Write a paragraph to describe the ways in which the new Norman system might have changed their lives.

**3** When a famous person dies, journalists usually write an obituary in which they detail the achievements of that person's life. William I died in 1087. Write his obituary, from the point of view of either an English person or a Norman.

## Checkpoint

**1** What was the feudal system?

**2** How did the feudal system help William keep control of England?

**3** Give two reasons why William ordered the Domesday survey to be carried out.

**4** How did the Domesday survey help the Normans control England?

**5** Give two ways in which the Domesday survey is useful to historians.

**6** List three ways in which the Normans brought change to England.

**7** List three ways in which the lives of English people stayed the same after 1066.

# How did William take control of England?

- The Norman Conquest affected some people very much and others hardly at all. How do you think the following people were affected:

  - a Norman knight who fought alongside William at Hastings

  - an Anglo-Saxon thegn who held land in the North of England

  - an Anglo-Saxon ceorl who grew wheat and barley and supplied milk to the nearby town

  - a monk who wrote parts of the *Anglo-Saxon Chronicle*?

  Put your ideas in a table with three columns headed 'Person', 'What changed' and 'What stayed the same'. Share your ideas with others in your class and draw up a class table with which you all agree.

- 'William took control of England by making sure everyone's lives were changed by the Normans.' Write a paragraph explaining whether or not you agree with this statement. Remember to back up your ideas with facts.

In this section, you have learned:

- that historians use sources to find out about the past.

What must I use to find out about Anglo-Saxon and Norman England?

Archaeological evidence of the ways in which people lived

The Bayeux Tapestry

The writings of Saxon monks and Norman noblemen

Paintings and drawings from the time

Buildings such as churches and castles

I must check my interpretation against the work of other historians. I might agree with them, or I might have discovered something new.

**Figure 1.13:** A historian gets to work.

## Your turn!

Historians can use a lot of different sources to help them find out about the past. Which type of source in Figure 1.13 would historians find the most useful if they were trying to find out about:

a the lives of ordinary Anglo-Saxon people

b what the Saxons thought about the Normans?

## Key term

**Inference\*:** Something you can learn from a source, which goes beyond the surface detail of what it says and on to what it suggests.

## Quick quiz

1 Give two ways in which England was a prosperous country before 1066.

2 What was a Witan?

3 Give two qualities a good medieval monarch had to have.

4 Who led the Vikings at the Battle of Stamford Bridge?

5 What happened on Christmas Day 1066?

6 What was the date of the harrying of the North?

7 Give two ways in which the Normans changed the lives of the Saxons.

8 Give two ways in which the lives of Saxons stayed the same after the Norman Conquest.

9 Who did the Normans say owned all the land in England?

10 In the feudal system:
    a what did the peasants have to do for their lord
    b what did their lord have to do for them in return?

11 Why did the Normans build castles? Give two reasons.

12 What was the Domesday Book for?

# Writing historically

Inference questions

How do historians use all the different kinds of sources to find out about the past? Two of the most important ways are comprehension and inference*.

**Comprehension** means understanding the source and being able to identify its key features.

**Inference** means working out something from the source which isn't actually stated or shown in it.

When you are asked to make an inference, you are being asked to explain what you think the source is suggesting. The inference can be about the situation described in the source, or about why it was made.

Look at Source A on page 30. What two inferences can you draw from this source about the Battle of Hastings?

### Student 1

> The Norman knights are wearing chainmail and they are fighting on horseback.

Student 1 is describing two features that can be seen in the source. This is comprehension; there are no inferences.

### Student 2

> The chainmail and helmets the Normans are wearing show that they were well prepared for battle. The Saxons aren't wearing armour at all, so would have been easier to kill.

Student 2 is drawing two inferences from the source – that the Normans were well prepared and that the Saxon soldiers were easier to kill. The student is giving reasons for drawing those inferences.

Now let's try using the same skill with a written source.

Read Source C on page 39. What two inferences can you draw from this source about the results of the harrying of the North?

### Student 1

> As a result of the harrying of the North, corpses were left to rot and no villages between York and Durham were lived in.

Student 1 is describing two results of the harrying of the North. This is comprehension; there are no inferences.

### Student 2

> People were forced to eat human flesh – this suggests that all the food and farm animals had been taken or destroyed by the Normans. The fact that a monk wrote about the harrying of the North so long afterwards shows that it was such a terrible event that people remembered it for a long time.

Student 2 is drawing an inference from the fact that people ate human flesh – that all other food sources had been taken or destroyed. The student is also making an inference by thinking about who wrote the source and why.

## Your turn!

Read Source A on page 15.

What two inferences can you draw from this source about the Saxon invasions of England in about AD 440?

# Why was the Church so important in people's lives?

Most medieval people led short lives, dying at the age of around 35. As a result, they thought a lot about what would happen after they died. Fear of the terrors, and possible rewards, of life after death drove their actions. Would they be rewarded in heaven or face eternal tortures in hell? What could they do to affect this fate? Many would go to church once a week; some would dedicate their lives to the Church as priests, monks or nuns, while others were prepared to kill for it.

But why was the Church so important in people's lives? This section of the book will look at:

- the medieval Christian belief in life after death (the afterlife)

- individuals who dedicated their lives to religion, including priests, monks and nuns

- the influence of religion on medieval ideas.

# Journey to the afterlife

## Learning objectives

- Understand the key features of medieval Christian belief.
- Learn how to use evidence to make claims about the past.

## What do you think?

What do you think most medieval Christians knew about their religion?

**Source A:** A description of people being tortured in purgatory from the story of the knight Owein. It was written in 1184 by an English monk.

Some were hanging from blazing chains by the feet with their heads turned upside down in flames. ... Others were burning in furnaces of sulphur; yet others were frying as if on pans; others were placed on blazing spits which were turned by demons. They were all beaten with whips by demons running in every direction. There one could see all the kinds of torture that one could imagine.

A popular medieval story tells of the knight Owein, who had done many bad deeds in his life. He was worried he would go to hell after he died, so he went to his bishop for help. Owein wanted to do something so challenging that it would make up for all his bad deeds. He chose to visit the afterlife* to find out what awaited him once he died.

He began his journey on a small island, where there was a door to the afterlife. From there, he walked through a dark cave to a place called purgatory*, where he met some angels. They told him he would meet many demons on his journey through purgatory, but if he prayed to Jesus Christ he would survive. If he gave up, he would die and disappear forever.

On his journey, Owein passed through many places of torture (see Figure 2.1), but he asked for Christ's help and survived. Eventually, he reached a bridge that took him over hell to an earthly paradise. Here, he met others who had survived purgatory and told him of heaven. After he had seen the beauty of this paradise, he promised to lead a holy life so that he could return there after death.

# The afterlife

Today, many people do not believe in the afterlife described in Owein's story, but the story was often retold in medieval times to explain what happened when people died. This means it can tell us something about medieval beliefs. The character Owein saw the afterlife, where most people thought their souls* would go when their bodies died.

Their soul was damaged if the person committed a sin, like theft, jealousy or eating too much. However, sins were forgiven by God if the person wanted forgiveness and performed a punishment to make up for them. As a result, the way a person lived their life affected where their soul went after death. They would end up in:

- **hell** if they had committed a mortal sin, like murder, and did not think it was wrong

- **heaven** if they had made up for all their sins during their lifetime

- **purgatory** if they had not yet been forgiven for all their sins.

Most people expected to go to purgatory first, waiting until they had been tortured enough to make up for their sins. After that, they would go to heaven.

## Key terms

**Afterlife*:** The experience some people believe they will have after death.

**Purgatory*:** A place where medieval Christians believed they would be tortured until they had made up for their bad deeds and thoughts. After this, they would go on to heaven.

**Soul*:** Christians believe this is a part of a person that can exist after death. The idea exists in some other world religions too.

**Key**

1 Owein began his journey to purgatory here.
2 Owein travelled through a pitch-black cave to the Magnificent Hall.
3 Angels warned Owein to protect himself by praying to Christ but demons tried to burn him on a fire.
4 The demons showed Owein how they tortured people.
5 The demons strapped Owein to a wheel of fire, then threw him into baths of flame and a well of fire but he escaped.
6 Owein had to cross a thin, slippery bridge to reach paradise, a resting place before heaven.
7 A churchman showed Owein the gateway to heaven.

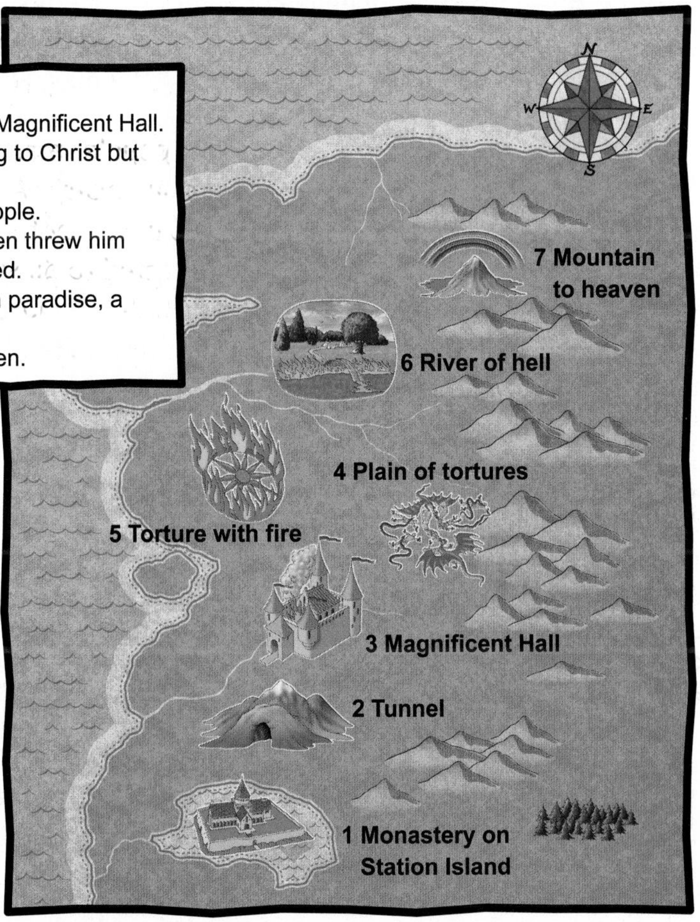

## Your turn!

1 Figure 2.1 retells a popular medieval story. List two things you can learn from it about the afterlife.

2 Source A is a small part of the story. Write a short explanation of why a contemporary source like this is helpful to a historian.

3 Create a question and answer guide for historians about the afterlife. It should include points from the story of Owein's journey.

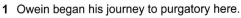

**Figure 2.1:** Knight Owein's journey through purgatory.

7 Mountain to heaven
6 River of hell
4 Plain of tortures
5 Torture with fire
3 Magnificent Hall
2 Tunnel
1 Monastery on Station Island

**Source B:** A 15th-century image of Saint Patrick in purgatory. He is said to have been shown purgatory by God.

## Getting to heaven

To get to heaven Christians believed they had to be forgiven for their sins. This involved confession of their sins to a priest, who would forgive them and give the sinner a penance* to make up for them. The most common penances were fasting*, giving to charity or reading parts of the Bible over and over again.

These penances were supposed to clean their soul of sin, but many worried that they had not done enough, and would spend years being punished in purgatory. To avoid this, they would do good works, giving food to the poor, helping the sick and burying the dead.

Many also went on pilgrimages, which involved a journey to a holy place. Some sites were fairly easy to get to, like Canterbury Cathedral in England, while others were far more difficult. The journey to the monastery* at Mount Sinai, where Moses received the Ten Commandments*, required a difficult trek through the Egyptian desert.

## Power of prayer

Medieval Christians also believed that prayer and religious services could help them. They were expected to attend mass* on Sundays and, if they were rich enough, could pay a priest to say mass for them. Again, it was thought this would help them get to heaven.

### Key terms

**Penance*:** A punishment for sin.

**Fasting*:** A commitment not to eat for either an entire day, or part of the day, or to avoid eating certain foods like meat.

**Monastery*:** The collection of buildings that monks live in.

**Ten Commandments*:** A list of rules given to Moses by God, which Jewish and Christian peoples are expected to obey.

**Mass*:** A Christian religious service performed by a Catholic priest.

**A saint:** ask a saint to protect you from evil.

**A relic:** buy a relic of a saint or biblical figure, or visit the place where one is kept.

**A pilgrimage:** visit a holy site linked to Christ's life, like Jerusalem, or a saint's life, like Canterbury cathedral.

**Seven Works of Mercy:** these include giving to charity, offering shelter, caring for the sick and helping prisoners.

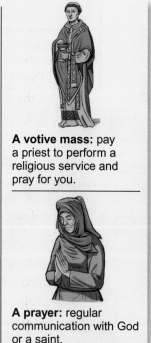

**A votive mass:** pay a priest to perform a religious service and pray for you.

**A prayer:** regular communication with God or a saint.

**Figure 2.2:** Getting to heaven catalogue.

However, people also wanted help on a day-to-day basis. If they were ill, or their crops would not grow, they turned to prayer. Usually, they would pray to a saint for help. These were people who had led holy lives or died for a religious cause. Medieval Christians hoped that, if you could get a saint to pray for you, then God might help by performing a miracle.

## Everyday life

People's beliefs changed the landscape. The desire to go on a pilgrimage meant churches, chapels and shrines* were built for pilgrims to visit. The need to do good works led rich Christians to set up alms* houses for the old and hospitals for the poor and sick. Finally, to ensure support from the local priest, churches were extended or improved using money donated by villagers.

Christian belief also affected people's behaviour. They would:

- **attend church** each week and on holy days: during the service, they heard mass, taking part in an act of worship with their community

- visit or buy **relics**: pieces of a dead saint's body or something they had used, often stored in a reliquary*, which could help to contact the saint

- **leave money or land to the church**: often in exchange for priests praying for them after they had died.

> **Source C:** A charm for curing toothache from *Rosa medicinae*, written by a doctor, John of Gaddesden, between 1305 and 1317.
>
> Also, on any day while the Gospel is being read at mass, as someone listens to the mass he should sign the [sore] tooth and his head with the sign of the cross. And let him say an Our Father and a Hail Mary for the souls of the father and mother of St. Philip. [If he prays] this continuously [as the Gospel is read] it preserves him from future toothache and cures the current one according to trustworthy men.

### Key terms

**Shrine\*:** A place dedicated to a saint. Pilgrims would visit shrines, hoping for a miracle or help after death to reach heaven.

**Alms\*:** A charitable gift to poor people, including money, food or a place to rest.

**Reliquary\*:** A container in which relics were kept.

**Source D:** A reliquary of Saint Foy in Conques, France. Medieval pilgrims who visited her relics believed that she could cure vision problems.

## Your turn!

 1   List evidence from this page that proves the claim that religion was important to medieval people.

 2   Write your own claim about medieval religion that could be proved by the evidence in this section: for example, 'Medieval people believed saints would help them'.

3   Imagine you are the designer of Figure 2.2. Create a front cover for the catalogue, showing why the actions described there were important to medieval people.

## Checkpoint

1   What did medieval Christians believe would lead them to end up in purgatory?

2   Describe two methods Christians used to help them get to heaven.

# Church career options

## Learning objectives

- Understand why priests, monks and nuns were important to medieval people.
- Learn how to use sources to test claims about the past.

**What do you think?**

What do you think the main difference was between a priest and a monk?

**Source A:** From a handbook for parish priests written by a priest called William of Pagula in the 1320s. A cut-down version was written and widely distributed after 1385. It contains a set of instructions for priests.

First he should teach his parishioners the way to baptise infants without a priest if it becomes necessary.

Also he should teach them that no one should marry except in the presence of a priest.

Also he should ask anyone over the age of 14 to confess all his sins to his own parish priest at least once a year and to do the penance given him for his sins.

Also one day during Lent he should publicly preach the key features of Christian belief.

In the modern world, there are hundreds of career options for people who want to help others. If you want to help the sick, you could become a doctor. If you want to help people with their problems, you could become a counsellor. If you want to help the poor, you could join or run a charity.

A thousand years ago, if you wanted to help, you had fewer options. You could work for your local church as a priest, or you could join a religious order* as a monk or nun.

## Option 1: Priests

Most villages had a priest. He ran the local church and dedicated his life to helping his parishioners*. His primary job was to deliver sacraments* (some are shown in Table 2.1), helping his parishioners get to heaven.

All of these duties made a priest a very important person in his village. As such, people came to him for advice and he was expected to help them lead Christian lives (see Source A).

| Job | Details |
| --- | --- |
| Baptising children | A ceremony performed on a child, which meant they would go straight to heaven if they died in their early childhood. |
| Performing marriage ceremonies | Priests made sure that a wedding between a man and a woman obeyed Church law. |
| Performing mass | The main religious service was given on Sundays and parishioners were expected to attend. |
| Hearing confession | A priest would give a penance for the sins committed by a parishioner. |
| Delivering last rites | If a person was close to death, a final ceremony was performed to help them through the afterlife. |

**Table 2.1:** The main duties of a priest, called sacraments.

## Option 2: Monks and nuns

Some men chose to become monks and some women chose to become nuns. They made vows of:

- **poverty:** individual monks and nuns did not own property

- **chastity:** they could not marry or have sex

- **obedience:** they had to obey the abbot or abbess and the rules of their order.

Most also had to make a vow of stability, staying in the same monastery or convent (for nuns) for their entire life.

Figure 2.3 shows some of the different religious orders people joined. They did so for many reasons, but the most important were:

- **to live a religious life** and stand a better chance of getting to heaven

- **to get a comfortable job**: rich people would pay monks and nuns to pray for them

- **to have a safe place to live**: the children of nobles were sometimes taken in and educated at convents and monasteries.

### Key terms

**Religious order\*:** A group of monks or nuns, who live their life according to guidance written by their founder.

**Parishioner\*:** A person who lived in a priest's parish (the area for which he provided services).

**Sacraments\*:** The ceremonial actions of a priest or bishop. There are seven sacraments, including baptism and marriage.

**Benedictine**
**Type:** Men and women of all ages.
**Lifestyle:** Most of the day spent in prayer, but plenty of time for eating, resting and reading.

**Anchorite**
**Type:** Mostly older women.
**Lifestyle:** Lived in a small building attached to a church, praying and reading.

**Franciscan**
**Type:** Mainly adult men, but non-preaching women allowed in separate convents.
**Lifestyle:** Walked around towns to preach. Begged for food and shelter.

**Gilbertine**
**Type:** Women in charge, but men allowed to live separately.
**Lifestyle:** Similar to Benedictines, but spent more time on education for the nuns.

**Cistercian**
**Type:** Mainly adult men, but some women were allowed later in its history.
**Lifestyle:** A very simple life, with most of the day spent farming or praying.

**Carthusian**
**Type:** Mostly adult men, but some women.
**Lifestyle:** Lived mostly alone in a cell, spending their day working on their own projects.

**Figure 2.3:** Types of monks and nuns.

### Your turn!

1. Use Source A to sum up in two words the main jobs a parish priest did for their community.

2. Listed below are some different reasons why individuals chose to become a monk or a nun:
   a. 'My children have grown up and I want to dedicate my last years to God.'
   b. 'My family are rich merchants, but I'm worried being rich will encourage me to sin.'
   c. 'I am the son of a nobleman, but my older brother will inherit all the land. I want a comfortable life.'
   d. 'I am a quiet person and want to dedicate my talents to God.'
   Copy the list and match each point to an appropriate religious order (see Figure 2.3) and give reasons for your choice.

## Your turn!

4th Look at Figure 2.4. List the sorts of things that happened in a monastery.

## Life in a monastery or convent

Most monks and nuns spent their day in silence and within the walls of their order, getting up at midnight to read the first prayer of the day. The rest of their day was organised around eating, sleeping, studying and reading more prayers.

Monks and nuns used their spare time to do jobs, like growing food or writing religious and historical books (see page 15). They were also expected to help the sick and look after travellers. However, as more and more people expected monks and nuns to pray for them and look after them, they had to get lay brothers\* and lay sisters\* to do some of these jobs.

## Helping the local community

By the end of the medieval period, monks spent most of their time saying masses for the dead. It was believed this would help shorten their time in purgatory. Although women were not allowed to do this, both monks and nuns did do two other important jobs.

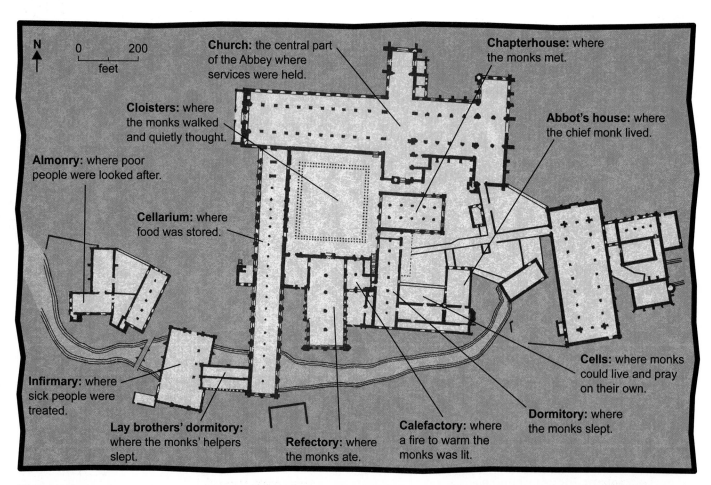

N

0    200

feet

**Church:** the central part of the Abbey where services were held.

**Chapterhouse:** where the monks met.

**Cloisters:** where the monks walked and quietly thought.

**Abbot's house:** where the chief monk lived.

**Almonry:** where poor people were looked after.

**Cellarium:** where food was stored.

**Cells:** where monks could live and pray on their own.

**Infirmary:** where sick people were treated.

**Lay brothers' dormitory:** where the monks' helpers slept.

**Refectory:** where the monks ate.

**Calefactory:** where a fire to warm the monks was lit.

**Dormitory:** where the monks slept.

**Figure 2.4:** Plan of a medieval Cistercian monastery called Fountains Abbey, outside the city of York.

- Firstly, they provided care for the sick, elderly and terminally ill. These were not like modern hospitals, where doctors give prescriptions and pharmacists make medicines. Instead, they were more like places of rest, where some people recovered and others died.

- Secondly, monks and nuns performed good works. They were expected to treat the poor and travellers as if they were Jesus Christ. As a result, they gave food to the poor who came to their gates and they provided a bed for the night to travellers who were far from home. Figure 2.5 shows some of the other services they provided.

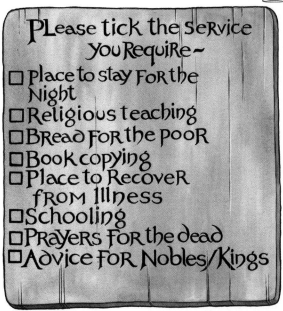

**Figure 2.5:** Services provided by monks and nuns.

> **Interpretation 1:** From *The Medieval Realms*, written by Nigel Kelly and published in 1991.
>
> The monks could read and write. They produced most of the books. Books were written, or copied, by hand and decorated. Many monasteries had schools, mostly for the children of the nobility. So they could influence powerful people from an early age. Also, many monks were from rich families; they could influence their relations. There were no hospitals at the time. Often it was the monks who cared for the sick. They grew herbs, and kept records of cures that worked. They also helped the poor and sheltered travellers.

**Source B:** A 13th-century picture of monks, from a Spanish monastery, offering a traveller a place to stay.

## Your turn!

1 The historian who wrote Interpretation 1 gives a reason why monasteries were important. Write down what you think it is.

2 Make a bullet-point list of contemporary sources that a historian might use to support or challenge your previous answer.

## Checkpoint

1 Who performed sacraments for their local community?

2 Which religious order gave women the most important roles?

3 What jobs did monks and nuns do for their local community?

# Religion and ideas

## Learning objectives

- Understand how religion influenced ideas about crime, science, medicine, warfare, society and architecture.
- Learn how to use a source to make an inference.

## What do you think?

What do you think medieval people wanted God's help for?

## Did you know?

**A famous trial by ordeal**

One story tells of Queen Emma, the mother of Edward the Confessor, who was not popular with the king's advisers. To get her out of the way, an earl accused her of adultery and Edward agreed to put her on trial. To prove her innocence, she chose a trial by iron, walking across nine red hot irons. She did so without even noticing. Edward was convinced of her innocence, fell to his knees and begged her forgiveness.

The way medieval people saw the world was different from today. If you committed a crime, God would judge you. If you became ill, God might cure you. And, if you went to war, God might help you. As a result, it was important to get God's support. This is why people prayed, went on pilgrimages and paid for the building of magnificent churches.

## Crime

Sometimes medieval people asked God to judge a criminal in a trial by ordeal. The accused had to take part in a physical test to prove their innocence. During the trial, God would show his verdict in different ways. For example, in a trial by combat, he would help the innocent or weaken the guilty.

**Trial by hot water or iron**
The accused puts their hand in boiling water, or holds a red-hot iron bar. Their hand is then bandaged.
**Innocent:** hand heals instantly, or has begun to heal after three days.
**Guilty:** burn is infected.

**Trial by cold water**
The accused is tied to a rope and thrown into cold water.
**Innocent:** sinks into water.
**Guilty:** floats.

**Trial by combat**
The accused fights his accuser. They are armed with weapons that have been kept in a church overnight.
**Innocent:** accused kills the accuser or forces them to give up.
**Guilty:** accused is killed or gives up.

**Figure 2.6:** Common types of trial by ordeal.

## Your turn!

4th Medieval people thought trial by ordeal was fair. Write a short explanation of the religious belief they held that meant they thought it was fair.

## Science

Medieval Christians believed that God created the world. When he did so, he set up natural laws for the world to follow. Chickens would lay eggs, sheep would grow wool and apple trees would grow apples. A medieval scientist would not ask *how* they did this but, instead, asked *why*. Christians would look for the purpose God had given a plant or animal. For instance, a sheep might grow wool for people to wear and a tree would grow apples for them to eat.

Instead of looking for scientific explanations, like evolution and photosynthesis, medieval people looked to God for explanations.

## Medicine

After God had created the world, medieval Christians believed, he continued to take an active role in it. If he chose to, God might act directly and perform a miracle. He could cure a headache, give sight to the blind or help a paralysed man walk. People prayed, or visited shrines, hoping for such miracles.

God was also believed to be responsible for disease. Leprosy*, for example, was seen as a punishment for sin. As a result, lepers were separated for religious reasons from their community. They would have to view mass through a special lepers' window in church, or carry a bell to warn people they were coming. Some were even forced to live in separate leper communities.

**Did you know?**

Christianity affected how medieval people thought the universe was organised. They believed that below the ground was hell and above them was a zone called 'the sphere of the Moon'. Further out from this were the planets, including the Sun and the Moon. Above them were the stars, a layer of sky called 'the firmament' and finally heaven itself.

Why do you think Christianity had such a big effect on the way people mapped out the universe?

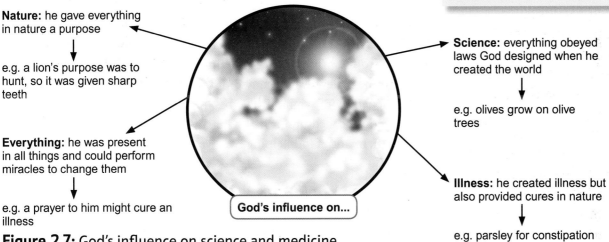

**Nature:** he gave everything in nature a purpose

e.g. a lion's purpose was to hunt, so it was given sharp teeth

**Everything:** he was present in all things and could perform miracles to change them

e.g. a prayer to him might cure an illness

**Science:** everything obeyed laws God designed when he created the world

e.g. olives grow on olive trees

**Illness:** he created illness but also provided cures in nature

e.g. parsley for constipation

**God's influence on...**

**Figure 2.7:** God's influence on science and medicine.

**Your turn!**

 **1** Write a medieval explanation for one of the following:
  **a** humps on a camel
  **b** use of willow bark (which contains aspirin) as a cure for headaches
  **c** a paralysed man who is able to walk again.

**2** Medieval people believed God set some things up so that they continued without his interference, while at other times he took an active part in the world.
  **a** List two examples of things medieval people thought God had set up.
 **b** List two examples of the belief that God acted directly in the world.

**Key term**

**Leprosy*:** A disease affecting the skin and nerves that can cause lumps to appear on the skin and result in the loss of body parts like fingers and toes.

Is it the enemy's fault? Have they done you harm? Yes/No

Is it approved by your monarch or pope? Yes/No

Are you doing it to help others? Yes/No

If you answered 'Yes' to all of the above, then the Church approves of your war.

[Terms and conditions: you may still have to do penance for any violence used during the war.]

**Figure 2.8:** Church checklist for war.

### Key term

**Just war*:** A Church theory about what made a war acceptable in the eyes of God. A holy war, or crusade, was considered just, but it had a religious purpose too.

### Your turn!

You can use sources to make inferences. This means you go beyond what the source *says* to what it *suggests*.

1 Read Source A. Sum up what it says in one sentence.

2 Explain what you could learn about what medieval people thought about God's role in a battle from the source.

## Warfare

Warfare was very common in medieval times. The Church could not stop people from fighting, so it came up with the idea of a 'just' war* (see Figure 2.8) to try and control it. If a war was just, the pope might give it his blessing. For example, the pope blessed William of Normandy's invasion of England in 1066, so his knights believed God would help them.

To many medieval knights, such help was essential. They would carry relics into battle, hoping these would provide them with practical support. For instance, at the Battle of Antioch in 1098 (see Figure 3.8 on pages 86–87), God reportedly sent saints to help the Christians defeat their enemy (see Source A). Such stories encouraged people to believe that God would interfere in events on Earth.

**Source A:** From the *Gesta Francorum*, an account of a battle fought during the First Crusade, written around 1100 by one of the crusaders.

There came out from the mountains armies with white horses, whose flags were all white. When our leaders saw this army, they recognized the help from Christ, led by St. George, Mercurius and Demetrius. This is to be believed, for many of our men saw it. These men, strengthened by the sign of the cross, together attacked the enemy first. Then we called upon the Living and True God and charged against them and, God helping, we overcame them.

## Structure of society

The feudal system (see page 42) helped organise the leaders and workers of society, but Christianity divided its members into two halves. The first half was called 'the clergy', which was led by the pope. Other members of the clergy included bishops, priests, monks and nuns. They organised the Church, ran its services and prayed for people's souls.

The other half of society was called 'the laity', which was divided into communities led by kings or emperors. Their power over day-to-day issues like law and order was authorised in the Bible, although they were supposed to obey the pope too. Other laymen included lords, who led, knights, who fought, and peasants, who worked.

## Religious architecture

Examples of Christian architecture can still be found across the landscape today. For example, simple stone crosses (see Source B) were built as waymarkers, pointing out the path for travellers, while at the same time reminding them of their faith. Around 350 examples can still be found in England today.

## Parish churches

Rich and poor Christians donated money to help build a local church. These were often stone buildings split into two parts. On one side was the nave, where parishioners stood during services. On the other was the chancel, where the priests performed the mass.

During the medieval period, parish churches grew larger. Inside, they contained features like stained glass windows illustrating Bible stories, to help people understand their faith better.

## Cathedrals

The most important churches were called cathedrals or minsters. These had more features, including:

- **a choir:** this separated the parishioners and the priest saying mass

- **side chapels:** often dedicated to important saints

- **accommodation:** for a bishop or other cathedral clergy

- **a large tower:** with bells to celebrate services and summon people to church.

**Source B:** A medieval stone cross near Edale, on Kinder Scout, in the Peak District. Its main purpose was religious, but it also helped show travellers they were on the correct route over the mountain.

### Your turn!

4th Imagine you are a rich lord who has decided to pay for a new church to be built. Create a design brief for the building that considers: how big or small it should be, what images you want, any extra chapels and who will use it. Explain your reasons.

### Checkpoint

1 How did medieval people believe God would demonstrate a criminal's guilt?

2 List two ways medieval people thought God might help them.

3 What impact did religion have on the landscape of England?

# Why was the Church so important in people's lives?

In a group, divide up the following roles between you: peasant, monk/nun, knight, criminal and architect. Write a one-sentence answer to the enquiry question from your chosen point of view.

Read out your sentences to each other. Then write an explanation for why the Church was central to a range of people's lives.

# What have you learned?

In this section, you have learned:

- about medieval religious beliefs, the different people who joined the Church and the influence of religion on ideas

- how evidence can be used to make inferences and test claims about the past.

Inference and utility questions

**Source A:** From the memoirs of Abbot Guibert of Nogent, written around 1112. In this excerpt he describes a tour around France and England, displaying the relics at Laon Cathedral.

There was a woman who had married as a little girl, and had worn the ring placed on her finger without ever taking it off. As years went by, her flesh had almost covered the metal, and she had given up all hope of getting it off. When the relics came to her city and she went to make her offering, as she held out her hand to place the money on the relics, the ring slipped from her hand. When the people saw that the Virgin Mary had helped the woman, the offering of money was beyond description.

## What is reliability?

Reliability means how much you trust someone or something. In everyday life, the reliability of something is seen in quite a simple way. For example, a person might say a car that breaks down on long journeys is unreliable. To a historian, reliability can change depending on purpose. A historian would say a car they need for short journeys is reliable even if it breaks down on long journeys.

## Bias

Reliability can be affected by bias. This means that your point of view might affect what you say. For example, if you love where you live, you might tell someone it is amazing. They might visit your local area and disagree. However, just because a person might be biased, it does not make them unreliable. In fact, your view could help historians infer reliably what residents think about your local area. What it does not do is give an idea of what people from outside your area might think.

### Your turn!

1 Source A is biased towards the belief that relics have healing powers. Write a short explanation of why it cannot tell historians the truth about the healing powers of relics.

2 Write an explanation of why the source could be reliable in telling historians about what medieval people believed relics could do.

3 Write down one other question the source could answer reliably even though it has an obvious bias.

# Writing historically

You are going to improve an answer to the question 'Give two things you can infer reliably from Source A about the popularity of the medieval Church.' This is an inference question, so it is asking you what the source suggests. It also asks you to make inferences that are reliable. The activities on this page will help improve your ability to use evidence in your answers.

## A basic answer

A basic answer will look for true and false information in a source and begin to comment on its reliability. Look at the example answer below and try to improve it, using the suggestion provided.

> Source A is unreliable. The writer is biased towards the belief that the relics could perform miracles. This means he may have exaggerated or made up the story of the ring slipping off the woman's hand. It is therefore difficult to infer anything reliably. However, Source A does tell you that...

Now finish this paragraph, adding some information from Source A that might be true or false.

## Improving the answer

A better answer will not try to identify true or false information and it will not focus on the idea of bias. Instead, an answer will show an understanding that a historian can:

• take evidence from a source to support a claim they can reliably make from it

• go through a process of interrogation to find ways in which a source can be used reliably.

Look at the example answer below to see how this can be done.

> Source A can reliably tell us about the popularity of the medieval Church. It describes how the relics of Laon Cathedral went on a tour around England and France, which suggests that lots of people wanted to see them. Even though Guibert of Nogent was biased towards the relics having the power to heal, it is unlikely that he made up the tour itself.

## Your improved answer

Create your own improved answer. Try to include something from the content of the source and use it to make a reliable inference. You could begin your answer with:

> Another inference you could make from Source A is ...

Your improved answer should have an inference, evidence selected from the source and an explanation of why this is reliable.

Look through your answer and label these features. Compare your answer with a partner's and discuss the similarities and differences between them.

# Why was the Archbishop of Canterbury murdered?

King Henry II (reigned 1154–89) and Thomas Becket were close friends, but their friendship was destroyed by an argument over the Church when Henry appointed Thomas to be Archbishop of Canterbury. Henry wanted the state to have more power to control the Church and thought his friend, Thomas, would help. However, Thomas refused. It was a refusal that ended in his murder, shocking Christians throughout Europe.

But why was Thomas murdered? This section of the book will look at:

- the breakdown of the relationship between Henry II and Thomas Becket

- the story of Thomas Becket's murder and the reasons for it.

## Henry and Thomas argue

**What do you think?**

Why do you think the king would want to control the Church?

### Learning objectives

- Understand how the relationship between Henry II and Thomas Becket changed over time.
- Learn how to identify a number of causes and begin to categorise them.

**Key term**

Chancellor*: The king's chief servant. The chancellor had many jobs, including writing important documents, managing royal finances and judging some legal cases.

Look at Source A. It is a reliquary containing the remains of Thomas Becket. It is a beautiful box, showing just how important he was. But how did Thomas end up in such a box?

## Becoming archbishop

**1154:** Thomas is appointed royal chancellor. The two men become close friends.

**1154–1162:** Thomas lives a luxurious lifestyle working for the king. He even fights for him in France.

**1162:** Henry asks Thomas to become Archbishop of Canterbury. Thomas begins to live a more holy lifestyle. He studies religion and wears a hair shirt under his clothes.

**1162:** Thomas resigns as chancellor without asking Henry's permission. Henry is angry.

**1163:** Henry and Thomas begin to argue, first about a new tax Henry wants to raise.

**Figure 2.9:** The relationship between Henry II and Thomas Becket.

Thomas Becket's story begins at Christmas 1154. Around this time, King Henry II of England made Thomas his chancellor*. The pair quickly became close friends and Thomas, the son of a merchant, enjoyed a lifestyle beyond his wildest dreams. He had six ships kept ready to transport his personal belongings and even had his own travelling zoo.

As chancellor, Thomas had an exciting job. He helped manage the king's lands and fought in battle for him.

These actions proved to Henry that Thomas was very talented. As a result, Henry decided to use him to take control of the Church, which had powers Henry wanted to limit. When the Archbishop of Canterbury died in 1161, Henry asked Thomas to take on the role, but it took him months to give an answer. In the end, he accepted the job, but made it clear he would not be Henry's puppet.

**Source A:** A reliquary from around 1190, containing the remains of Thomas Becket.

## Early signs of trouble

Right from the start, there were signs that Henry and Thomas's friendship was in trouble. Henry had a fierce temper, expecting complete loyalty from his men. In contrast, Thomas was calmer but refused to do anything he disagreed with. For example, five months after becoming archbishop, Thomas gave up the chancellorship, believing he could not do both jobs. Henry disagreed and was furious, but Thomas did not change his mind.

**Source B:** From the chronicle of William Fitzstephen, a clerk who worked for both Henry II and Thomas Becket. It was written in 1173–74.

Thomas and the king would play together like young boys of the same age, in the hall, in church, in court and out riding. One day they were riding together through the streets of London. At a distance the king saw a poor old man and he said to Thomas, 'Wouldn't it be a great act of charity to give him a warm cape? To be sure, this great act of charity will be yours!', and taking hold of his hood, the king tried to pull off [Thomas's] fine new [cloak]. Eventually, Thomas gave up and let him take it.

### Your turn!

1. In groups of four, take the following roles: Henry II, Thomas Becket, Henry's inner voice and Thomas's inner voice. Plan and perform a role play in which Henry asks Thomas to become archbishop. The inner voice characters should say what Henry and Thomas are really thinking.

2. Create a table with two columns: 'Signs of a strong relationship' and 'Signs of a weak relationship'. Study Source B. Use the information in this source and on pages 62–63 to provide examples that show each type of relationship.

3. Based on your table, predict what Thomas and Henry may argue over in the future.

## Key terms

**Anoint\*:** To give spiritual power to a monarch or priest by pouring holy oil on them.

**Criminous clerk\*:** Any churchman, including priests and their assistants, who had committed a crime. They could claim the right to be tried in a Church court.

**Excommunication\*:** When a person is banned from church services and Christian burial. A medieval person believed they were at greater risk of going to hell if they died as an excommunicant.

**Legate\*:** A representative of the pope, with a lot of power. A legate could remove a bishop from their job and issue sentences of excommunication without asking the pope.

## Your turn!

**3rd** **1** Look at Figure 2.10. Make a bullet-point list of six things the head of state and head of the Church might argue over.

**4th** **2** Sort the six things you listed into two categories: related to money or to power.

**5th** **3** Identify one of the three that is to do with both money and power. Write a short explanation for your decision.

## Church and state

In medieval times, England was run by two separate powers: the Church and the state. The Church was led by the Archbishop of Canterbury, who ruled over bishops, priests, monks and nuns. The archbishop was responsible to the pope, but had a lot of money and power of his own because the Church owned so much land in England.

The other major power was the state. This was led by the king, who had barons to help him run the country. In theory, the king was answerable to no one except God. He also owned a huge amount of land, which provided him with some of the money he needed to run the country. Figure 2.10 shows the main rights and powers the Church and state each had.

The Church and state were also closely related. For example, the Church had the power to crown and anoint\* the king of England and the king usually chose people for the most important jobs in the Church. This overlapping power is what led to Henry and Thomas's biggest fall-out.

## Argument over the power of the Church

Henry and Thomas's argument was about power. Henry wanted more power over the Church, but Thomas would not give it to him.

**Job:** head of state

**Role:** to run the country

**Rights:**
- to try criminals
- to make laws
- to tax people
- to wage war
- to choose officials for powerful and well-paid jobs, including the archbishop.

**Power:** use physical force, for example using armed knights, to get own way

**Job:** head of the Church

**Role:** to run the Church and its lands

**Rights:**
- to try Church criminals
- to enforce religious law, for example over marriage cases
- to make money from Church lands
- to decide if a war is just
- to choose who gets powerful and well-paid jobs in the Church

**Power:** use religious force, like excommunication, to get own way

**Figure 2.10:** The relationship between Church and state.

Henry and Thomas argued over:

- who should **appoint churchmen**: Thomas thought the archbishop and pope should decide, Henry thought he should choose

- the right to **judge criminous clerks***: Henry wanted churchmen to be tried in the royal court, rather than the Church court; he thought their punishments were not harsh enough

- sentences of **excommunication***: Henry wanted the power to stop an excommunication of his barons, which could be issued by the pope, or his legate*.

The timeline shows how this argument developed between 1164 and 1170, destroying the friendship between Henry and Thomas.

## Timeline

**January 1164** Henry proposes limits on church power. Thomas agrees, but refuses to sign the documents.

**November 1164** Thomas meets the pope and is permitted to break his January promises.

**March 1170** Henry has his son crowned without Thomas conducting the ceremony.

**October 1164** Henry puts Thomas on trial for treason, but Thomas flees to France before the sentence is delivered.

**May 1166** The pope gives Thomas the power to excommunicate people. Thomas uses this power against some of Henry's supporters.

**July 1170** After the threat of excommunication, Henry finally makes peace with Thomas.

## Your turn!

1 Imagine it is now July 1170. Add a second scene to your role play from the activity on page 63.

2 After you have performed and watched the role plays, write a summary of what Henry and Thomas argued over.

**Figure 2.11:** The argument between Henry and Thomas.

## Checkpoint

1 What job did Henry want Thomas to accept in 1162?

2 Who was head of the Church and who was head of the state?

3 How did the pope help Thomas gain power over Henry?

4 What was the main reason Thomas and Henry fell out, and why was it important?

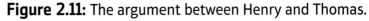

**Source C:** An illustration from a biography of Thomas Becket. It shows Thomas issuing a sentence of excommunication and arguing his case to Henry II and the French king, Louis VII.

# Murder of Thomas Becket

**Learning objectives**

- Understand the events of Thomas Becket's murder and the reasons that led to it.
- Learn how to plan and write up a narrative with supporting factual information.

**What do you think?**

What do you think would cause four knights to murder Thomas Becket?

## 1170: the year of the murder

On 24 November 1170, Thomas made the decision that would lead to his murder. He excommunicated the three bishops who had crowned and anointed Henry II's son, Prince Henry. If the king found out, he would be furious, as the bishops were acting on his orders.

However, in the short term, Thomas was safe in his palace at Canterbury. The bishops had chosen not to tell Henry straight away. Instead, they tried to have Thomas arrested in England for a made-up crime of planning a revolt against Prince Henry. When this plan failed, due to Thomas's popularity with the people of England, the three bishops set sail for France to speak to Henry II directly.

As soon as they arrived, on 21 December, they told the king that they had been excommunicated and that Thomas was planning a revolt. A day later, the king met with his barons and other knights and went into a rage. Legend says that he shouted 'Who will rid me of this turbulent priest?' and that four knights overheard him. Although we do not know for sure what he actually said, the four knights misunderstood his words. They thought he wanted Thomas murdered and set off to England.

**Source A:** From a biography of Thomas Becket written by Garnier of Pont-Sainte-Maxence, a travelling poet, in 1174. In this part of the story, Henry has just been told that Thomas has suspended his bishops.

'A man', the king said to them, 'who has eaten my bread, who came to me poor, and I have raised him high – now he draws up his heel to kick me in the teeth! He has shamed my family, shamed my kingdom; the grief goes to my heart, and no one has avenged me!' Then the whole court stirred and murmured; they began to blame themselves severely and to utter fierce threats against the holy archbishop. Several men started to join together by oath to take vengeance for the king.

## Murder in Canterbury Cathedral

On Tuesday afternoon, 29 December 1170, four knights burst into the Archbishop's Palace in Canterbury. Finding Thomas at his dinner table, they demanded he leave England forever. Thomas refused and the knights stormed out in anger.

Once outside, they began to arm themselves. At the same time, Thomas headed into the cathedral for a service. The monks, fearing that Thomas's life was in danger, tried to block the door, but the archbishop ordered it to be left open.

A few minutes later, the knights rushed in. Seeing their weapons, Thomas insisted that they leave his monks and clerks alone. In reply, they commanded him to go outside, but he refused, clinging on to a pillar. Realising he would not leave, the knights struck him five times, cutting off the top of his head. Then, as they left, one scooped out his brains and smeared them on the floor.

**Source B:** An illustration from the *Life of St. Thomas Becket*, c. 1180. It shows the arrival of the knights (top), the murder (bottom left) and the knights praying for forgiveness (bottom right).

**Source C:** An eyewitness account of the murder by Edward Grim, a clerk who was visiting Canterbury at the time. It was written between 1171 and 1172.

As he lay on the floor, the third knight struck Thomas with his sword. With this blow the crown, which was large, was separated from the head, so that the blood brightened the floor. The fourth knight held off those arriving on the scene so that the others could continue the murder. But the fifth, not a knight but a clerk, put his foot on the neck of the precious martyr, and scattered the brains with the blood over the pavement. 'Let us go, knights,' he called out, 'this fellow will not get up again.'

### Your turn!

1. In groups of three, recreate one of the three scenes in Source B. Each person should take on a different role and plan a short speech, explaining what they are thinking in the snapshot.

2. Join up with two other groups (covering the other two scenes) and present your snapshots to each other. Each character should take it in turns to come to life and give their speech.

3. Draw an earlier scene, using page 66 to help, showing another event leading to the murder.

## Key term

**Council\*:** A meeting of important officials. In medieval times, a council might include the king, members of his household, the barons and the bishops.

**Source D:** An early 14th-century picture of Henry II and Thomas Becket arguing.

## Why was Thomas murdered?

The short-term cause of Thomas's murder was a misunderstanding. Henry was furious that his bishops had been excommunicated and held a council\* to discuss Thomas's future (see Figure 2.12). During the meeting, four ambitious knights misinterpreted Henry's words as an order to kill Thomas.

However, this was only the immediate trigger for the murder. In the longer term, it was the argument between the Church and state that had led to it. Thomas's attempt to try and stop the king from taking power from the Church had resulted in Thomas fleeing to France, meeting with the pope and deciding to excommunicate the bishops. Without this background argument, Henry would have had no reason for his angry rant in December 1170.

## What happened afterwards?

The news of Thomas's murder shocked Europe. When Henry found out, he was stunned, locking himself in his room for three days. He knew his words had led to the murder and thought that everyone would blame him, so he asked the pope for forgiveness. To receive this, he had to promise to go on a crusade and give up his fight with the Church. Henry agreed, but he still had to convince his people he was sorry.

To do so, he went on a pilgrimage to Canterbury Cathedral in 1174, walking barefoot into the city.

Once inside the cathedral, Henry approached Thomas's tomb and begged forgiveness. As a penance, the monks and bishops present took it in turns to whip Henry.

**Four knights:** misinterpret Henry's call for vengeance and swear an oath to kill Thomas.

**Henry II:** accuses Thomas of treason and decides to have him arrested. During the council, he calls for revenge in a fit of anger.

**Three bishops:** accuse Thomas of planning to overthrow Henry's son, who had been crowned king.

**Barons:** call for Thomas to be executed or outlawed.

**Figure 2.12:** Events of 22 December 1170.

Once the beatings finished, Henry spent the whole night in prayer, leaving orders that pilgrims should be allowed inside to witness his act of penance. However, Henry was not the only one to be blamed for the murder (see Figure 2.13). There were consequences for the others involved.

- **Knights:** Henry encouraged the four knights to leave England and visit the pope. After that, they went to the Holy Land to live out their days praying for forgiveness.

- **Bishops:** the three bishops whose words had led to Henry's angry rant had to visit the pope and beg for forgiveness. The pope eventually forgave them.

- **Thomas Becket:** he died as a martyr* and miracles began to be reported at his tomb. As a result, the pope made him a saint in 1173.

**King Henry II**
- Made Thomas archbishop.
- Tried to take power from the Church.
- Called for revenge, leading to the knights' actions.

**Four knights**
- Killed Thomas in his own cathedral.
- Did not act on direct orders from the king.
- Misunderstood the king.

**Who was to blame for Thomas Becket's murder?**

**Thomas Becket**
- Did not ask the king before taking action.
- Refused to back down and give the king more power.
- Took actions that he knew would anger the king.

**Three bishops**
- Helped crown young Prince Henry without Thomas's permission.
- Lied about Thomas's plan to revolt.
- Refused an offer of a pardon from Thomas.

**Figure 2.13:** Who was to blame?

## Key term

**Martyr*:** A person who dies for their faith. A martyr could become a saint if the pope approved and miracles were linked to them.

## Your turn!

**3rd 1** Create a sequence of labels arranged like a timeline: Thomas becomes archbishop, Thomas flees to France, Thomas returns to England, Thomas is murdered and Henry goes to Canterbury.

**3rd 2** Fill in the gaps between these labels with any events from pages 62–68. There is no need to include specific dates.

**4th 3** Use your sequence to write the story of Thomas Becket's murder.

## Checkpoint

1 What does 'excommunicate' mean?

2 Where was Thomas murdered?

3 Who misunderstood Henry's demand for vengeance?

4 Who was most to blame for the murder and why?

# Why was the Archbishop of Canterbury murdered?

Imagine you could interview Henry II about the murder of Thomas Becket. In a group, think of three questions you would ask Henry to find out why the murder took place.

Swap your questions with another group. Try to guess what Henry II might say. Use your answers to write a brief judgement to explain why you think Thomas was murdered and send it back to the other group.

# Did the Church make everyone good?

In medieval times, people believed the Church controlled who went to heaven and who went to hell. It told them what to believe and how to behave. However, it would be a mistake to think everyone listened. Rulers fought popes, religious groups challenged Christian beliefs and many ordinary people called on magic for help or to do harm.

So did the Church make everyone good? This section of the book will look at:

- the limits to the Church's power over individuals, including ordinary people, criminals and rulers

- the way some people led unChristian lives.

# Limits to Church power

## Learning objectives

- Understand the limits to the power of the Church over individuals.
- Learn how to interrogate information with a particular purpose.

## What do you think?

Why do you think the monarch might have more power over individuals in their kingdom than the Church?

## Key terms

**Secular\*:** Not related to religious matters.

**Sanctuary\*:** A place of safety; a criminal could claim sanctuary in a church for 40 days, protecting them from arrest.

**Jury\*:** A group of local men who were considered respectable and owned land.

**Pillory\*:** A post to which a criminal was attached by the neck and hands. They were usually put in marketplaces where people could throw things at the criminal.

**Branded\*:** A mark (such as 'T' for a thief) was burnt onto the hand with a hot iron.

In 1285, Walter Eghe was put on trial for theft in a secular* court. He was found guilty and sentenced to hanging. Shortly afterwards, he was hanged and then taken to a local church for burial. However, there was a slight problem. Somehow Walter was still alive.

He took sanctuary* in the church for over a month. Inside its walls, he was safe from the king's judges. In the meantime, his friends tried to get him a royal pardon. They succeeded. As far as the king was concerned, God had given his judgement. How could the king argue with that?

## Who had more power over the individual?

The story of Walter Eghe suggests the Church was all-powerful, but this was not really the case. After all, it was the king, not a churchman, who decided to give Walter the pardon. He was in charge of the justice system and most criminals had their trials in his courts.

## Power of the state

A person suspected of a crime was reported to a local jury*. They would tell the king's judges, who then placed the accused on trial. They would usually receive a trial by jury. If found guilty, punishments included being fined, placed in the pillory*, imprisoned, branded*, mutilated or executed. Only those who could prove they were clerics could escape the king's courts.

# Power of the Church

The Church's main power was over priests, monks, nuns and others who had been ordained*. Thomas Becket had protected the Church's power to try criminous clerks (see pages 64–65 and Figure 2.10), making their maximum punishment life imprisonment in a monastery.

**Philip de Broi**

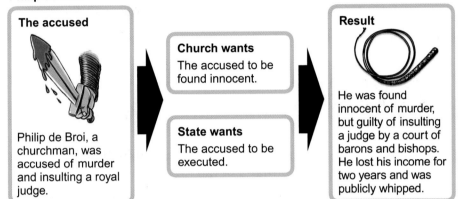

**The accused**

Philip de Broi, a churchman, was accused of murder and insulting a royal judge.

**Church wants**
The accused to be found innocent.

**State wants**
The accused to be executed.

**Result**

He was found innocent of murder, but guilty of insulting a judge by a court of barons and bishops. He lost his income for two years and was publicly whipped.

**Figure 2.14:** A famous church court case during Henry II's reign.

However, the Church did have some authority over other individuals. Its courts handled moral crimes, like sex outside marriage and adultery*. They also had power to decide on issues of marriage law and what happened to a person's property after death. A typical punishment issued by the Church courts was public penance, which meant standing in the church, dressed only in your underwear, holding a lit candle.

## Key terms

**Ordained*:** Clerics who had taken part in a ceremony which allowed them to perform the sacraments.

**Adultery*:** Sex between a married person and someone who is not their husband or wife. It was punished with a whipping in a public place.

## Did you know?

The Church would not protect everyone. In 1322, Isabella Bury killed a clerk in a London church. She claimed sanctuary in the church, but the bishop denied it. She was put on trial and hanged for her crime.

**Interpretation 1:** From *Religion in the Medieval West* by Bernard Hamilton, written in 1986.

The church continued to make a considerable impact on the everyday activities of lay people. All the rural population paid tithe [a Church tax] to support it, while church law, administered by the church courts, affected everybody because it regulated marriage, the making of wills and public behaviour. In addition a high proportion of the rural population lived on church land.

## Your turn!

1   Look at the court case in Figure 2.14. What evidence does it provide that the Church was important in medieval society? Write a short explanation.

2   Read Interpretation 1. Pick one piece of evidence the historian uses to prove the Church was important. Explain how it proves the Church was important.

3   Create a table with two columns: 'Evidence that suggests the Church was important' and 'Evidence that suggests the Church was not important'. Look back through this chapter and find evidence to add to your table.

## Key terms

**Fornicator\*:** A person who has sex outside of marriage.

**Deadly sin\*:** The Church organised sins into seven categories: pride, envy, anger, sloth (laziness), greed, gluttony and lust.

**Gluttony\*:** Eating or drinking too much.

**Heretic\*:** A person with religious views that disagree with official Church teaching.

**Adjuration\*:** A command ordering sickness or a demon to leave a sufferer.

**Leechbook\*:** A medical textbook containing natural remedies, magical charms and rituals used by medieval healers, known as leeches.

**Source A:** A magical prescription for skin disease from the *Leechbook of Bald*. It was written in the tenth century.

Take goose-fat, and the lower part of [the herbs] elecampane and viper's bugloss, bishop's wort, and cleavers. Pound the four herbs together well, squeeze them out, and add a spoonful of old soap. If you have a little oil, mix it in thoroughly and lather it on at night. Scratch the neck after sunset, and silently pour the blood into running water, spit three times after it, then say, "Take this disease and depart with it." Go back to the house by an open road, and go each way in silence.

## UnChristian lives

Some people did not lead Christian lives. The Church courts spent most of their time punishing fornicators\* and adulterers. Other groups also ignored part of the Church's teachings.

- **Knights:** the Church accused them of the deadly sin\* of taking too much pride in their actions.

- **Rich lords:** they were criticised for the deadly sins of greed and gluttony\*.

- **Priests:** some were absent from their parish church, collecting the income but failing to look after their parishioners. Others had sexual relations with women, which was banned by the Church.

- **Nuns and monks:** some broke their vows. One Gilbertine nun had sex with a lay brother and fell pregnant. As a punishment, she had to live alone and her partner had his testicles removed.

Another group, called heretics\*, also led unChristian lives in the eyes of the Church. They still thought of themselves as Christian, but each different group of heretics had slightly different Christian beliefs, practices or organisation from the official Church. A person convicted of heresy was forced to abandon their beliefs or be burnt at the stake.

## Magicians, diviners and alchemists

The Church disapproved of magic, but that did not stop ordinary people from trying to use it.

- **Healers:** they would gather herbs, applying them to the patient using a magical ritual (see Source A). They also used adjurations\* from leechbooks\* to command diseases to leave the victim.

- **Diviners:** believed they could predict the future from dreams, bird calls, palm readings or dice rolls. Diviners could also help to choose the best day for an event (see Source B).

- **Witches**: most were women, who tried to use black magic to harm people or livestock. They used curses or other magical potions and rituals.

- **Alchemists:** they tried to turn lead into gold. Their science was based on the idea that the planets and metals were somehow connected to each other.

## Defiant kings

Medieval kings believed that they had been chosen by God. This belief gave them spiritual power, which they sometimes used to defy the Church. For example, King Henry II argued with Thomas Becket and the pope over criminous clerks (see pages 64–65). Even though Henry later abandoned some of his demands, he still gained more power over the Church.

1. Magical amulets can protect you from disease or attack.
2. Diviners can predict the future.
3. The planets and stars affect people's actions.
4. Alchemists can turn base metals into gold.
5. Necromancers can summon demons to work for them.

An amulet owned by King Charlemagne, said to contain a fragment of the cross Jesus was crucified on.

**Figure 2.15:** Top five medieval superstitions.

### Your turn!

 1 Use the information on pages 72–73 to add evidence to your table from question 3 on page 71.

 2 Write a report investigating the question: 'Who had more power over the individual: the Church or the state?' Organise it under the headings: 'Criminals', 'People's lives', 'Power'. Add another heading and include it in your report.

### Checkpoint

1 Who might execute a criminal: the Church or the state?

2 Over which type of cases did the Church have power?

3 Name two types of people who might lead unChristian lives and describe what they might do.

4 Why do you think magic was important to medieval people?

**Source B:** An example of medieval fortune-telling from a 15th-century leechbook. It says there are 32 evil days each year and describes what could happen on them.

Whoever weds a wife on any of these days, he shall not long have joy of her. And whoever undertakes any great journey shall never come back again, or some misfortune shall befall him. And he that begins any great work shall never finish it. And he that has a medical operation shall soon die, or never be well.

# Did the Church make everyone good?

Create a table with two columns headed: 'The Church made everyone good' and 'The Church did not make everyone good'. Add evidence to support the claims made in the headings.

Imagine you are a chronicler writing a section on people's behaviour. Use evidence from your table to help write the section, exploring whether the Church made everyone good or not.

# What have you learned?

In this section, you have learned:

- about the argument between King Henry II and Thomas Becket
- the ways in which the power of the Church was limited
- how to categorise causes and plan a narrative.

**Analytical narrative**

## Your turn!

**1** Look at Figure 2.16. Write down the statements in chronological order.

**2** Label each statement as 'long-term cause' (years before), 'short-term cause' (months or days before) or 'outcome' (the event itself).

**3** Look at the phrase bank. Select and use a word or phrase to link a long-term cause from Figure 2.16 to a short-term cause of Becket's murder.

## Quick quiz

1 Where did medieval people believe their souls went after death?

2 Give one example of a job that a medieval person could do to lead a religious life.

3 What might a medieval person carry into battle to help them succeed?

4 Which group of criminals did Henry II want the power to judge?

5 In what year was Thomas Becket murdered?

6 Name one of the seven deadly sins.

## Writing narratives

When historians tell a story about the past, they create analytical narratives. The most important feature is that they are written in chronological order, so that the story makes sense. The narrative is also written in the third person and the past tense, as the historian is not pretending to have seen the events. Instead, they are trying to look back and describe them from an outsider's point of view.

To make their writing analytical, historians do a number of things. This section will explore how they sometimes:

- write about the long-term and short-term causes of an event: they sometimes put a long-term cause first and follow it with a short-term cause that is linked to it

- deal with things that happen at the same time: they show that events overlap with one another, using some of the words in the phrase bank below.

| Phrase bank: words... | | |
| --- | --- | --- |
| ...for the start | ...for events that follow | ...for events that overlap |
| Before | After | At the same time |
| At first | Then | Simultaneously |
| Initially | Later on | Alongside this |

Henry II made Thomas Becket the archbishop to get more power over the Church.

The knights murdered Thomas in Canterbury Cathedral.

The knights demanded Thomas leave England.

Henry went into a rage that four knights misunderstood.

Thomas excommunicated three bishops loyal to Henry.

King Henry II wanted the power to judge criminous clerks and stop excommunications.

**Figure 2.16:** Pieces of the Thomas Becket story.

# Writing historically

You are going to explore how to answer the question 'Write a narrative account of the events in the years 1162–70 leading up to Thomas Becket's murder.' This is asking you to construct a narrative, so you will need to plan your response as shown below.

## Stage 1: creating a plan

The first stage is to pick out the events you want to cover in your narrative, so that you have something to write about. Look at the example plan below and make your own copy, adding in one further event from pages 62–69.

- *1154: Henry makes Thomas the royal chancellor.*

- *1162: Henry asks Thomas to become archbishop.*

- *1164: Henry and Thomas argue, so Thomas flees to France.*

- *1170: Henry and Thomas have another serious argument over excommunications.*

- *1170: Henry's knights murder Thomas in Canterbury Cathedral.*

## Stage 2: checking the plan

A common mistake students make when writing a narrative is choosing the year in which it should start. This question gives a date range, so cross out the event that does not fit in and stick to the range you have been given. Then you are ready to write a basic narrative. This means a simple version of the story like the example below.

> 'King Henry II and Thomas Becket were friends. They argued over the Church. Thomas ran away. They had another argument. This time it was very serious. Thomas was murdered by Henry's knights.'

## Stage 3: improving a simple narrative

To improve your narrative, you need to include detail. Try adding the events from your list:

> 'King Henry II and Thomas Becket were friends. In 1162, Henry decided to make his friend the archbishop of Canterbury. They argued over the Church. In...'

Now finish the narrative, including all the events from your list.

Your narrative probably has a lot of examples of 'in XXXX, this happened'. To improve your answer still further, you need to start to link it together. Use some of the words from the phrase bank, for example:

> 'King Henry II and Thomas were friends. **Then**, in 1162, Henry decided to make his friend the archbishop of Canterbury. **Soon after**, they argued over the Church. **Following that**, in...'

Now try and rewrite your narrative, using some of the ordering words from the phrase bank to help you.

# Why was Jerusalem worth dying for?

In AD 1096, in response to a request by the pope, 60,000 Christians left Europe to try and take Jerusalem from Muslim control. Most were prepared to die on the four-year march they embarked on, in what became known as the First Crusade.

But was Jerusalem worth dying for? This section of the book will look at:

- the rise of the Islamic World and the capture of Jerusalem before the First Crusade

- the threats facing the Byzantine Empire and Jerusalem in the 11th century

- why Christians joined the First Crusade and its consequences for Jerusalem.

# The rise of Islam

## Learning objectives

- Understand the key features of Islamic civilisation during its golden age.
- Use a range of sources to find out about Islamic civilisation.

## What do you think?

What do you already know about Jerusalem?

## Key terms

**Calligraphy\*:** An artistic form of handwriting.

**Mosque\*:** A place of worship for Muslims.

**Caliph\*:** The ruler of an Islamic empire.

**Dynasty\*:** A term for rulers who all come from the same family. The Umayyads set up the first Muslim dynasty and passed on the position of caliph to members of their own family.

**Pilgrim\*:** A person who is on a religious journey. Muslims are expected to go on a pilgrimage to the holy city of Mecca in modern Saudi Arabia at least once in their lifetime.

The Islamic golden age began in the eighth century and continued until the 13th. It was a period of great change in culture, science and technology. Source A is typical of this period. It is an ivory casket from the tenth century used to store jewellery. The images on it are intricately carved, demonstrating many features of Islamic culture such as calligraphy\*, music and exploration.

Buildings that survive from the period can also tell us a lot about the golden age. For example, the Great Mosque\* in Damascus (see Source B), was built in the eighth century. The mosaic on the front shows how skilled the artists were. The design of the mosque, with its dome, arch and courtyard, is typical of Islamic architecture during the period.

## Growth of Islam

The Islamic faith was founded by the prophet Muhammad in the seventh century and he ruled over its followers. When he died in 632, caliphs\* took over the leadership of Muslim people. These rulers first spread Islam to Arabia's tribes and then attacked other countries. By 661, the first dynasty\* was set up, which fought to expand Islamic civilisation even further. By 756, it had grown into a huge empire (see Figure 3.1).

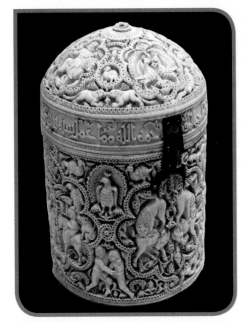

**Source A:** Casket made for a member of the royal family in Islamic Spain in the tenth century.

**Source B:** A mosaic, made from small pieces of glass, on the outside walls of the Great Mosque at Damascus.

## Jerusalem in the golden age

Jerusalem was an important city in the Islamic world. It was conquered by Muslims in 638, who valued it for the following reasons:

- Muhammad is said to have gone on a journey to Jerusalem and then to heaven to see God.

- Many parts of the Jewish and Christian faiths were accepted by Muslims, which meant that Jewish and Christian holy places were important to Muslims too.

- Muslims built the Dome of the Rock in Jerusalem on a site linked to the Christian and Jewish story of Abraham. Muslims saw the story as part of their history, making this a site for pilgrims*.

Jerusalem became an important place for Christians, Jews and Muslims to meet and share ideas. Most of the time, they lived in peace with one another.

**Your turn!**

4th Sources A and B are both sources that historians could use to find out about the Islamic world. List some other types of sources you could use to find out about Islamic culture.

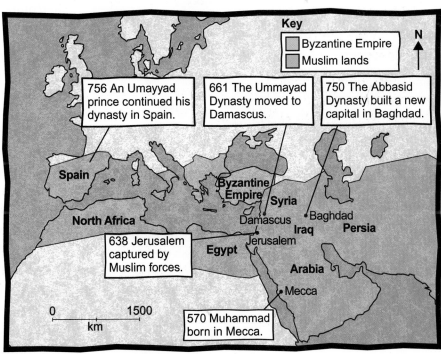

**Figure 3.1:** A map of the Islamic empire in 756.

Key
- Byzantine Empire
- Muslim lands

N

756 An Umayyad prince continued his dynasty in Spain.

661 The Ummayad Dynasty moved to Damascus.

750 The Abbasid Dynasty built a new capital in Baghdad.

Spain

Byzantine Empire

Syria

North Africa

Damascus

Baghdad

Iraq

Persia

Jerusalem

638 Jerusalem captured by Muslim forces.

Egypt

Arabia

Mecca

0    1500
km

570 Muhammad born in Mecca.

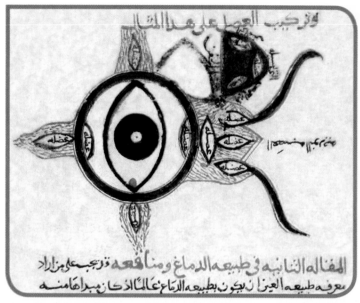

**Source C:** The earliest known medical description of the eye. It was drawn by Hunayn ibn Ishaq, who worked in Baghdad in the ninth century.

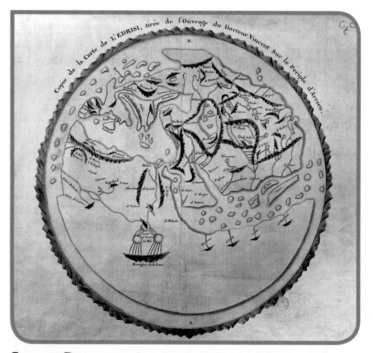

**Source D:** A copy of Muhammad al-Idrisi's map of the world, which was originally produced in the 12th century.

## Top travel destination: Baghdad

Baghdad was built by Abbasid Caliph al-Mansur in 762, who made it the capital of the Islamic world. Travellers and traders came from around the world to visit. They brought their ideas with them. For example, Chinese travellers taught the people of Baghdad to make paper. By 795, the city was the first in the Islamic world to have a paper factory. Other examples of the skills of Baghdad's residents are shown in Figure 3.2.

## The brains of Baghdad

Caliph al-Mansur wanted to protect and develop ancient knowledge that had been ignored since the fall of the Roman Empire (see pages 80–81). He set up the House of Wisdom. Here, experts in Hindu, Persian and Greek translated books of learning into Arabic.

The House became an important library, a place for study and a translation centre. The scholars who worked in the House of Wisdom helped to improve the study of several subjects.

- **Maths:** Hindu books introduced the idea of zero. Greek books provided the advanced maths needed to make tools like the astrolabe, which could help work out time, date and location.

- **Science:** Ancient books led to improvements in medicine, as doctors looked for physical causes of disease, rather than blaming God.

- **Geography:** Translations of work on geometry* and astronomy* helped Muslim geographers to work out the size and shape of the world.

### Your turn!

1   Look at Sources C and D. With a partner, discuss the different approaches Christian and Islamic civilisations took to science.

2   In your pairs, decide why the two civilisations were different. Write a summary of your discussion.

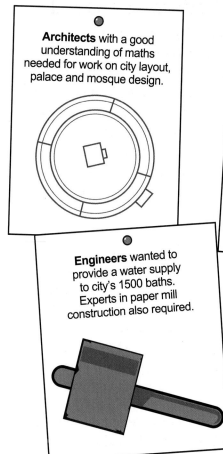

**Architects** with a good understanding of maths needed for work on city layout, palace and mosque design.

**Doctors** wanted to staff hospital, or teach in city's medical school. Opportunities to develop new medicines also available.

**Engineers** wanted to provide a water supply to city's 1500 baths. Experts in paper mill construction also required.

**Town crier** to call people to prayer needed. Should be good at astronomy and able to write a calendar of prayer times.

**Figure 3.2:** Jobs in Baghdad.

## Key terms

**Geometry\*:** A type of mathematics that involves studying lines, shapes and the relationship between points.

**Astronomy\*:** The study of the planets and stars. Astronomy helped Muslims work out prayer times and the dates of religious holidays.

## Your turn!

Imagine that a medieval Christian student from Europe is applying for one of the jobs in Figure 3.2. They have asked you to research life in Baghdad for them.

1. Create a table with two columns: 'Questions' and 'Notes'.

2. In the Questions column, write the following questions:
   a. Will I be allowed to live peacefully in the Islamic empire?
   b. Is it really a golden age for Islam?
   c. Would I get a job there?

3. Use the information and the sources on pages 76–79 to find out answers to each of these questions. You will need to refer back to the information on medieval Christian ideas on pages 56–59 to help with question 2c.

4. Write a short report explaining whether you think the student should apply for a job. Use three pieces of evidence to support your view.

## Checkpoint

1. Why was the period from the eighth to the 13th century known as the golden age of Islam?

2. Name three modern countries that were part of the medieval Islamic world.

3. How did the House of Wisdom help to improve the study of maths, science and geography?

4. Imagine you have been asked to write another advert for Figure 3.2. Write one for an artist, a translator, an astronomer or a mapmaker.

# Threats to the Byzantine Empire

### Learning objectives

- Learn what the Byzantine Empire was and how it was threatened by the Turks.
- Understand that causes can have a number of consequences.

### What do you think?

What do you think happened to the Roman Empire?

### Key terms

**Crusader*:** A person who made a promise to help capture and protect Jerusalem. The first crusaders were a mixed group of people, including knights, peasants, monks, priests and women.

**Mercenary*:** A soldier who is paid to fight in a foreign army. The Byzantine army contained Germans, Englishmen and Normans, amongst others.

**Seljuk Turks*:** A group of Muslims led by Seljuk, who built up a powerful empire in the 11th century. By 1095, control of the Seljuk lands was divided between different rulers.

Have you ever advertised a party on a social media site? It's a big mistake if you forget to make it 'private' – a lot more people can turn up than you expect. In 1096, something like this happened to the Byzantine emperor, Alexius I. He asked for military help from the pope to deal with the threats his empire faced, hoping a few hundred knights would turn up. This is not what happened.

In 1096, tens of thousands of crusaders* arrived in the Byzantine Empire's capital city, Constantinople. They all wanted to help, but they were uncontrollable. There were riots across the city as supplies ran short. Why had all these people come to Constantinople?

## What was the Byzantine Empire?

By the third century, the Roman Empire had grown so large that it was split into two. In the west, Rome was the capital and in the east, it was Constantinople. Historians call the eastern half the 'Byzantine Empire' after Constantinople's earlier name, Byzantium.

In the fifth century, the western section of the Roman empire fell apart, but the Byzantine Empire survived and even grew over the next few centuries. At its most powerful, in the early seventh century, the Byzantine emperor ruled over a huge empire which stretched from the Middle East to southern Italy.

However, by the 11th century, the Byzantine Empire was much smaller. It was also experiencing problems that might make it even weaker.

- The empire could not afford to look after its powerful army, so it reduced the size of this force and relied on mercenaries* instead.

- Emperor Alexius I was not very popular. In 1094, a leading nobleman even tried to assassinate him.

- To protect the empire, Alexius relied on military help from Europe.

- Alliances with Muslims that Alexius had made for defence against the Seljuk Turks* were breaking up.

**Source A:** A ninth-century mosaic called *The Mosaic of the Donors* in the Hagia Sophia church, Constantinople. It shows the Virgin Mary being presented with a model of the church by one emperor and a model of the city by another.

**Your turn!**

4th Draw your own copy of one part of Source A. Give it a caption that describes what the Byzantine people thought was important.

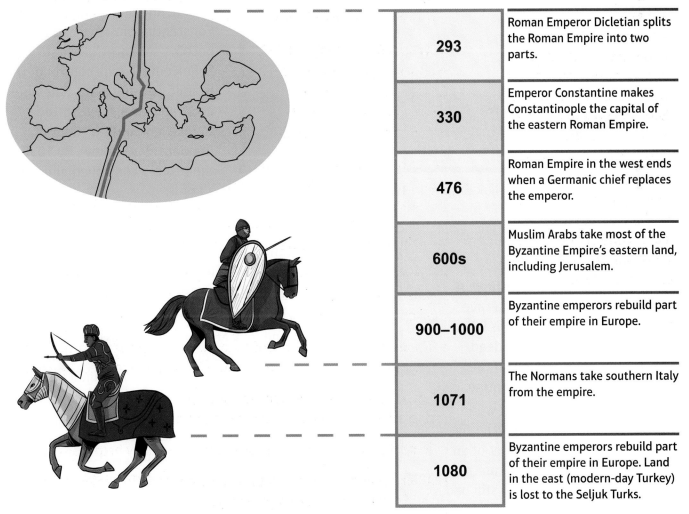

| | |
|---|---|
| **293** | Roman Emperor Dicletian splits the Roman Empire into two parts. |
| **330** | Emperor Constantine makes Constantinople the capital of the eastern Roman Empire. |
| **476** | Roman Empire in the west ends when a Germanic chief replaces the emperor. |
| **600s** | Muslim Arabs take most of the Byzantine Empire's eastern land, including Jerusalem. |
| **900–1000** | Byzantine emperors rebuild part of their empire in Europe. |
| **1071** | The Normans take southern Italy from the empire. |
| **1080** | Byzantine emperors rebuild part of their empire in Europe. Land in the east (modern-day Turkey) is lost to the Seljuk Turks. |

**Figure 3.3:** A very short history of the Byzantine Empire.

## The threat to Jerusalem

It had been a long time since the Byzantine Empire had governed Jerusalem, but this was hardly a disaster for Christians. There were still churches in the holy city, Christians were allowed to worship and pilgrims were allowed to visit. Even though Caliph al-Hakim destroyed their holiest site, the Church of the Holy Sepulchre*, in 1009, the next Islamic ruler returned things to normal.

The real problem for Christians did not begin until the Seljuk Turks took over much of the Middle East. Before then, Jerusalem had been a hugely popular pilgrim destination. Seven thousand Germans visited in the 1060s, during one of the biggest pilgrimages of the 11th century. But, when the Turks took over, the roads became more dangerous and pilgrims were too afraid to visit.

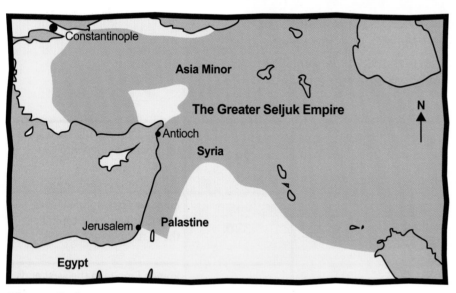

**Figure 3.4:** A map of the Seljuk Empire in 1095.

## The Turks take over

Before 1037, no one had heard of the Seljuk Turks, but within 50 years, their forces had pushed into the Byzantine Empire and almost reached Constantinople. How had they become so powerful? First, Seljuk emirs* took control of the Islamic world in Syria, Palestine and Iraq. Then, they started to take land in Asia Minor: (modern-day Turkey). By 1090, their forces controlled almost all of it.

## Key terms

**Church of the Holy Sepulchre*:** A church built on the site of a cave tomb. Christians believe it is where Jesus Christ rose from the dead. It was built on the orders of the Byzantine emperor Constantine.

**Emir*:** A lord in the Islamic world. By 1095, emirs were ruled over by a caliph, the symbolic leader of an empire, and a sultan, who ran the empire. Despite this, emirs still had a lot of power.

**Source B:** From the speech of Pope Urban II at Clermont in 1095. This version was written by Robert of Rheims in 1107. He may have been an eyewitness to the speech.

From Jerusalem a horrible tale has reached our ears. The Turks have invaded the lands of Christians and destroyed the churches of God. When they wish to torture people, they cut their navels and pull out their intestines. They then beat them until they fall to the ground. Others they attack with swords to try and cut through their neck with one blow. The Byzantine Empire has now lost so much land that it would take more than two months to walk across what they have lost.

In the short term, the Seljuk Turks were only an irritation to the Byzantine Empire. They made trade more difficult, because the roads were blocked and Muslim pirates attacked Byzantine ships. However, the last time Muslim forces had been this close to Constantinople, in 674, the city had faced a four-year siege*. This was not something it wanted to experience again, which is why Alexius found himself asking for help in 1095.

**Key term**

**Siege*:** An attack on a fortified site, such as a castle or a walled city, cutting it off from supplies to force it to surrender. Sieges could last a long time if the site was well defended.

Loss of Byzantine land in Asia Minor.

Growing power of the Seljuk Turks.

Land near Constantinople under control of the Turks.

Trade difficulties.

Pirate raids on Byzantine ships.

Failure of peace talks with the Turks.

**Figure 3.5:** Reasons why the Byzantine emperor was worried.

**Your turn!**

1. Create your own copy of the spider diagram in Figure 3.5. Colour code the branches to show which are:
   - to do with land
   - to do with trade.

2. Pick one of the groups you have colour coded. List as many consequences of the developments as you can. Why would they make the emperor worried?

3. Write a short explanation for why Emperor Alexius I asked for help in 1095.

**Checkpoint**

1. What was the Byzantine Empire? Include two dates, two places and one name in your definition.

2. Why did the weakness of the Byzantine Empire affect Christians in Europe?

3. In what ways did the Turks threaten the Byzantine Empire?

4. A mood board is a page covered in pictures and key words related to a topic. Create a mood board for the threats to the Byzantine Empire, including at least six pictures and three words.

# The First Crusade

**Learning objectives**

- Understand the reasons why people joined the First Crusade, its key features and consequences.
- Identify and use a range of historical terms in your writing.

**What do you think?**

What do you think people in medieval times would have been willing to fight and die for?

## Key terms

**Holy Land\*:** An area of land in the Middle East that is important to Christians, Muslims and Jews. It includes places like Jerusalem that are linked to the life of Jesus Christ.

**Indulgence\*:** The grant of a reduction in punishment for sins.

In November 1095, Pope Urban II launched the First Crusade. Gathering many important churchmen around him, he gave a powerful speech. He told tales of Turks torturing Christians, cutting open pilgrims to see if they had hidden gold in their intestines and spreading their blood across holy sites. He begged his audience to help their fellow Christians. These were strong words and they spread quickly. Soon, 60,000 people prepared to march to Jerusalem. There were a number of reasons that led people to become crusaders.

## Fighting for God

One reason was to fight a war with a religious goal. The aim was to capture Jerusalem from the Muslims and take control of the Holy Land\*. In return, they were offered an extraordinary reward.

Whether they succeeded or not, anyone who went on crusade would receive an indulgence\* (see Figure 3.6). An indulgence was one of the best rewards the Church had to offer medieval people.

**Figure 3.6:** What is a crusade indulgence?

**Source A:** From Pope Urban II's speech to the Council of Clermont in 1095. It was written by a monk who may have been present when the speech was delivered.

Jerusalem, situated in the middle of the world, is now held captive by God's enemies and is made servant, by those who know not God, for the ceremonies of the heathen. It looks for help from you [knights], especially, because, as we have said, God has given glory in arms upon you more than on any other nation. Undertake this journey, therefore, for the [forgiveness] of your sins, with the promise of 'glory which cannot fade' in the kingdom of heaven.

Every week, priests reminded Christians of the awful things that happened to sinful people in hell. The only escape was to do penance, but it was difficult to know if they had done enough to avoid hell. Without this confidence, many lived in fear. However, an indulgence was a guarantee that all their bad deeds would be forgiven. It was like a Christian get-out-of-hell-free card.

## Chivalry

Another reason for joining the crusades was chivalry*. Pope Urban II launched the First Crusade in November 1095. He made it clear that a crusade was like a pilgrimage for knights. They could use their skills in battle and siege warfare and earn a place in heaven.

## Land and booty

Some crusaders went to the Holy Land in search of booty*, hoping to return home with great riches. Others wanted land. For example, Bohemond of Taranto, whose family land in Europe had been lost, hoped to capture some in the Holy Land. When the crusaders took the important city of Antioch on the way to Jerusalem, Bohemond made himself its prince. He had achieved his personal aim and he abandoned the crusade.

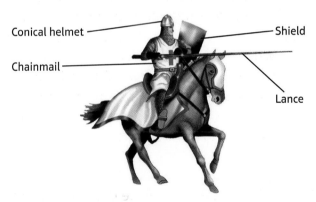

Conical helmet — Shield

Chainmail —

— Lance

**Figure 3.7:** A knight at the time of the First Crusade.

**Your turn!**

1. Sum up Anna Comnena's message in 140 characters for a social media site.
2. Read your message out to a partner. Ask them to explain why Anna Comnena thinks the crusaders went to the Byzantine Empire.
3. Bohemond had attacked the Byzantine Empire in the 1080s. Discuss with your partner how this might affect the reliability of the source.

**Your turn!**

1. a Rewrite Source A using modern language.
   b Present your speech to a partner. They should note down any words that Urban would definitely not have used.
2. Pick out five historical terms from this page and use them to try to convince your partner to go on crusade.

**Key terms**

**Chivalry*:** The way a knight was supposed to behave. Knights were expected to be strong, brave and skilled in warfare.

**Booty*:** The valuable items stolen by the winner after a siege or battle.

**Source B:** From the *Alexiad* written by Anna Comnena between 1143 and 1153. She was the daughter of Emperor Alexius I.

There were among the crusaders such men as [Bohemond] and his fellow advisers, who, eager to take the Byzantine Empire for themselves, had been looking with greed upon it for a long time. Seeing an opening for their plans in the expedition to Jerusalem, they stirred up this huge movement and, in order to trick the more simple, they faked a crusade against the Turks to regain the Holy Sepulchre and sold all their possessions.

## Events and consequences of the First Crusade

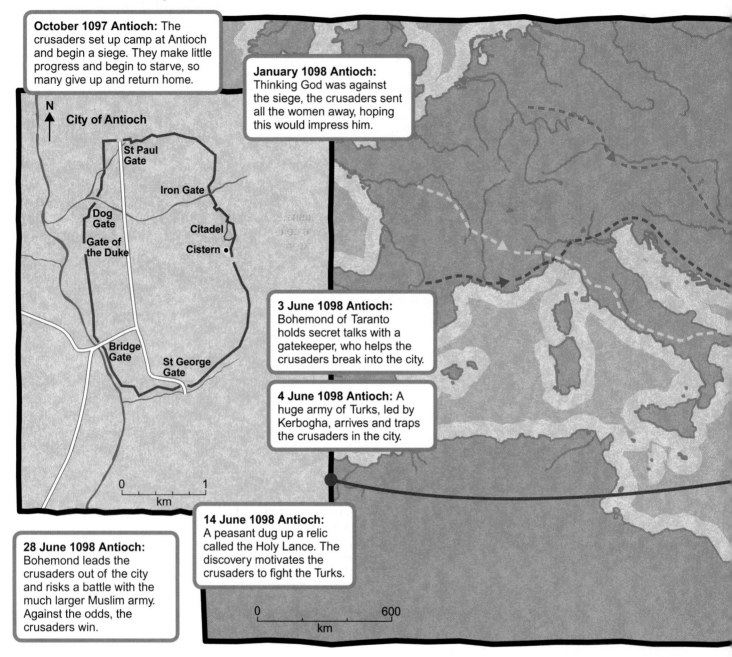

**October 1097 Antioch:** The crusaders set up camp at Antioch and begin a siege. They make little progress and begin to starve, so many give up and return home.

**January 1098 Antioch:** Thinking God was against the siege, the crusaders sent all the women away, hoping this would impress him.

N

City of Antioch

St Paul Gate

Iron Gate

Dog Gate

Citadel

Gate of the Duke

Cistern

**3 June 1098 Antioch:** Bohemond of Taranto holds secret talks with a gatekeeper, who helps the crusaders break into the city.

Bridge Gate

St George Gate

**4 June 1098 Antioch:** A huge army of Turks, led by Kerbogha, arrives and traps the crusaders in the city.

0 — 1 km

**14 June 1098 Antioch:** A peasant dug up a relic called the Holy Lance. The discovery motivates the crusaders to fight the Turks.

**28 June 1098 Antioch:** Bohemond leads the crusaders out of the city and risks a battle with the much larger Muslim army. Against the odds, the crusaders win.

0 — 600 km

**Figure 3.8:** Events and consequences of the First Crusade.

## Short-term consequences

The First Crusade was a success, but the immediate consequence was that the crusaders had to look after what they had won. There were a number of problems.

- **Protecting captured land:** Edessa, Antioch and Jerusalem were now under Christian control, but they were surrounded by Muslim forces who wanted the cities back.

- **The loss of crusaders:** After Jerusalem was captured, most crusaders went home. Few were left to protect their new possessions.

- **A new crusade failed:** In 1101, the pope asked those who had run away from the First Crusade to go on a new one. It was unsuccessful, leaving the Holy Land defenceless.

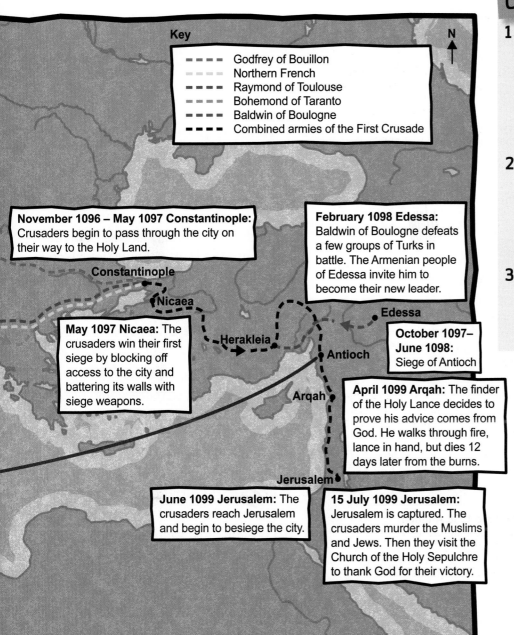

**Key**

- – – – Godfrey of Bouillon
- – – – Northern French
- – – – Raymond of Toulouse
- – – – Bohemond of Taranto
- – – – Baldwin of Boulogne
- – – – Combined armies of the First Crusade

N

**November 1096 – May 1097 Constantinople:** Crusaders begin to pass through the city on their way to the Holy Land.

**February 1098 Edessa:** Baldwin of Boulogne defeats a few groups of Turks in battle. The Armenian people of Edessa invite him to become their new leader.

Constantinople

Nicaea

**May 1097 Nicaea:** The crusaders win their first siege by blocking off access to the city and battering its walls with siege weapons.

Herakleia

Edessa

**October 1097– June 1098:** Siege of Antioch

Antioch

**April 1099 Arqah:** The finder of the Holy Lance decides to prove his advice comes from God. He walks through fire, lance in hand, but dies 12 days later from the burns.

Arqah

Jerusalem

**June 1099 Jerusalem:** The crusaders reach Jerusalem and begin to besiege the city.

**15 July 1099 Jerusalem:** Jerusalem is captured. The crusaders murder the Muslims and Jews. Then they visit the Church of the Holy Sepulchre to thank God for their victory.

## Checkpoint

1 Explain why people volunteered to join the First Crusade. Use at least one of the following words in your answer: penance, chivalry, booty.

2 List three places that were important in the First Crusade and write a short description of what happened at each.

3 Create a recruitment poster to encourage people to help protect the Holy Land after 1099.

# Why was Jerusalem worth dying for?

- In groups of three, identify three groups who were prepared to die for Jerusalem.

- Each person should represent a group, researching the reasons why they would fight and die for Jerusalem. Write up the research onto small cards.

- Put all the cards on the table. Move cards that have a similar point on them near to each other.

- Use the cards to help write an answer to the question: 'Why was Jerusalem worth dying for?'

# What have you learned?

In this section, you have learned:

- about Islamic civilisation, the Byzantine Empire and the First Crusade
- how to use historical sources to find out about the past.

Utility questions

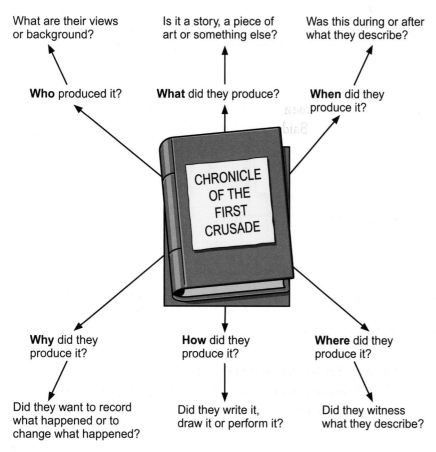

What are their views or background?

**Who** produced it?

Is it a story, a piece of art or something else?

**What** did they produce?

Was this during or after what they describe?

**When** did they produce it?

**Why** did they produce it?

Did they want to record what happened or to change what happened?

**How** did they produce it?

Did they write it, draw it or perform it?

**Where** did they produce it?

Did they witness what they describe?

**Figure 3.9:** Using 5Ws and an H with historical sources.

## What is provenance?

The provenance of a source is the background detail about the person who produced it and the circumstances in which it was produced. Figure 3.9 shows how you can use the H and W questions (see page 36 in Chapter 1) to identify these details.

## Importance of provenance

The provenance of a source can help historians. It can be used to decide what enquiries a source would be reliable for. For example, Source B on page 85 is from Anna Comnena, the daughter of the Byzantine Emperor. Her father was an important individual in the First Crusade, but he did not like how the crusaders behaved. Consequently, Source B can give a reliable view of the Byzantine attitude to the crusaders, but an unreliable view of the crusader's motives.

## Your turn!

1 Copy out the '5Ws and an H' questions from Figure 3.9, then answer each one using Source A.

2 Choose one of your answers. Explain how it would affect the reliability of Source A in helping to find out how Baldwin became ruler of Edessa.

**Source A:** From *The Chronicle of Fulcher of Chartres*, written between 1101 and 1128. Fulcher was a cleric who travelled with the crusaders to Edessa, where he joined Baldwin of Boulogne and became his chaplain.

Baldwin was invited to go to Edessa, so that he and the ruler of the city would become friends. It was agreed that if the Edessan duke should die, Baldwin would possess the city and his whole land in inheritance forever. It was decided because they were unable to defend themselves from the Turks and the duke wished to have his land defended by Baldwin and his soldiers, who he had heard were brave warriors. After we had been there fifteen days, the citizens of the city wickedly plotted to kill their prince, whom they hated, and to put Baldwin in the palace to rule.

# Writing historically

You are going to write an answer to the question 'How reliable is Source A for an enquiry into how Baldwin became ruler of Edessa?' This is a reliability question, so it is asking you to think about the provenance of Source A in order to make a decision. The activities on this page will help you to construct a strong answer.

## Introduction

The introduction should demonstrate that you understand what the question is about. As it is a reliability question focused on a specific enquiry, you should briefly describe the enquiry. An example introduction might say:

'Source A describes how Baldwin of Boulogne became ruler of Edessa. In 1098, Baldwin was made heir to the ruler of Edessa. When the heir was murdered shortly after this, Baldwin took over as ruler.'

## Paragraphs

A good answer to this question will refer to the provenance of the source. To do so, it will:

- begin with a reliable or unreliable feature
- give some evidence to describe the reliable or unreliable feature
- explain why this evidence makes it reliable or unreliable for the enquiry in the question.

An example of a good answer could look something like this:

'Source A is reliable because the writer was present when Baldwin became ruler of Edessa. It is written by Fulcher of Chartres, who travelled with Baldwin of Boulogne and worked for him. This makes it reliable for an enquiry into how Baldwin became ruler, because he saw the events and so is able to describe them.'

The problem with the answer above is that it assumes that being present at an event somehow makes you more reliable. A better answer would also consider an unreliable feature of the provenance. Have a go at producing your own strong answer.

You could begin your answer with:

'Source A is less reliable because the writer worked for Baldwin of Boulogne...

## Conclusion

This is where you give a judgement that answers the question. It asks 'how reliable', so use a measuring word in your conclusion. Some choices are 'very', 'partially' or 'not at all'. You should then try to explain your choice of measuring word. You could begin your conclusion with:

'Source A is ... reliable for an enquiry into how Baldwin became ruler of Edessa.'

You could then write a paragraph about a reliable or unreliable feature of the content of the source. The 'Writing historically' section on pages 60–61 explains how you can select reliable content from a source.

# Did the Crusades change the Holy Land?

After the First Crusade, some crusaders and other settlers from Europe took over the Holy Land. Just under 100 years later, they were forced to abandon most of it.

During that time, did anything really change in the Holy Land? This section of the book will look at:

- how life changed in the crusader states for Muslims and those who settled there
- the way the Muslim world changed in response to the new crusader states
- ways in which individual leaders, like Richard I and Saladin, changed the Holy Land.

# Living with the enemy

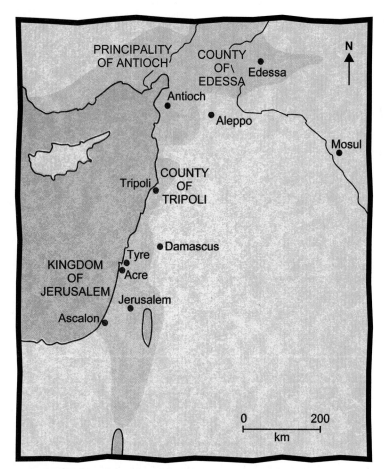

**Figure 3.10:** The crusader states of Outremer.

## Outremer

Outremer is French for 'beyond the sea' and is the name used for the crusader states* captured by Christians during and immediately after the First Crusade – Edessa, Antioch, Jerusalem and Tripoli (see Figure 3.10). There were very few Christians to govern and protect them, so the Christian rulers accepted that Muslims were needed to farm the lands and to trade with. To survive, the Christians had to accept living alongside the same group of people they had attacked during the First Crusade.

Most Christians who came to settle in Outremer lived in towns. Markets were held, selling food, clothing and luxury goods like spices. Business with visitors such as traders and pilgrims helped to make townspeople rich, but it also meant they were at risk from Muslim attack. To protect them, towns were surrounded by walls, guarded by towers and could only be accessed through gates.

Life in the countryside was even more risky. Christian settlers lived in small communities, using large plots of land to grow their own food and produce goods for sale. In return for their land, villagers were expected to defend it. They had no walls, towers or gates to protect them, so they had to fight if attacked.

## The Kingdom of Jerusalem

The most powerful state in Outremer was Jerusalem. In 1099, the Kingdom of Jerusalem was set up with a crusader, Godfrey of Bouillon, as its leader. At this point, the Christians only controlled a few cities within the kingdom and needed to make some changes to survive. These included the following.

- **Conquest:** The new rulers attacked and captured the seaports of Acre and Tyre first. This meant European help could come by ship and traders could buy and sell overseas.

- **Powerful lords:** The lords of Jerusalem were given a lot of land and power. In return, they would protect the kingdom from attack.

- **Settlers:** Europeans were offered land with low taxation and cheap rent. It was important they came so that they could help lords if the Muslims invaded.

**Source A:** From *A History of the Expedition to Jerusalem, 1095–1127* by Fulcher of Chartres, who wrote about events in the crusader states between 1095 and 1127.

We who were once westerners have now become easterners. He who was of Rheims or Chartres has now become a citizen of Tyre or Antioch. Some have taken wives not only of their own people, but Syrians, Armenians or even Muslims who have converted to Christianity. Words of different languages have become common property to each nationality, and shared faith unites us. He who was born a stranger is now as one born here; he who was born a foreigner has become a native.

**Interpretation 1:** From *God's War* by Christopher Tyerman, written in 2006.

In cities where Christians lived side by side with Muslims, they adapted to each other. At Acre, where the two faiths shared a converted mosque as well as a shrine, Muslim visitors were treated fairly. Mosques still operated openly in Tyre and elsewhere. Important Muslims were able to travel through the lands of Outremer. Although banned from living there, in 1120 Arab traders were encouraged by the king to sell food in Jerusalem. In large parts of the countryside Muslim villagers farmed the land under Christian ownership paying taxes without protest.

## Key term

**Crusader states\*:** The lands taken by the crusaders and ruled by the Christians.

## Your turn!

 **1** Read Interpretation 1. In bullet points, note two things that changed for Muslims in the Holy Land because Christians took over and one thing that stayed the same.

 **2** Read Source A. Find one piece of evidence in Source A that agrees with one of your bullet points from question 1 and write it down.

**3** Think of a question you could ask Fulcher of Chartres to find out if Interpretation 1 is correct. Write it down and discuss, with a partner, what his answer might be.

**Source B:** The remains of the castle at Saone. It was built by a Muslim emir in the mid-tenth century, but the crusaders gave it a major overhaul in the mid-12th century.

## Taking control: crusader castles

One big change a Muslim living in Outremer would have noticed in the 12th century was that a lot more castles were built. These had different designs (see Figure 3.11) and a range of purposes, which included the following.

- **Defence**: They were garrisoned* by knights, who protected key cities and defended main roads. Their role was to fight off invaders and protect traders.

- **Showing off**: The castles were like an advert, proving how much power the Christians had. This helped convince villagers to pay their taxes and force traders to pay them too.

- **Attack**: Castles could be used as a base from which to launch attacks. One was built near Tripoli to supply troops during the long siege to capture the city.

### Key term

**Garrison*:** The knights who defended a castle. A lord usually expected his knights to do this for a fixed number of days each year.

### Your turn!

1   In pairs, prepare a sales pitch to encourage one of the following to settle in Outremer: an adventurous lord, a young knight, a trader or a farmer.

2   Present your pitch to a small group, without mentioning who your target audience is. Ask them to work out who you were pitching for.

3   After your pitch, ask the group to list two ways your target settler might change life for Muslims in Outremer.

**(a)**                          **(b)**                          **(c)**

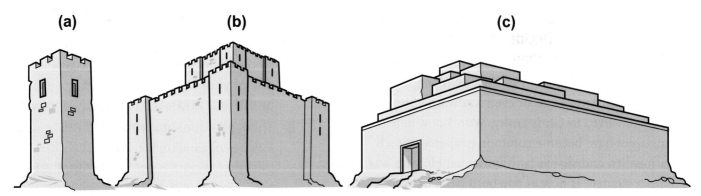

**Figure 3.11:** Crusader defences. (a) Fortified tower. (b) Concentric enclosure. (c) Walled town.

**Source C:** Two Templars, from the chronicle of Matthew Paris, written in the mid-13th century.

## Keeping control: Templars and Hospitallers

A few hundred knights signed up to join the military orders in the 12th century. A military order was made up of men who lived like monks, following most of the same rules, but they were allowed to fight. The first group, the Templars, was founded around 1120 because of attacks on pilgrims on their journey to Jerusalem. They were based in Jerusalem and had about 500 members living across Outremer.

The other order was called the Hospitallers. Before they became a military force, they had run a hospital in Jerusalem, providing care for the poor and sick. In 1130, they started to take on similar jobs to the Templars. Both would defend castles and cities, provide military advice to the rulers of Outremer and help them out in battle. Without them, Outremer would have been much easier to invade.

**Source D:** From *In Praise of the New Knighthood*, written in the 1130s by the preacher Bernard of Clairvaux. It was written to encourage support for the Templars.

When war is announced they arm themselves on the inside with faith and on the outside with iron, not gold, so that they strike fear into the enemy by their arms and do not encourage greed by their gold. They choose their horses for their strength and speed, not their colour or their accessories. Their thoughts are on the battle and victory, not display and glory. Their aim is to bring fear, not admiration. They are not impulsive, but they assemble and form their battle formation thoughtfully and carefully.

### Checkpoint

1 How did Christians change the Holy Land?

2 What did Christians keep the same in Outremer?

3 How was Outremer protected from attack?

4 Create an information leaflet for European Christians who plan to move to Outremer. Include a description of the people who live there, the jobs and how the newcomers will be protected.

### Your turn!

1 Sources B and C show two different ways Outremer was defended. Decide which one you think would lead to the biggest change. Write a short explanation for your decision.

2 Imagine you are a lord who lives near Muslim land. Design a plan to defend your land, including a diagram and a list of resources needed.

3 List three changes you think your plan will lead to. Try to rank them in order of importance.

# The Muslim fightback

### Learning objectives

- Understand the idea of jihad and the importance of the unification of the Muslim world.
- Find out how the actions of key individuals can cause changes, which are not all as important as each other.

### What do you think?

How do you think Muslim leaders responded to the First Crusade?

### Key term

**Jihad*:** A holy war fought against Christians and other non-Muslim groups. The term can also mean a personal struggle to improve a believer's faith in Islam.

The Islamic civilisations in the Near East were not ready for the First Crusade. Instead, they argued and fought with each other. When the crusaders arrived at their first target, Nicaea, its Muslim ruler was busy fighting a rival Turk. When the Christians got to Antioch, the Muslim leader in charge could not convince his allies to help him. Finally, as the crusaders marched south, some Muslim leaders guided them to Jerusalem. This was a huge help to the crusaders, but a disaster for the Muslim world.

## Jihad

After the First Crusade, it took a while for the Muslim world to recover from the shock of four new Christian states on its doorstep. When it did, a jihad* was launched against the Christians. This was a holy war with the aim of forcing the Christians out of Outremer.

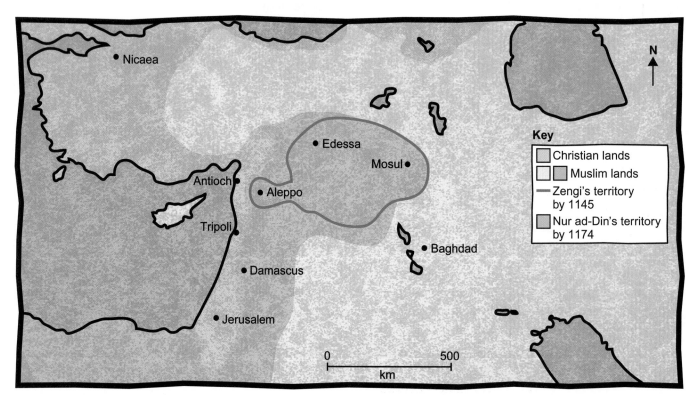

**Figure 3.12:** Map of the Muslim lands after the First Crusade.

At first the jihad was led by a ruler called Zengi, who realised the best way to defeat the Christians was to unite Muslims under one leader. This process meant Zengi had enough soldiers to capture Edessa from the Christians in 1144. However, shortly after this, he was stabbed to death by one of his own slaves. It was now up to his son, Nur ad-Din, to finish what Zengi had started.

> **Source A:** A eulogy* to Zengi by Ibn al-Athir. He was a Muslim chronicler who wrote 13 volumes of history in the early 13th century.
>
> Before Zengi came to power the absence of strong rulers, and the presence of the Christians nearby, had made the country a wilderness, but he made it flower again. The population increased, and so did its wealth. During his reign he was entirely surrounded by hostile states, all doing their best to seize his kingdom. But he never let a year pass without taking over a piece of enemy territory. At his death he had taken over a lot of land from his neighbours.

Nur ad-Din's first task was to scare the Christians, who thought they were safe now that Zengi was dead. To do this he crushed a revolt in Edessa, killing 30,000 rebels. Then he attacked Antioch, killing its Christian prince. These attacks gave Nur ad-Din time to unite most of the Muslim world around Outremer, providing the next leader with enough strength to defeat the Christians.

## Did you know?

The Second Crusade was launched after Zengi captured Edessa. It was a disaster for the crusaders. The leaders did not work together and spent ages arguing over the crusade's goal. In the end, they gave up after an unsuccessful siege on Damascus in 1148.

## Key term

**Eulogy*:** A piece of writing that praises a person. It is usually written or spoken after their death.

## Timeline

**Unification of the Muslim world under Zengi and Nur ad-Din**

**1127:** Zengi becomes governor of Mosul

**1128:** Zengi takes control of Aleppo

**1144:** Zengi's forces capture Edessa

**1146:** Zengi is stabbed to death and replaced by Nur ad-Din

**1154:** Nur ad-Din attacks and captures Damascus

**1169:** Nur ad-Din's commander, Shirkuh, captures Cairo

## Your turn!

1. List three changes that happened in the Muslim world after the First Crusade.

2. Use Figure 3.12 and the timeline to help you to write a description of the progress made by the Muslim world after the First Crusade.

3. Read Source A. Give one way that Zengi contributed to this change.

4. Look at Figure 3.12 and the timeline. Give one way that Nur ad-Din contributed to this change.

## Who was Saladin?

Saladin is the most famous leader of the jihad against the Christians. This is partly because of his personality. He was thought of as generous and deeply religious. He was also ambitious and worked hard to become the vizier* of Egypt when his commander, Shirkuh, died unexpectedly.

These qualities made him a memorable figure, but his actions against the Christians are the main reason he is significant. Figure 3.13 shows how Saladin took over Egypt and then spent the years 1174–86 taking control of Nur ad-Din's old lands. Once he had done this, he was ready to take on the Christians.

## Reconquest of Jerusalem

Saladin's plan was to try and get the Christians to fight an all-out battle with him. In 1183, he raided the Kingdom of Jerusalem, hoping to anger Outremer's leaders and make them fight back. However, the Christians did not fall for Saladin's trick, so he returned to his own territory. A few years later, he was more successful.

In 1187, while the Christians were in disagreement over who should be king, Saladin marched into the Kingdom of Jerusalem with 30,000 men. He had been able to do so because a Christian, one of those who wanted to be king, had asked for Saladin's help. This gave the Muslim leader a chance to attack targets deep within Outremer.

**1167:** Saladin's first invasion of Egypt fails.

**1169:** Successful attack on Egypt. Saladin soon becomes its new ruler.

**1174:** Nur ad-Din dies. Saladin begins to take over his empire. Two years later, he marries Nur ad-Din's widow.

**April 1187:** Makes a treaty with a Christian, using it as an excuse to start an invasion of Outremer.

**July 1187:** Saladin leads some Christians into a trap, where they cannot get water, and defeats them at Hattin.

**October 1187:** Jerusalem is defended by a small force of recently knighted teenagers. Saladin captures it.

**Figure 3.13:** Saladin's rise to power.

**Source B:** A description of Saladin's victory at the Battle of Hattin in 1187 by Imad al-Din, who was Saladin's secretary and friend.

Our army stood between the Christians and Lake Tiberias. Devastated by thirst the Christians stood patiently. Saladin moved among his soldiers, encouraging them and promising them the victory they expected from God. Our army was strengthened by the sight of him. They blocked the enemy's attack and threw them back. Some of our holy warriors set fire to the grass. The heat became intense. No matter how hard they fought the Christians were beaten back. They retreated to Mount Hattin but they were surrounded.

**Interpretation 1:** Saladin's statue in Damascus. It was commissioned by President Hafez al-Assad of Syria in 1992 and emphasises Saladin's military skill as leader of a jihad.

Saladin captured the town of Tiberias, hoping the crusaders would try and take it back. If they did, the Christians would be falling into a trap because Saladin controlled all the water supplies in the area. When 20,000 Christians headed for the small town, Saladin's troops surrounded them, cutting off their access to water, and defeated them at the Battle of Hattin.

Most of Outremer's knights were now dead or prisoners of Saladin. With few men left to defend it, Jerusalem was captured in 1187. Saladin then moved from castle to castle, gradually destroying Christian defences. The situation in Outremer was now so bad that the pope launched the Third Crusade.

**Source C:** A picture of Saladin produced around 1180. It shows him as a pious leader and in a position that suggests he is deep in thought.

## Your turn!

1. Study Interpretation 1. List two qualities it suggests that Saladin had.
2. Look at Source C. Add a third quality to your list that is missing from Interpretation 1.
3. Next to one of the qualities in your list, write how this might help reverse the changes made by the crusaders.

## Checkpoint

1. What was a jihad?
2. How did Zengi and Nur ad-Din unite the Muslim world?
3. What actions did Saladin take to reverse the changes made by the crusaders?
4. Imagine you are a Christian chronicler living in Outremer. Write a short history of the 12th century, describing the growth of Muslim power. Include words that describe your reaction to it.

# Changes to the Holy Land

- Understand the ways in which the Crusades changed the Holy Land.
- Learn how a person's actions can make them significant.

**What do you think?**

What could make a leader significant?

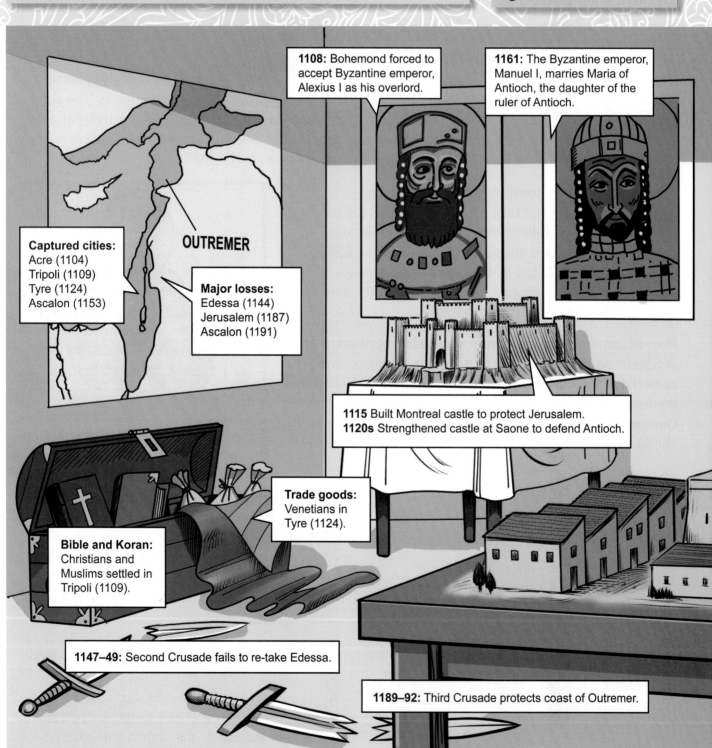

**Figure 3.14:** Escape the room: changes in the Holy Land during the 12th century.

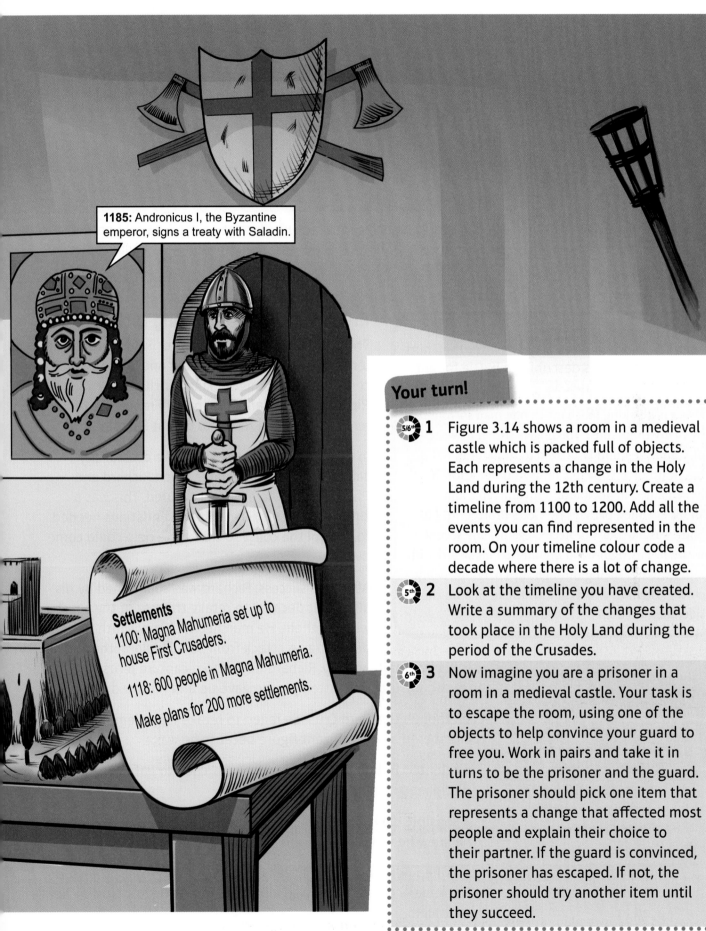

**1185:** Andronicus I, the Byzantine emperor, signs a treaty with Saladin.

**Settlements**
1100: Magna Mahumeria set up to house First Crusaders.

1118: 600 people in Magna Mahumeria.

Make plans for 200 more settlements.

**Your turn!**

**1** Figure 3.14 shows a room in a medieval castle which is packed full of objects. Each represents a change in the Holy Land during the 12th century. Create a timeline from 1100 to 1200. Add all the events you can find represented in the room. On your timeline colour code a decade where there is a lot of change.

**2** Look at the timeline you have created. Write a summary of the changes that took place in the Holy Land during the period of the Crusades.

**3** Now imagine you are a prisoner in a room in a medieval castle. Your task is to escape the room, using one of the objects to help convince your guard to free you. Work in pairs and take it in turns to be the prisoner and the guard. The prisoner should pick one item that represents a change that affected most people and explain their choice to their partner. If the guard is convinced, the prisoner has escaped. If not, the prisoner should try another item until they succeed.

## Key terms

**Formation\*:** The way a military force is organised. During Richard's march to Jaffa, he split his army into divisions (sections) and columns (lines) to protect the soldiers carrying supplies.

**Truce\*:** An agreement to stop fighting for a certain period of time. Richard's truce with Saladin was arranged in 1192.

**Source A:** An early 14th century illustration of Richard I fighting Saladin in the Third Crusade. Although shown together, it is unlikely the two ever met.

**Source B:** From the chronicle of Richard de Templo, written around 30 years after the Third Crusade. Here he is describing a battle fought during the Third Crusade.

What of the king [Richard I], one man surrounded by many thousands? The fingers stiffen to write of it and the mind is amazed to think of it. Who has heard of anyone like him? I do not know how he remained invincible and invulnerable among all his enemies, perhaps by God's protection. His body was like brass protected against any sort of weapon. His right hand brandished his sword with rapid strokes, slicing through the charging enemy, cutting them in two as he met them, first on this side, then on that.

## Your turn!

 1  Look at the information and sources on this page. List Richard I's actions during the Third Crusade.

 2  Next to each item on your list, add any changes his actions led to.

## Crusader case study: King Richard I

The Third Crusade, planned after Saladin captured Jerusalem in 1187, was the last one in the 12th century. Several mighty kings, including Richard I of England, Philip II of France and Guy of Jerusalem, joined forces to defeat Saladin.

In 1189, Guy began the siege of a coastal city called Acre. Two years later, when Richard and Philip arrived, Acre was recaptured. This was a significant victory because the Christians needed to control the coast so that extra help could come by ship.

After this success, Richard was abandoned by his allies, but decided to retake the rest of the coast without them. He marched his army south to Jaffa, defeating an attack from Saladin along the way. It was his last major victory. Richard hoped to recapture Jerusalem, but after two unsuccessful attempts, he gave up and returned home.

Even though the Third Crusade failed to retake Jerusalem, Richard is remembered as a significant figure because he was:

- **a talented military leader**: his army marched to Jaffa in a disciplined formation\*

- **a sensible decision-maker**: he did not capture Jerusalem because he knew he would not be able to defend it against Saladin

- **a skilled peacemaker**: in 1192 he agreed a truce\* that protected Outremer's coastal cities and allowed pilgrims to visit Muslim-held Jerusalem.

## Did the Crusades change anything?

The First Crusade had captured the key cities that became Outremer. In the short term, more land was taken and the crusader states expanded. However, once the Muslim world united, the situation changed. As Muslim forces attacked Outremer, the crusader states shrank to a small series of states on the coastline. Figure 3.15 shows how much had really changed by the end of the century.

In the longer term, the Crusades caused even less change. There were a number of failed crusades in the 13th century, but none managed to recapture Jerusalem permanently. Instead, Outremer faced repeated Muslim invasions. In 1291, Acre was the last major city to fall. After that, Outremer was abandoned by the Christians.

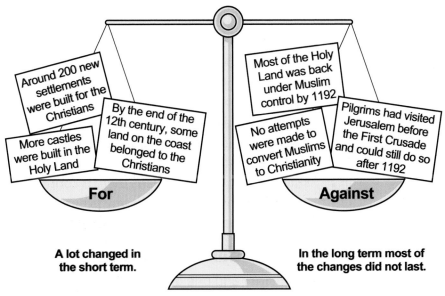

**Figure 3.15:** Did the Crusades change the Holy Land?

### Checkpoint

1 List one way the Crusades changed the landscape of the Holy Land and one way they changed the people who lived there.

2 Why is King Richard I a significant person in the history of the Crusades?

3 How were the following people affected by the Third Crusade:
   a pilgrims
   b the people of Acre
   c Saladin?

4 Plan your own ideas for an 'Escape the room' activity, using items that represent Richard I's actions during the Third Crusade.

# Did the Crusades change the Holy Land?

Create a table comparing the situation before the First Crusade with the situation after the Third Crusade. In the first column, headed 'Before First Crusade', write the following statements.

• In 1095 there were no crusader states.

• In 1095 there were no defences for Christians in the area surrounding Jerusalem.

• In 1095 the Muslim world was disunited.

• In 1095 Jerusalem was under Muslim control.

In the second column, headed 'After Third Crusade', write your own entries for 1192, using the material from this section. Then write an explanation of whether you think the Crusades really changed the Holy Land.

# What have you learned?

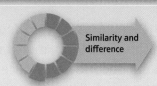

Similarity and difference

In this section, you have learned:

- about changes in the Holy Land between the 11th and 12th centuries
- how events and the actions of individuals can result in change.

## Your turn!

 1 Other than the examples in Figure 3.16, give one similarity and one difference in the Holy Land over this period.

2 Think of an event or action that led to each of the changes below. Write explanations for your choices.

   **a** An event that increased either Muslim or Christian control in the Holy Land.

   **b** An event that strengthened or weakened relations between the Christians in Outremer and the Byzantine Empire (see Figure 3.14).

   **c** An event that improved the unity of the Muslim world.

## Quick quiz

1 Name the important library, place for study and translation centre in Baghdad.

2 Which people threatened the Byzantine Empire?

3 What reward did Christians receive for joining the First Crusade?

4 Name a group who protected Outremer.

5 Which city did Saladin capture in 1187?

6 Who led the Third Crusade?

## Change and continuity

One of a historian's jobs is to look at the bigger picture, rather than focusing on one event or individual. To do this they sometimes look at similarities and differences between two points in time. Then they explore why and in what ways some things have stayed the same, while others have not.

If there has been a change, then historians look for events or the actions of individuals that have led to that change. For example, an event might make a situation better or worse, or an individual's actions might make the position of their group stronger or weaker. If a situation has stayed the same that means there is continuity and historians try to explain why events or individuals have not changed it.

## Similarities and differences in the Holy Land

Figure 3.16 shows one similarity and one difference in the Holy Land between the 11th and 12th centuries, demonstrating how events have led to that continuity or change.

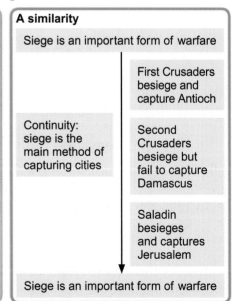

**Figure 3.16:** Change and continuity in the Holy Land.

# Writing historically

You are going to analyse similarities and differences questions. This will help you to write answers to these types of question. Figure 3.16 will help with both of the questions that follow. The first question asks you to 'Explain one way in which the unity of the Muslim world in the 11th century was different from the unity of the Muslim world in the 12th century'. This is a differences question, as it is asking you to explain one difference that you can identify.

## An average answer

An average answer will describe events as if they were the difference. It will use correct factual information, but it will not be very detailed. Study the example answer below and write a short explanation of why it is an average answer.

> 'In the First Crusade the Muslims lost. They were defeated at Nicaea, at Antioch and then at Jerusalem. At the end, the Christians took over the Holy Land. In the Third Crusade the Muslims did a lot better. Saladin had captured Jerusalem a few years before and he kept control of it during the Third Crusade.'

## A better answer

A better answer to this question will have the following features:

- it will show an understanding that the difference results from an event or an individual's action

- it will give some features of the period studied to explain the difference.

Look at the example answer below and write an explanation of why it is a better answer.

> 'In the First Crusade the Muslim world was divided. For example, instead of fighting the crusaders at Nicaea, the Muslim ruler in charge was busy fighting a rival Turk. This shows the Muslim world did not even work together when it was under attack. In the Third Crusade the Muslim world was united. Saladin had captured Egypt in 1169 and then went on to bring Syria under his control. Then, during the Third Crusade, he was able to use these armies together to protect Jerusalem. This showed their unity had made them stronger.'

## Writing your own answer

Now write your own answer to the question 'Explain one way in which the fighting in the crusades at the end of the 11th century was similar to the fighting at the end of the 12th century'. This is a similarities question, as it is asking you to explain one similarity that you can identify. In your answer, try to focus on using features of the period you have studied. You could begin your answer in the following way:

> 'One similarity between the fighting at the end of 11th century and at the end of the 12th century is that both involved siege warfare. In the First Crusade...'

# What happened to England's medieval monarchs?

There were 18 monarchs in England between 1066 and 1485. Only ten of them died a natural death. Some were murdered, others were killed in battle and some died in mysterious circumstances.

This section of the book will look at:

- the way in which each medieval monarch met his end

- what the various violent deaths had in common

- case studies of a strong and a weak king.

**What do you think?**

Why was it risky to be a medieval monarch?

# How did their reigns end?

**Learning objectives**

- Learn the chronology of medieval monarchs.
- Understand what the fates of the medieval monarchs had in common.

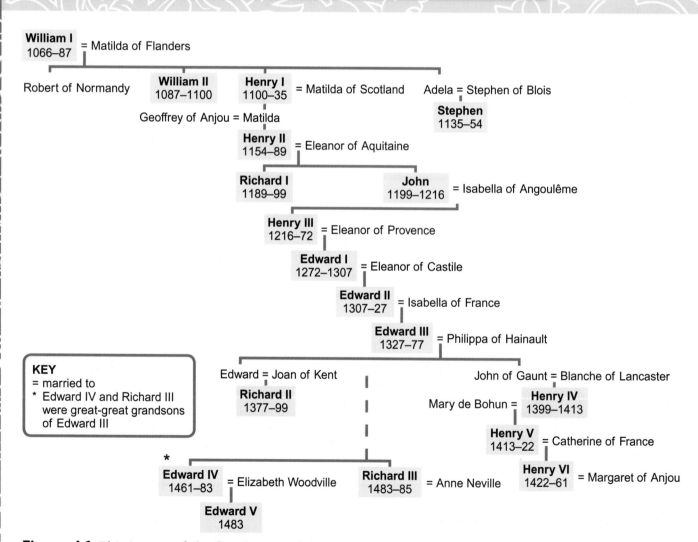

KEY
= married to
* Edward IV and Richard III were great-great grandsons of Edward III

**Figure 4.1:** This is part of the family tree of the kings of England between 1066 and 1485.

Some medieval monarchs had long and successful reigns; others had disastrous reigns that did not end well, as you will see from Table 4.1.

In medieval times, a monarch needed the following qualities:

- be physically strong

- be able to travel around his kingdom on horseback and lead his armies in battle

- have a strong personality

- be in control, and win the respect of powerful nobles

- give justice to everyone, even if it upset the rich and powerful

- keep control of the government.

## Your turn!

**4th** **1** Use the family tree of the kings of England (Figure 4.1) to draw a timeline of all monarchs from 1066 to 1485.

**4th** **2** The first Norman king was William I and the first Plantagenet king was Henry II. Colour the timeline to show which monarchs were Normans and which were Plantagenets.

**6th** **3** Discuss in your class whether how a monarch dies indicates whether they were strong or weak. Talk about whether you can find any patterns. For example, did the monarchs who were murdered, or possibly murdered, fight in civil wars or lose wars against foreigners? What other patterns can you find?

**5th** **4** Use all the information you have gathered to write a paragraph beginning: 'It was risky being a medieval monarch because…'.

## Key term

**Civil war\*:** A war between people within the same country.

| King | Reign | Wars fought | Cause of death |
|---|---|---|---|
| William I | 1066–87 | Conquered England | Died of illness/injury while on campaign |
| William II | 1087–1100 | Won wars against Scotland, Wales and brother | Killed while hunting, possibly murdered |
| Henry I | 1100–35 | Won civil war* against brother | Died after eating too much |
| Stephen | 1135–54 | Won civil war against cousin | Heart attack |
| Henry II | 1154–89 | Won land in Ireland and France. Lost civil war against wife and sons | Fever |
| Richard I | 1189–99 | Successful in Crusades and in wars against France | Killed in war |
| John | 1199–1216 | Lost civil war | Serious diarrhoea |
| Henry III | 1216–72 | Lost and then won civil war against barons. Lost land in France | Old age |
| Edward I | 1272–1307 | Won wars against Wales and Scotland | Old age |
| Edward II | 1307–27 | Lost wars against Scotland and France and civil war against wife | Murdered |
| Edward III | 1327–77 | Won wars against France. Hundred Years' War (HYW) starts | Old age |
| Richard II | 1377–99 | Lost wars in France and against cousin | Probably murdered |
| Henry IV | 1399–1413 | Won civil war and wars against Scotland, Wales and France | Serious skin disease |
| Henry V | 1413–22 | Won wars and land in France | Serious diarrhoea |
| Henry VI | 1422–61 | Lost land in France. Lost throne in civil war. HYW ends | Murdered |
| Edward IV | 1461–83 | Won throne and lost it for a while in civil war | Died after eating too much |
| Edward V | 1483 (not crowned) | Forced off throne by uncle | Probably murdered |
| Richard III | 1483–85 | Won war against Scotland. Lost civil war | Killed in battle |

**Table 4.1:** Medieval kings: who they were and how they died.

Edward did not punish his mother. She lived in luxury for the rest of her life, but was not allowed to come to his court and mix with the noblemen.

# Edward III: a strong king?

Edward III is often considered a very successful medieval king. However, his reign did not begin well. His mother Isabella forced his father (Edward II) to give up the throne, and he later died in Berkeley Castle, probably murdered on the orders of Roger Mortimer, Isabella's lover. The young Edward was crowned king of England in 1327 when he was 14 years old. He was considered too young to govern England by himself, and so his mother and Roger Mortimer governed for him. This was not a good arrangement. In 1330, Edward III had Mortimer arrested. He was thrown into the Tower of London and executed without trial. Edward was now in control.

**Good at war**
He defeated the French at the Battle of Crécy and the Scots at the Battle of Neville's Cross (1346). In 1356, he captured the king of France and kept a large part of southern France.

**Behaved like a king**
He wore expensive clothes and valuable jewels; he held jousts and tournaments, calling the bravest knights the Knights of the Garter. He ordered the rebuilding of Windsor Castle.

**Increased the power of the House of Commons**
Edward needed the approval of the Commons for raising taxes to pay for his wars. This gave them some power and control.

**Revived the English language**
He ordered the use of the English language in the law courts, parliament and schools.

**Family man**
There was no opposition to Edward from any of his five sons when they became adults. His eldest son, Edward the Black Prince, died in 1376. None of his surviving sons challenged the crown passing to Richard, the Black Prince's son, even though he was a child.

**Popular with the nobles**
The nobles supported him because he consulted them before he took action. They joined his army because he was successful at winning wars, bringing them land and money.

**Sympathetic to merchants**
He understood the importance of trade in bringing wealth to England. He listened to merchants' complaints and dealt with them generously.

**Strengthened justice**
He expanded the role of justices of the peace so that they could investigate crimes, make arrests and try cases.

**Figure 4.2:** Edward III and details of his reign.

# Henry VI: a weak king?

Henry VI is often considered a very weak medieval king. He was nine months old when his father, Henry V, died from dysentery (severe diarrhoea) while campaigning in France. The baby Henry inherited the throne of England.

**Powerful nobles**
When he was a child, a council of nobles ruled for him. This council, and individual nobles, especially Richard of York from 1450, were very strong. Henry could not control them.

**Deeply religious**
He was a deeply religious man who was trusting and faithful. He hated rich clothes and jewels, and avoided hurting anyone. He would not dismiss ministers even when they were incompetent.

**Family man**
He married Margaret of Anjou, a strong-willed and determined woman, and had one child. He valued the children from his mother's secret marriage to Owen Tudor, and made two of his half-brothers earls.

**King of two countries**
In 1429, when he was eight years old, Henry was crowned king of England. A year later, he was crowned king of France.

**Hated war**
He was a king who hated violence in any form. By 1453, all land in France held by England had been lost, except Calais.

**Mentally unstable**
He had bouts of mental illness throughout his life, during which time Richard of York governed England.

**Civil war**
Civil war broke out in 1460 between two noble families, the Yorkists and the Lancastrians. Henry's son was killed, probably by Yorkist nobles, after the Battle of Tewkesbury in 1471. In the same year, Henry was imprisoned in the Tower of London, and murdered there. The civil war was later called the Wars of the Roses.

**Supported education**
He founded Eton College and King's College, Cambridge and was deeply interested in education.

**Figure 4.3:** Henry VI and details of his reign.

## Your turn!

1 Look at Figure 4.2 about Edward III's reign. All of the issues listed played a part in making him a strong king. Work with a partner to list these in order of importance. Compare your list with those of the rest of your class and decide on a list with which you all agree. Write a paragraph explaining why Edward III was a strong king.

2 Look at Figure 4.3 about Henry VI. What one thing would you pick out as being the most important in making him a weak king? Write a paragraph to explain why you chose this.

3 Have a class discussion about whether luck played a part in being a successful monarch. For example, it was good luck if a new monarch inherited a peaceful country and bad luck if he inherited the throne when he was a baby. How could a monarch overcome bad luck?

## Checkpoint

1 Name two medieval kings who were murdered.

2 Name two medieval kings who died naturally.

3 Name three things that made Edward III a strong king.

4 Name three things that made Henry VI a weak king.

# How important were England's medieval queens?

Most of England's medieval queens were faithful and somewhat shadowy figures, whose marriages brought land and wealth to the Crown and who did what they were expected to do – produce healthy heirs. Two were different. One was the daughter of a king, who asserted her right to be queen on her father's death, plunging England into civil war; the other married a king and supported her sons in their rebellion against their father.

This section of the book will look at:

- Matilda's claim to the throne, her personal qualities and fitness to rule

- Eleanor of Aquitaine's influence and limitations

- contemporary and later interpretations of the roles of Matilda and Eleanor.

# Matilda's opportunity

### Learning objectives

- Learn what Henry I did to try to make sure there was a peaceful succession after his death.
- Understand why Matilda's attempt to become queen of England led to a long civil war and how it ended.

### What do you think?

How do people react to women in powerful positions today?

**Source A:** A painting from the early 1300s. It shows Henry I and the sinking of the *White Ship*.

In November 1120, the *White Ship* left Normandy to cross the English Channel. About 250 young noblemen and women were on board, including William, the son of Henry I and heir to the English throne. They were all very drunk. They persuaded the crew to race the *White Ship* against a ship carrying Henry I and senior nobles, which had set off before them. The sea was calm and the moon was bright. What could possibly go wrong? Suddenly, the *White Ship* hit a rock that could only be seen at low tide. The ship sank quickly. There was only one survivor – and it was not Henry's son William.

This was Henry's nightmare. Not only was his son dead, but there was only a girl – his daughter Matilda – to succeed him. Legally, there was no reason why a woman couldn't be a monarch. But a monarch had to be physically strong, lead the country's armies, win the respect of powerful earls and provide justice for everyone, even if it upset the strong and wealthy. Most people in medieval times believed a monarch had to be a man.

## Making sure Matilda would be queen

Daughters were as useful to monarchs as sons, but in a different way. Sons were brought up to inherit their father's throne, whereas daughters could be married to powerful foreign monarchs and so make useful alliances. It was particularly good if their marriage resulted in healthy sons because these sons could become possible heirs.

In 1114, when she was about 12 years old, Matilda was married to the Holy Roman Emperor, Henry V of Germany. The marriage produced no children and Henry V died in 1125.

Matilda, a childless widow aged about 23, returned to her father's court*. What could Henry do to make sure she succeeded him? Time was running out. In 1127, he made all the barons swear they would support Matilda as their queen when he died. However, Henry knew this was risky. Barons could easily change their minds when the time came.

In 1128, Matilda was married to Geoffrey of Anjou, a French prince. Matilda was not happy with the arrangement – Geoffrey was ten years younger than she was, and she didn't really like him. Nevertheless, arranged marriages were usual for the time and Henry had arranged this one, desperate for Matilda to have children, which would secure his succession. He was lucky. Matilda and Geoffrey had three sons.

However, there was a problem. Matilda's cousin, Stephen, was waiting to seize his chance.

**Source B:** A picture of Matilda from a medieval manuscript.

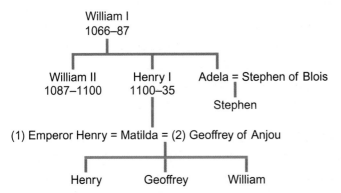

**Figure 4.4:** Matilda's family tree.

### Key term

**Court\*:** A monarch's household, where all those who meet regularly with the monarch gather.

### Your turn!

1   Write two or three sentences to explain why the shipwreck of the *White Ship* was such a disaster for Henry I.

2   Imagine you are Matilda. Write a paragraph about the story of your life from 1114 to 1128. Don't just give the facts: describe how you felt. You might, for example, say how you felt about being sent away from home to a foreign country when you were only 12, how you felt about your father arranging your marriages and whether you thought you really would inherit the throne when he died. Remember to stay in role as a 12th-century young woman.

3   Who had the better claim to the throne of England, Matilda or Stephen? Discuss this in your class.

Did you know?

**Did you know?**

The civil war between Matilda and Stephen is sometimes called 'the Anarchy'. Nineteenth-century historians gave it this name. Anarchy means disorder, lawlessness or chaos.

## Civil war, 1135–53

Stephen was one of Henry's favourite nephews. Henry gave Stephen so much land that he became the wealthiest man in England. While Henry was alive, Stephen swore publicly to support Matilda as the rightful heir to the English throne. However, he was secretly gathering support among the barons for his own claim to the throne.

On 1 December 1135, Henry died. Stephen moved quickly before Matilda returned to England from France, expecting to be crowned queen. Stephen gained the support of most of the barons and the pope. On 22 December 1135, Stephen was crowned king in London. Matilda was furious, and so were the barons who had remained loyal to her. They gathered together an army to fight Stephen and his supporters. The result was a bloody civil war.

1. Matilda and her half-brother Robert invaded England. Several skirmishes occurred, but Stephen was unable to defeat Matilda.

2. 1141: The Battle of Lincoln. Stephen was captured and imprisoned.

3. Just before her coronation was due to take place in London, Matilda announced a new tax. Londoners were so angry that they chased her out of the city. Stephen was freed and declared king again.

4. Christmas 1142: Stephen trapped Matilda inside Oxford Castle. She climbed down the castle walls and crossed the frozen Thames at night on foot. She fled to Normandy, where she remained for the rest of her life.

The civil war years (1135–53) were terrible ones for England. Barons fought barons and their armies killed people and destroyed villages and towns. New castles were built and old ones strengthened. Law and order broke down. Finally, in 1153, Stephen and Matilda reached an agreement. Stephen would remain king of England and, when he died, Matilda's son Henry would succeed him. When Stephen died in 1154, Henry was crowned King Henry II.

## Who was fit to rule: Matilda or Stephen?

Both Matilda and Stephen had a claim to the throne, and they fought each other over it. But which of them was fit to be monarch? What did their contemporaries think of them?

**Source C:** A portrait of King Stephen from a medieval manuscript.

**Source D:** From *The Deeds of King Stephen*, written by an anonymous monk, in the 1100s.

Matilda sent for the richest men and demanded from them a huge sum of money, not with gentleness, but with the voice of authority. They complained that they did not have any money left because of the war. When they said this, Matilda, with a grim look, her forehead wrinkled into a frown, every trace of a woman's gentleness removed from her face, blazed into unbearable fury.

**Source E:** From the *Anglo-Saxon Chronicle*, written by monks.

In the days of this king [Stephen] there was nothing but strife, evil and robbery, for quickly the great men who were traitors rose up against him. When the traitors saw that Stephen was a good-humoured, kindly and easy-going man who inflicted no punishment, then they committed all manner of crimes. And so it lasted for nineteen years while Stephen was king, till the land was all undone and darkened with such deeds, and men said openly that Christ and his angels slept.

### Checkpoint

1 Why did Henry have to make sure there was a smooth succession after his death?

2 Who was crowned king of England after Henry's death?

3 What happened when Matilda claimed the throne?

4 What agreement did Stephen and Matilda reach about the succession?

5 Matilda needs support. Design a poster that will encourage people to join her cause.

### Your turn!

 **1** Matilda's decision to come to England in 1139, four years after her father's death and Stephen's coronation, started a terrible civil war. Was her decision the right one? Discuss this with a partner and make a list of points for and against her decision being correct.

 **2** Read Sources D and E. Using these as evidence, write a paragraph to explain whether you think Matilda would have made a better monarch than Stephen.

**3** Do the troubles that hit England in the years 1139–53 prove that medieval monarchs should always be men? Discuss this in your class.

# Eleanor of Aquitaine: a strong-willed queen

**Interpretation 1:** A modern painting of Eleanor of Aquitaine entering Constantinople in 1147.

Why did the richest and most powerful woman in the world ride into Constantinople with armed knights in 1147? In order to answer this, we have to go back ten years.

## Eleanor, queen of France (1137–52)

In April 1137, on the death of her father, Eleanor became the rich and powerful Duchess of Aquitaine. She was 15 years old and the most sought-after bride in Europe. Her father had entrusted the care of his daughters to the king of France, Louis VI. Louis decided that the best way to take care of their vast fortunes and extensive lands was to marry the eldest and richest daughter, Eleanor, to his son Louis. The old king died less than a week after the wedding, making the young Louis and Eleanor king and queen of France.

The marriage was not a success. Louis had been brought up by monks and was quiet and scholarly, and the French court was old-fashioned. Eleanor was used to the lively Aquitaine court, where music and art flourished, along with a very open attitude to romantic relationships. At the start, Eleanor seems to have made the best of the situation.

She welcomed poets and troubadours* to the French court and encouraged music, dancing and fashionable clothes and manners. The French court became the most popular in Europe.

In 1145, she gave birth to a daughter, Marie. She had proved that she and Louis could have children, and there was every expectation that boys (always preferable as heirs) would follow. In 1151, they had another daughter, called Alix.

**Key term**

**Troubadour*:** A poet who writes verse to music.

# Eleanor goes on the Second Crusade

Eleanor was not prepared to spend her life in the French court, producing babies. When Europe began preparing for the Second Crusade in 1147, she was determined to join in. Interpretation 1 shows her doing just that!

**1.** Eleanor and other noble ladies ride around France, whipping up support for the Crusade.

**2.** Eleanor sets off for the Holy Land...

**3.** Eleanor and Louis reach Constantinople. Eleanor wants to head for Odessa first but Louis insists she goes with him directly to Jerusalem.

**4.** The crusade fails. Eleanor is furious and she and Louis return to France in separate ships.

Tensions between Eleanor and Louis got worse and they divorced in 1152. Their two daughters stayed in France, but Eleanor kept all the Aquitaine land she had brought into the marriage.

**Interpretation 2:** From *Eleanor of Aquitaine* by Alison Weir, published in 1999.

Eleanor was renowned for her loveliness, but was also headstrong and wilful. Her behaviour was scandalous. Rumours of her many affairs in France and during the Second Crusade were circulating throughout Europe.

## Your turn!

**1** Look at Interpretation 1. Write down one thing the artist got right, and one they might have made up.

**2** Look at Interpretation 2. Which parts of this interpretation are facts and which are the writer's own interpretation of the facts? Discuss this in your class and see if you can reach an agreement.

**3** What do you think were Eleanor's most important achievements as queen of France? Discuss this in your class. Write a paragraph beginning 'Eleanor's most important achievement as queen of France was …' to explain why you have chosen this achievement.

## Eleanor, queen of England (1154–89)

Two months after the ending of her marriage to Louis, Eleanor married again. This time, aged 30, she married 19-year-old Henry, Duke of Anjou. This was a significant marriage: Henry was Matilda's son, and in 1154 he became King Henry II of England with Eleanor as his queen. Henry's strength of purpose and fiery temper combined with Eleanor's wildness and determination meant that the marriage was a stormy one.

**1.** 1154: Henry and Eleanor ruled over a great empire that stretched from the borders of Scotland to the Pyrenees.

**2.** Eleanor gave birth to five sons (William, Henry, Richard, Geoffrey and John) and three daughters (Matilda, Eleanor and Joan); Richard was her favourite child.

**3.** In 1173, Eleanor led three of her sons, Henry, Richard and John, in a rebellion against their father, Henry II.

**4.** The rebellion failed and Henry imprisoned Eleanor for 16 years.

**Figure 4.5:** Eleanor, queen of England.

When Henry died in 1189, his son Richard inherited his father's throne. He immediately ordered the release of his mother. At 67, she was an old lady by medieval standards, but she wasn't ready for retirement.

Eleanor helped rule England when Richard I was away on the Third Crusade (see page 100) and organised armies to defend his lands in France. She raised vast sums of money to pay his ransom when he was captured. Travelling throughout Europe, Eleanor managed her armies and estates, and chose a wife, Berengaria, for Richard. When Richard died in 1199, Eleanor transferred her energies to supporting his younger brother, John, when he became king. Eleanor died in 1204, aged 82, at Fontevrault, her favourite religious community, where older aristocratic women went for spiritual comfort.

**Interpretation 3:** *The Lion in Winter* is a film about Eleanor, Henry II and their sons. It is a fictional story, and few of the events in the film happened in real life. It won many awards. Katharine Hepburn played the part of Eleanor of Aquitaine, and Peter O'Toole played Henry II.

**Interpretation 4:** From *Eleanor of Aquitaine* by Katherine Bailey, published online in 2006.

Eleanor resented Henry's relationships with other women, particularly his with Rosamund, a beauty much praised by English poets. Yet more important than Eleanor's resentment was her overwhelming ambition for personal power. She believed that with one of her sons on the throne, she herself would rule England.

**Interpretation 5:** From *A History of Britain* by Simon Schama, published in 2000.

Eleanor greeted the death of Henry II with dry eyes. For her, it was an occasion for rejoicing. When Richard, with his blue eyes and red-gold hair, and with his character formed by Eleanor, was finally seated on the throne, she could once again assert herself in governing the kingdom.

**Your turn!**

**1** Think about Interpretation 3. There are many films made and stories written with historical themes. Does it matter if the history is wrong as long as the story is good? Discuss this in your class.

**2** Read Interpretation 4. Write a sentence to say what impression this gives you of Eleanor. Now do the same for Interpretation 5.

**Checkpoint**

1 Who was Eleanor's first husband?

2 Name one change Eleanor made to the French court.

3 Name two things that happened when she went on crusade.

4 Who was Eleanor's second husband?

5 Name two things Eleanor did to support him.

6 Why did Eleanor's husband lock her up for 16 years?

# How important were England's medieval queens?

- Imagine a conversation between Matilda and Eleanor. What advice would they give each other about playing an important part in governing a kingdom? Work with a partner and write out the conversation. You could act it out in front of your class.

- A company is making a TV series about England's medieval queens. They want you to advise them about how they should portray Matilda and Eleanor. Write a paragraph of advice.

In this section you have learned:

- that there can be many different interpretations of events and people in the past.

### Your turn!

1. You have been asked to design a poster for the local tourist board to attract visitors to your area.

   a  Decide what you will include in the poster and what you will leave out.

   b  Now design your poster. Compare your poster with others in your class. Have you all decided to include and leave out the same things?

Studying history involves working with all kinds of different source material. Source material can be divided into two main groups.

- **Sources:** These come from the time of the person or event you are studying. If you are working with sources, you need to evaluate them. This means asking, for example, whether the person who created them was in a position to know what they were describing. You need to assess them for reliability and usefulness, and investigate their nature, origin and purpose. You read about how to do this on page 88.

- **Interpretations:** These are made later, by people who did not know the individuals, or were not involved in the events. These need investigating in a different way from sources. You need to check interpretations against what you know about the person or event. This means you need to work out what the author or artist has decided to include, and what they have left out; you need to decide what impression the interpretation gives – is it positive or negative, gloomy or upbeat? What message is the author or artist trying to get across? Then you will be able to say how far you agree with a particular interpretation.

## What is an interpretation?

Anything where a person is trying to recreate some part of the past is an interpretation (see Figure 4.6). One of the most important interpretations is what historians have written about the past.

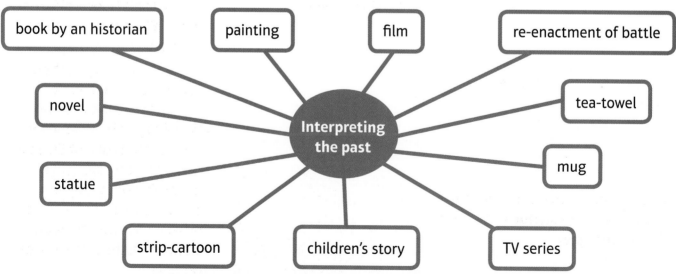

book by an historian · painting · film · re-enactment of battle · novel · tea-towel · statue · **Interpreting the past** · mug · strip-cartoon · children's story · TV series

**Figure 4.6:** Ways of interpreting the past.

# Writing historically

In designing your poster, you had to decide what to put in and what to leave out. This created an impression of your local area, which in turn gave out a message to those looking at the poster. This is exactly what anyone creating any sort of an interpretation does. So when you are analysing* an interpretation, there are four questions you must ask.

- What has been included?
- What has been left out?

- What impression does the interpretation give?
- What is the message of the interpretation?

You could think of these as the four Qs: *In, Out, Impression and Message – IOIM.*

Students were asked to analyse the interpretation of Eleanor of Aquitaine in Interpretation 1 on page 112. We will look at two answers and consider how well each answers this question.

**Student 1**

> Eleanor of Aquitaine is riding in between two knights. You can tell they are going to Constantinople because of the misty image of the city in the background.

Student 1 is describing what can be seen in the picture; there is no analysis.

**Student 2**

> Eleanor of Aquitaine would have been accompanied by far more than just two knights. The artist has drawn a cross on the banner being carried by Eleanor to show that they are going on a crusade.

Student 2 is starting to analyse the picture by noting what has been included and what has been left out, but has not gone far enough.

You can do better than these students! Remember the four Qs, and copy and fill in the following boxes.

**Box 1: What has the artist chosen to show?**

**Box 2: What has the artist left out?**

**Box 3: What impression has the artist given of Eleanor's entry into Constantinople?**

**Box 4: What message is given by this interpretation?**

### Your turn!

Choose an interpretation of Queen Matilda, or a different one of Eleanor of Aquitaine, from this chapter.

Analyse the interpretation using the four Qs. You can set out the analysis in four boxes as you have done for the interpretation of Eleanor entering Constantinople, or you can write it up in a paragraph. Remember that written interpretations are analysed in the same way as pictures.

# How powerful were English monarchs?

Monarchs, in order to become strong, needed the support of their nobles, a strong army and a contented population. This combination was not always easy to achieve. A strong monarch could then exercise their power, often by defeating enemies and gaining land. This increased their strength and made them even more powerful.

In this section, you will look at two monarchs: one who tried to exercise his power and failed, and one who tried to exercise his power and succeeded.

This section of the book will look at:

- the failures of King John and the reasons for them
- the successes of King Edward I and the reasons for them
- the limitations of the power of English monarchs.

## What do you think?

What do you think stopped medieval monarchs becoming all-powerful?

# King John: unlucky or useless?

## Learning objectives

- Learn about what King John did to make himself so unpopular that the barons rebelled against him.
- Understand the significance of Magna Carta.

In 1199, King John inherited the Angevin Empire from his brother, Richard I. The empire was prosperous and flourishing. It included rich farming land, busy ports and trade routes, prosperous towns and a growing population.

What could possibly go wrong?

- In order to take possession of his French lands, John had to promise to be loyal to the king of France. But the king of France didn't want John to be king. He and the French barons wanted Arthur, John's nephew.

- John's brother, Richard I, had left huge problems for John to sort out. Richard had been away from England a lot, fighting in the crusades (see page 100), and leaving the barons and the Church to run the country for him. Now they didn't want to give up their power.

- Richard's crusades had been expensive and he had run up big debts paying for them. Somehow, John had to pay back the money Richard had borrowed.

**Source A:** From the *Barnwell Chronicle*, written by monks in Barnwell Abbey, Cambridgeshire, at the end of the 1220s.

[John] was a great prince but hardly a happy one. and he experienced the ups and downs of fortune. He would have thought of himself as happy and successful had he not lost his continental possessions and suffered the Church's curse [excommunication].

**Source B:** Written by Matthew Paris in 1235. Matthew was a monk based in St Alban's Abbey, Hertfordshire.

John was a tyrant, not a king; a destroyer, not a governor, crushing his own people and favouring foreigners. He lost the duchy of Normandy and many other territories through laziness. As for Christianity, he was unstable and unfaithful. Foul as it is, hell itself is defiled by the fouler presence of King John.

He married Isabella of Angoulême. This should have helped secure his lands in France, but it upset the king of France because Isabella had been promised to one of his nobles.

He taxed his barons heavily in order to pay for his wars. They had to pay more tax to him than they had to pay any other king. This upset them, particularly since he was defeated.

He tried to run the country without the barons. Instead of appointing the most powerful ones to important positions, he ignored them and their advice.

He ordered the murder of his nephew, Arthur. This should have removed any possible threat to his throne, but it disgusted barons in Britain and France. French barons were happy to support the French king in his wars against John.

He went to war twice against France in order to defend his French lands, and lost both times. By the end of his reign, he had lost almost all England's lands in France.

He quarrelled with the pope about who was to be the next archbishop of Canterbury. The pope banned all church services in England. People were afraid they would go to hell. John was excommunicated, which meant that all his nobles were absolved from their oaths of loyalty to him, allowing them to rebel.

**Figure 4.7:** How King John became unpopular.

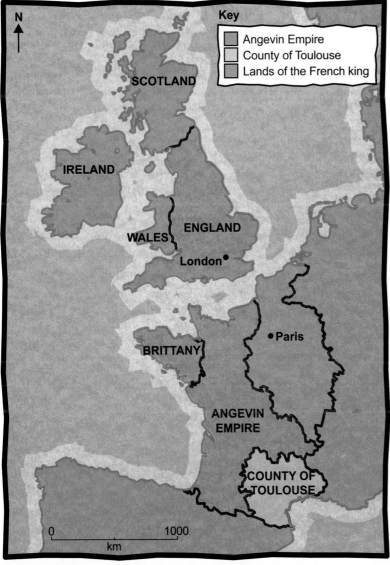

**Figure 4.8:** Map of the Angevin Empire in 1199.

**Your turn!**

1 Look at all the reasons why John became unpopular. List them in order of importance. Write a sentence to explain which, in your opinion, was the most important and a sentence to explain which was the least important.

2 Read Sources A and B. Work in a small group. Imagine you are going to interview both Matthew Paris and the monks who wrote the *Barnwell Chronicle*. Write down a list of questions to ask them about why they held the views they did about John. Swap your list with the group next to you. Each group should then try to work out the answers that might have been given. You could act out a question and answer session.

# Barons hit back: Magna Carta 1215

**Interpretation 1:** A 19th-century painting of King John putting his seal on Magna Carta. Today, this painting hangs in the Houses of Parliament.

By 1215, the barons had had enough. They believed that John was ruining the country and was being disrespectful to them and to their position in his kingdom. About 40 barons met in Bury St Edmunds, Suffolk. They chose Robert Fitzwalter to lead them and marched with their armies on London. They did not intend to overthrow the king – they simply wanted John to negotiate with them. Since John couldn't raise an army without the support of the barons, he was forced to negotiate. Finally, on 15 June 1215, John met with the barons at Runnymede, close to the River Thames, near Windsor. The barons presented him with a charter that listed all their demands. Reluctantly, John agreed to them all and put his seal on the charter. He had no choice. In return, the barons promised to be loyal to King John.

## What did the charter say?

The charter contained 63 promises.

**Did you know?**

The barons called the charter the 'Charter of Liberties'. This was later called Magna Carta, which is Latin for 'Great Charter'.

The English Church shall be free to choose its own bishops and archbishops.

No freeman can be seized or imprisoned, or stripped of his rights or possessions, or outlawed or exiled, except by the law of the land.

No freeman shall be imprisoned without a proper trial by a jury.

Justice will not be refused to anyone, nor will it be delayed or sold.

All merchants shall be free to buy and sell goods in England without paying extra taxes.

The advice of the Great Council must be sought before the king raises taxes.

A baron's son shall inherit his lands on payment to the king of £100 and no more.

25 barons are to be elected by the other barons to keep the peace and liberties granted by this charter.

**Key term**

**Great Council\*:** An assembly of church leaders and wealthy landowners who met with the king from time to time to discuss national affairs.

**Figure 4.9:** Some of the most important promises within the charter presented by the barons, written in modern English.

## What happened next?

John may have put his seal on Magna Carta, but he didn't like it one little bit. He particularly hated having to call the Great Council* whenever he wanted to raise taxes. He had no intention of keeping the promises he had made to the barons.

He got the pope to agree that no one could force a monarch to do anything. This was because people believed monarchs were chosen by God, and so were above the law.

Civil war broke out and John was successful in defeating the rebels.

In desperation, London rebels offered the throne of England to the king of France. In 1216, he landed in England with his armies, and many English barons joined him.

At this critical moment, in October 1216, John died. There was no mystery about his death: it was from natural causes. John was succeeded by his son, who became King Henry III. Henry was nine years old when John died, so until he was 18 he was guided by his guardians, William Marshal and Hubert de Burgh. There were two problems that needed to be dealt with quickly.

**Problem 1: end the civil war.** The rebel barons were defeated at Lincoln in 1217 and the French fleet destroyed at the Battle of Sandwich. The French king went back to France.

**Problem 2: Magna Carta.** The pope, who had told John he didn't have to carry out the Magna Carta agreement, had died. The charter was discussed and agreed to by the barons, the king and the pope, and reissued in the name of Henry III.

The new reign had started well. The troubles of King John's reign were over, and the fact that they were over so quickly shows just how far King John had overstepped what had become acceptable in a monarch.

### Your turn!

1 Look at Interpretation 1.
   a What impression has the artist given of the scene at Runnymede in 1215?
   b Use what you know about the events surrounding Magna Carta to write a few sentences to explain whether you think the artist got it right.
   c Have a class discussion on why the painting hangs in the Houses of Parliament today.

2 Write two or three sentences to explain how the following people would have been affected by Magna Carta: Wulf, a peasant who worked for his lord as a shepherd; Mary, a widow who had taken over her husband's woollen business; Richard, a priest; Joan, who brewed ale and had never left her village; Thomas, the son of a nobleman.

3 Magna Carta was written to put right bad things that were happening. For example, saying that no freeman should be imprisoned without a fair trial indicates that some were being imprisoned without a fair trial. Look at the examples given and write a paragraph to say what England was like before Magna Carta.

### Checkpoint

1 What were the dates of King John's reign?

2 Give one problem Richard I left for John to sort out.

3 Name two things John did that made him unpopular.

4 Name the baron who led opposition to King John.

5 Where did John and the barons meet?

6 What is the date of Magna Carta?

7 Give one way in which Magna Carta affected freemen.

8 What happened to Magna Carta after John's death?

# Edward I: a popular monarch

**Interpretation 1:** A modern interpretation of the Battle of Evesham, 1265.

In 1265, the Battle of Evesham was fought between rebel barons, who were trying to put limits on royal power, and the armies of Henry III. Henry's son, Prince Edward, led the royal armies. Edward led his men into one of the bloodiest battles ever to be fought in England. No hostages were taken; the rebels were killed mercilessly as Edward successfully asserted royal authority. So, even before he became king in 1272, Edward had a reputation as an ambitious and ruthless leader, who would ferociously punish his enemies.

## Learning from others' mistakes: parliament

Edward was determined not to make the mistakes of his father and grandfather, and end up with barons rebelling against his rule. He decided to encourage them to work with him.

He often called meetings of parliament (the new name for the Great Council) so that they knew what he wanted to do, and he knew their opinions. In this way, he could avoid trouble.

In 1275, he invited two men from each county (knights) and two important people from each city or town (burgesses) to attend parliament along with the nobles and clergy. This deepened Edward's understanding of what people wanted, and how they would react to his wishes.

Edward's strength was that he knew that if he was to govern well and have the money he needed, he had to give in to parliament occasionally. For example, in 1303, Edward gave merchants the right to trade freely in return for accepting a new taxation system.

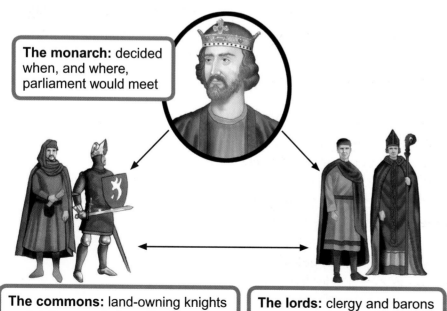

**The monarch:** decided when, and where, parliament would meet

**The commons:** land-owning knights and richer people from the towns

**The lords:** clergy and barons

**Figure 4.10:** Parliament in 1275.

## Learning from others' mistakes: the Church

King John, Edward's grandfather, had huge problems with the pope which resulted in the pope closing all the churches in England (see page 119). Edward learned from this. In 1296, the pope tried to impose his authority on the English Church. He told all the clergy in England that they needed his permission before they paid taxes to King Edward. Edward would have none of this! He got the support of parliament and then told the clergy he would take away their land if they did not pay their taxes. Faced with opposition from parliament and the king, the pope backed down. Edward had won the day.

**Source A:** An illustration from a medieval manuscript showing Edward I and parliament together with the rulers Llywelyn (Wales) and Alexander (Scotland).

### Did you know?

Unlike Christians, Jewish money-lenders were allowed to charge interest* on the loans they made. Edward taxed the Jews heavily. When they could no longer pay these taxes, Edward accused them of disloyalty. He took away their right to charge interest on the money they loaned. He made all Jews over seven years old wear a yellow badge on their clothes. He ordered the heads of Jewish households to be arrested. Three hundred were taken to the Tower of London and executed. In 1290, he expelled all the Jews from England.

### Your turn!

1 Write a paragraph to describe the changes that Edward made to the Great Council that used to meet in his father's time.

2 What were the advantages of having a parliament for (a) the king and (b) the barons, clergy, knights and burgesses? Write two or three sentences in explanation.

3 Do you think that Edward's actions showed he was a weak king or a strong one? Discuss this in your class, and make a list of points that could show he was weak and a list of points that could show he was strong. Reach a conclusion with which most of you agree.

4 Source A shows Edward attending parliament together with the rulers of Wales (Llywelyn) and Scotland (Alexander). This never happened. There could be many reasons why the medieval artist painted Edward's parliament like this. With a partner, decide what you think was the most likely reason.

### Key term

**Interest*:** A fee for lending someone money, usually a percentage of the money lent.

# Taking over Wales

**Source B:** Written by Gerald of Wales in 1194. He was a priest who worked as a royal clerk and for two archbishops. His father was a Norman and his mother a Welsh princess.

They [the Welsh] may not shine in open combat and in fixed formation, but they harass their enemy by ambushes and night-attacks. In a single battle they are easily beaten, but they are difficult to conquer in a long war. They are not troubled by hunger or cold, and fighting does not seem to tire them. They do not lose heart when things go wrong, and after one defeat they are ready to fight again and face once more the hazards of war.

**Source C:** *The Chronicle of Lanercost*, written by monks at the time, describes the death of Dafydd ap Gruffydd.

Dafydd had his entrails cut out of his stomach for being a traitor. He was then hanged. His arms and legs were cut off, for being a rebel. They were then sent to four parts of England as a warning and a celebration. The right arm was sent to York, the left arm to Bristol, the right leg went to Northampton and the left to Hereford. His head was bound with iron to stop it falling apart as it rotted. It was sent to London and put on show on the city walls.

William I (1066–87) wasn't particularly interested in conquering Wales. He was more worried that Wales would attack England. In 1066, Wales was a country almost entirely different from England. It had its own language, laws and customs, and was run by a number of princes who each controlled different regions. In order to keep the Welsh princes inside Wales, William chose strong, loyal lords to run the lands along the Welsh border. They were known as the Marcher Lords. Unlike other lords, they had the right to build castles and call up armies. Gradually they extended their control into south Wales. They didn't attempt to take over Gwynedd, a region of rugged mountains, in north Wales. There, the princes were determined and strong, and never swore loyalty to the English kings as other Welsh princes had done.

## Enter Edward I

Edward's father, Henry III, had allowed the most powerful prince in Gwynedd, Llywelyn ap Gruffydd, to call himself 'Prince of Wales'. When Edward became king, Llywelyn refused to do homage to him. Edward called a meeting of parliament and got their agreement to raise money for a war with Llywelyn.

King Edward I, 1277

sends army into Gwynedd | sends ships to stop food getting from Anglesey into Gwynedd

Llywelyn surrenders

Peace of Treaty of Aberconwy 1277
Llywelyn restricted to land in Gwynedd, west of River Conwy
Llywelyn's brother, Dafydd, restricted to land in Gwynedd, east of River Conwy

1282 Llywelyn and Dafydd rebel against Edward

Edward's armies invade Gwynedd; the rebellion is brutally put down; Llywelyn is killed and Dafydd captured

1283 Edward starts building castles throughout the Welsh kingdoms

**Figure 4.11:** The pathway to English control in Wales.

After taking control of Wales, Edward enforced English law and language, and divided Wales into seven counties, following the feudal system. Wales was never again to be an independent country.

## Owain Glyndwr (1359–1415)

Many Welsh people resented being ruled from England, but could do nothing about it because English kings were too powerful. However, their chance came in 1400 when a dispute between two great landowners in Wales led to one of them, Owain Glyndwr, leading a revolt against Henry IV. By 1403, Owain, who called himself the Prince of Wales, had gained control of most of Wales. He called a Welsh parliament and invited the Irish and Scots to join with him in a Celtic alliance. He asked France for support and, in 1405, around 2600 French soldiers landed on the coast of Wales to support Owain. Gradually, however, English armies defeated the rebels and by 1410 Owain was a fugitive on the run. England was once again in control.

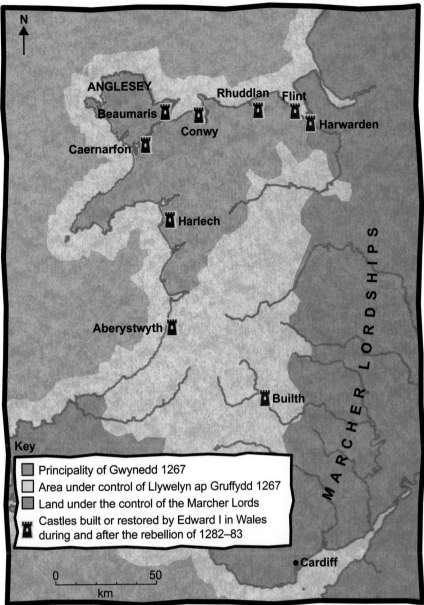

**Figure 4.12:** Wales at the time of Edward I's conquests.

## Checkpoint

1 When did Edward I's reign begin?

2 Give two changes Edward made to his father's Great Council.

3 What did the pope want the clergy to do in 1296, and how did Edward stop this happening?

4 When did Edward expel the Jews from England?

5 Name the leaders of the Welsh revolts against Edward in 1277 and Henry IV in 1400.

6 Give two reasons why Wales failed to gain independence.

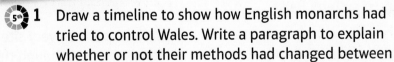

## Your turn!

1 Draw a timeline to show how English monarchs had tried to control Wales. Write a paragraph to explain whether or not their methods had changed between 1066 and 1410.

2 Why were neither Llywelyn ap Gruffydd nor Owain Glyndwr able to keep Wales independent of England? Write three or four sentences in explanation.

3 Read Sources B and C. Discuss in your class whether Source B explains why Edward I went to the trouble of having Dafydd ap Gruffydd hanged, drawn and quartered.

# Changing castle designs

**Learning objectives**

- Learn about the ways in which Edward I's Welsh castles were designed for defence.
- Understand why the ways in which castles were used changed over time.

1. Gatehouse with three portcullises.
2. Arrow slits letting archers fire at attackers while staying protected.
3. Round towers, which are stronger than square ones.
4. The 'killing ground' where trapped attackers could easily be killed.

**Interpretation 1:** A modern reconstruction of Harlech Castle, painted by Terry Ball.

## Edward I's castles

Harlech was a fantastically strong castle built in 1282–89 as part of Edward I's strategy for taking over Wales. In the 200 years since William I built the first motte and bailey castles, stone had taken over from wood as the favoured building material. Wooden motte and bailey castles were quick to build and helped William I establish Norman rule in England (see pages 40–41). They were replaced by stone keep and curtain wall castles, which took longer to build, but lasted far longer and were more difficult to attack.

Edward only built castles in Wales. He employed one of the greatest castle architects of the Middle Ages, James of St Georges d'Espéranche, to come over from Europe to design the most up-to-date castles in the western world.

Edward inspected every site personally, and was usually there when building began. Although the Welsh castles designed by James were all very different, they had some features in common.

- All were near the sea or tidal rivers to take advantage of Edward's sea power.

- They were so well designed that they could be defended by very few men.

- They were built to fit the geographical features of their sites perfectly.

**Did you know?**

Edward's colossal new stone castles of Conwy, Harlech, Caernarfon and Beaumaris were known as the Iron Ring of Snowdonia.

## Beaumaris Castle

Beaumaris Castle, started in 1295 and finished around 1330, was the last castle built by James in Wales. Although never fully completed, it is a perfect example of a symmetrical, stone concentric castle: that is, one featuring walls within walls. Labour costs were enormous, as building stone castles needed skilled workers. These workers were brought in from all over England.

### Your turn!

**5th 1** Look back at the picture of the motte and bailey castle on page 40 and compare it with the picture of Harlech Castle on page 126. How many similarities and differences can you find? Make two lists.

**2** Imagine you are a Welsh spy. You have managed to get into Harlech Castle. Your task is to advise Welsh rebels as to how they could attack the castle. Make notes telling them what they should, and should not, do.

**3** James was an architect who was always working to improve his designs. In what ways is Beaumaris Castle an improvement on Harlech Castle? Discuss this in your class.

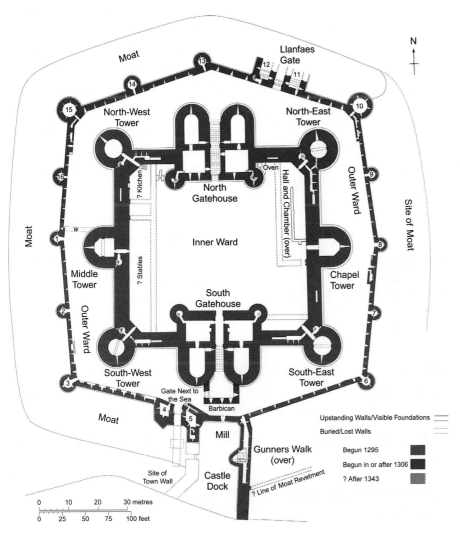

**Figure 4.13:** A plan of Beaumaris Castle.

**Source A:** Part of a letter written by James to the Treasurer and barons of the Exchequer in February 1296.

In case you should wonder where so much money went in one week, we would have you know that we have needed, and shall continue to need, 400 masons, both cutters and layers, together with 2000 less skilled workmen, 100 carts, 60 wagons and 30 boats bringing stone and sea coal; 200 quarrymen, 30 smiths and carpenters. The men's pay has been and still is very much in arrears and we are having the greatest difficulty in keeping them because they simply have nothing to live on.

And, Sirs, for God's sake be quick with the money.

# Changing castle use

If you were able to take a trip around England and Wales in the 1400s, looking for castles, you would find more ruins than standing castles. How had this happened?

## Centres of local government

In the 1300s, England and Wales were more or less peaceful and castles were used differently. They became the centre of government for the local area. The monarch's judges, tax collectors and civil servants were based there. Barons began to convert them into homes.

## Changes in warfare

Early cannons were not much use. They kept falling apart when they were fired. They were heavy and difficult to pull around on a muddy battlefield. By the 15th century, however, cannons were strong and gunpowder was easier to use. Cannonballs could smash a castle wall. They were even more useful in defending a castle. They were set at fixed points and fired through gun ports.

Castles became so well defended that it was almost a waste of time to attack them. This changed the way in which armies fought. Warfare became more about battles between armies and less about besieging castles.

Lord's solar – the private rooms of the lord and his wife

Garderobe

Great hall

Chapel

Kitchens

Cellars

Dungeons

**Figure 4.14:** Life inside a castle in the 1300s.

## Changes in society

It wasn't just changes in warfare that altered the way castles were used. Society changed, too.

Government gradually came to be more centred in London. The monarch didn't need to travel around the country so much and so didn't need to stay in well-defended castles.

Barons stopped acting as local judges and tax collectors. These jobs were done by the monarch's own judges who toured the country, or by the monarch's sheriffs in each county.

**Source B:** A photograph of Herstmonceux Castle, Sussex.

Castles were uncomfortable, draughty places in which to live. Barons began to want a higher standard of living than was possible in a castle.

This didn't mean that castle building stopped! Herstmonceux Castle in Sussex was built in the 1440s by Sir Roger Fiennes, the king's treasurer.

At first glance, Herstmonceux looks very like any other castle. But look more closely. It is built from bricks, and the windows are not arrow slits, but large enough to let in the light.

### Checkpoint

1 Who was the architect who designed Edward I's castles?

2 Name two castles designed by Edward's architect.

3 Give two features that Edward's Welsh castles had in common.

4 What was the Iron Ring of Snowdonia?

5 Give one way in which cannons changed castles.

6 Give one change in society that affected the way in which castles were used.

### Your turn!

1 The baron who lives in the castle on page 128 needs a tutor to teach his sons to read and write. He wants to write to the monks in the nearest monastery to ask them to find someone suitable and who would like living in a castle. Write the letter for him. You'll need to be positive about the living conditions!

2 Draw a mind map to show how changes in society and in warfare led to changes in the ways in which castles were used.

3 Which were the more important in changing the ways in which castles were used: changes in society or changes in warfare? Have a class discussion.

# Losing Scotland

**Source B:** A stained glass window in Lerwick town hall, showing the princess Margaret.

**Source A:** Part of the Declaration of Arbroath, 1320.

As long as but a hundred of us remain alive, never will we on any conditions be brought under English rule. It is in truth not for glory, nor riches, nor honours that we are fighting, but for freedom – for that alone.

What was it that made 51 Scottish barons put their seals to the Declaration of Arbroath and send it to the pope? This part of the shared history of Scotland and England begins with the death of a child.

## The death of a child

In September 1290, a ship travelling between Norway and Scotland was hit by a violent storm. It was blown off course and landed on Orkney. One of the passengers, a child aged seven, died – supposedly from severe sea-sickness. This child was Margaret, granddaughter of King Alexander III of Scotland, and his only heir. She was to have been crowned as Scotland's queen and then married to Edward of Caernarfon, the son of Edward I of England. Margaret's death left Scotland without a monarch and England without the opportunity to control Scotland.

## Enter John Balliol

The Scottish nobles asked Edward I to judge the claims of the 13 barons who each wanted to be king of Scotland. Edward dismissed the claims of all of them except John Balliol, who held land in Scotland, England and France, and Robert the Bruce, who was the great-grandson of David I, king of Scotland 1124–53. Edward chose John Balliol, because he thought that John would be more likely to agree to England's demands than Robert. He was wrong.

### Did you know?

Scottish kings were always crowned sitting on the Stone of Scone. In 1296, Edward I removed the stone and took it to London. It was put underneath a specially built throne on which English monarchs were crowned. It wasn't returned to Scotland until 1996.

| John Balliol refuses to do homage to Edward I. | ▶ | John Balliol makes an alliance with France, England's old enemy. | ▶ | Edward I invades Scotland. | ▶ | Edward I defeats John Balliol at the Battle of Dunbar, 1296. | ▶ | Edward I declares himself king of Scotland. | ▶ | Edward I forces the Scots to pay heavy taxes and fight in the English army. |

**Figure 4.15:** Timeline showing how Edward I becomes king of Scotland, 1296.

## William Wallace's chance

It didn't take long for the Scots to revolt against English rule. William Wallace was a Scottish knight and a member of the lesser nobility. He and the Scots defeated the English at the Battle of Stirling Bridge in September 1297. He then invaded England, getting as far as Newcastle.

Edward I, in retaliation, invaded Scotland. In 1298, he defeated William Wallace's army at the Battle of Falkirk. Wallace was forced into exile and Edward continued with his campaign to conquer Scotland.

By 1304, the conquest was complete. Scottish nobles were forced to give up their fortresses; Scotland was run by an English lieutenant, with the power to change Scottish laws.

William Wallace was betrayed by some Scottish nobles who thought they would have a better future if they were allied with England. William was arrested and in 1305 was hanged, drawn and quartered as a traitor.

**Source C:** Part of William Wallace's response when being accused of treason against Edward I in 1305.

I cannot be a traitor, for I owe him [Edward I] no allegiance. He is not my Sovereign; he never received my homage, and while life is in my body, he shall never receive it. To the other points of which I am accused, I freely confess them all. I have slain the English; I have opposed the English king; I have stormed and taken the towns and castles which he unjustly claimed were his. I repent me of my sins, but it is not of Edward I of England I shall ask pardon.

### Your turn!

1. Write a paragraph to explain how the death of a child created problems for Scotland and also for England.

2. Edward I was called the 'Hammer of the Scots'. What did he do that led to people calling him this? Think of three things and write them down.

3. Read Source C. Was William Wallace correct in saying he could not be accused of being a traitor? Imagine you are taking part in his trial. Work with a partner; one of you must prepare a case in William's defence and the other, a case for the English accusers. You could act this out.

4. Thousands of people saw the film *Braveheart* and it won many awards. However, it is full of historical mistakes. For example, William Wallace never painted his face blue. Does this matter? Discuss this in your class.

**Interpretation 1:** A still from the film *Braveheart*, starring Mel Gibson as William Wallace.

# Robert the Bruce triumphs

### Did you know?

Robert the Bruce decided to lead the Scottish fight against the English because English soldiers put his sister, Mary Bruce, in a wooden cage, then hung the cage from the walls of her castle.

In the early 1300s, a new leader emerged in Scotland: a knight called Robert the Bruce. Edward I had almost succeeded in destroying the Scottish army before his death in 1307 and Robert was forced to fight English soldiers in small skirmishes. However, under his leadership, the Scots largely succeeded in pushing the English out of Scotland.

## The Battle of Bannockburn, 1314

By 1314, just two fortresses remained under English control: Berwick and Stirling. It was left to Edward I's son, Edward II, to bring Scotland back under English rule.

1. Edward II leaves Berwick, heading for Stirling castle, at the head of his army of 2000 heavily-armed cavalry and 15,000 infantry, consisting of many longbow men.

2. Robert the Bruce prepares to face the English army: digs hundreds of holes that will snap the horses' legs during a cavalry charge, and hides his army in woods the other side of the Bannockburn (a stream).

3. An early encounter: an English knight, Henry de Bohun, spots Robert the Bruce, lowers his lance and charges his war horse at him. Robert twists his horse at the last moment, stands in his stirrups and with his axe, splits Henry's head, killing him instantly.

4. Edward II crosses the Bannockburn with his troops. Robert's forces emerge from the wood and kneel to pray. Edward thinks they are surrendering. He's wrong!

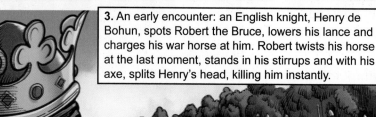

5. The battle begins. Edward's troops are packed in too tightly to use their cavalry or longbows effectively. The Scottish pike formations (schiltrons) do terrible damage to the English army.

6. Edward and his bodyguards flee the battlefield, with the Scottish army in hot pursuit.

Despite the humiliation of Bannockburn, Edward II would not acknowledge Robert as king of Scotland. So, Robert took the war to England, raiding lands on the borders. Six years after Bannockburn, the Scots sent the Declaration of Arbroath to the pope (see Source A on page 130) in an attempt to persuade him to acknowledge Scotland as an independent country. Edward II was deposed and killed in 1327, leaving his son Edward III to sign the Treaty of Edinburgh–Northampton, in 1328. By this treaty, Edward III recognised Robert the Bruce as king of Scotland.

But the war flared up again in 1332. After many years of fighting, Edward III's armies defeated the Scots in the Battle of Neville's Cross in 1346. The Scottish King, David II was captured and held for 11 years, until the war was ended by the Treaty of Berwick in 1357. By the terms of the treaty, Scotland remained an independent country, though it had to pay a large fine.

Busy fighting the Hundred Years' War in France, English kings avoided further wars in Scotland. After 1603, England and Scotland had the same king, and in 1707 the governments of both countries were united.

## Your turn!

1 Robert the Bruce desperately needs recruits! Design a poster that will attract people to his cause.

2 Do you think it was the leadership of Robert the Bruce or the death of Edward I that was more important in the English accepting Scottish independence? Write a paragraph to explain your answer.

## Checkpoint

1 Who did Edward I choose to be king of Scotland in 1290?

2 Name the Scottish leader who defeated the English at the Battle of Stirling in 1297.

3 Who won the Battle of Falkirk in 1298?

4 What was the date of the Battle of Bannockburn?

5 Who led the Scottish army at Bannockburn?

6 What was the date of the Declaration of Arbroath?

7 Give two ways in which the Treaty of Edinburgh–Northampton in 1328 settled problems between England and Scotland.

# How powerful were English monarchs?

- Write a paragraph to explain which monarch, King John or King Edward I, was the more powerful. Remember to back up what you say with evidence.

- In 1513, an Italian called Niccolò Machiavelli wrote a short pamphlet called 'The Prince' in which he described the ways rulers should behave. It looks as though English monarchs could do with some special advice! In a group, put together a booklet of advice for English monarchs, telling them how to be powerful.

- Imagine that King John and King Edward I were having a conversation about which of them was the most powerful. King John could start by saying 'How can you call yourself powerful when you let parliament control what you do?' Or King Edward could start by saying 'Call yourself powerful? You had the barons in revolt!' With a partner, take on the roles of each monarch and continue the conversation.

In this section you have learned:

- that whether monarchs are successful or unsuccessful depends on the way they manage events

- that events have many causes, some of which have existed for a long time, and some of which are more recent.

## Causation

Historians are interested in why particular events, like the Norman Conquest, happened. They like to show how a sequence of small events (like a broken promise) could lead to a huge event like the Norman Conquest. Historians also like to divide causes into different types. Two important types are:

- **Long-term** – These are the causes of an event that have existed for a long time. Whether this is a month, a year or several years depends on the event.

- **Short-term** – These are the causes of an event that have existed for a short time only. Whether this is an hour, a day or several weeks depends on the event.

Some historians add a **trigger**, which is what starts off the whole sequence of events. The trigger for the Norman Conquest was the death of Edward the Confessor.

### Your turn!

Why did Edith have nothing to sell at the market? Sort the causes into long-term and short-term causes. To help you do this, copy and complete the table below. The first two lines have been filled in for you.

| Cause | Long-term | Short-term | Trigger |
|---|---|---|---|
| King John imposed heavy taxes on people | ✓ | | |
| Seth had not mended Edith's shoes | | ✓ | |

Did everyone in your class have the same long- and short-term causes? What were the triggers? Discuss this until you have a completed table with which you all agree.

Read through the following story.

> *It is 1214 and Edith is walking the 12 miles to market. She is carrying two heavy baskets full of eggs and homemade bread and cheese. She is getting tired. She is also worrying about money instead of watching the path. She needs to make more money than usual because of the heavy taxes King John expects people to pay. Her husband, Seth, is a shoemaker and was caught and fined for trapping rabbits on the lord's land. He has been working harder than ever to pay the fine and feed the family. Indeed, Seth had been working so hard that he hasn't had time to mend Edith's shoes. Suddenly, Edith catches her toe on a tree root and the sole comes off one shoe. Edith trips and falls. The eggs smash and the bread and cheese roll into the mud. She has nothing to sell in the market.*

### Quick quiz

1. What did Henry I make the barons swear in 1127?

2. What decision ended the civil war of 1135–53?

3. When was Eleanor of Aquitaine queen of England?

4. Name two promises in Magna Carta.

5. What was the 'Iron Ring of Snowdonia'?

6. When was the Battle of Bannockburn and who was it between?

# Writing historically

## Using long- and short-term causes to answer a question

Students were asked to answer the question 'Explain why Edward I was able to take over Wales'.

**Student 1**

> One of the reasons why Edward was able to take over Wales was that his armies were stronger than those of the Welsh rebels. Another reason was that he employed a good castle designer and built strong castles to subdue the Welsh people. The Marcher Lords helped, too.

Student 1 is starting to focus on the reasons why Edward I was able to take over Wales. The reasons are valid, and some explanation has been given for the first two. The answer needs organising into long- and short-term reasons, with an explanation for each of them as to why they helped his takeover of Wales.

**Student 2**

> One long-term reason why Edward I was able to take over Wales was the existence of the Marcher Lords. A short-term reason was parliament's willingness to let him raise taxes. Finally, the trigger for the takeover was probably the refusal of Llywelyn to do homage to him.

Student 2 has focused on the reasons why Edward was able to take over Wales, and has correctly identified a long- and a short-term cause as well as a trigger. However, the student has not explained why these causes helped Edward's takeover of Wales.

You can do better than these two students!

You need to organise the causes into long-term and short-term causes. Copy and complete the following table, the first two lines of which have been filled in for you. How many more reasons can you find?

| Cause | Long-term | Short-term | Trigger |
|---|---|---|---|
| The Marcher Lords controlled the border between England and Wales | ✓ | | |
| Edward I persuaded parliament to give him money to fight Llywelyn ap Gruffydd | | ✓ | |
| | | | |
| | | | |

**Your turn!**

1   Use the table you have completed and the comments about the two student responses to answer the question 'Explain why Edward I was able to take over Wales'.

2   Now complete a new table and use the same technique to answer to the question 'Why did King John quarrel with the barons?'

135

# Was 1348 the end of the world?

In 1348, many parts of the world were devastated by a mysterious and terrifying disease – the Black Death. Millions died, villages were abandoned and crops were left to rot in the fields. But was 1348 the end of the world? In this section of the book, you will learn:

- what the Black Death was, and where it came from

- how medieval people tried to avoid the Black Death and treat the sick

- the short-term consequences of the Black Death.

## What do you think?

Why did diseases spread so easily in medieval times?

# The Black Death

## Learning objectives

- Understand where the Black Death came from.
- Know how it spread across the known world in 1348.
- Understand the explanations medieval people gave for the Black Death.

## Did you know?

Some accounts say that in 1343, Black Death victims were catapulted into cities during sieges. Clearly people even then knew that the disease was deadly.

## Your turn!

Look at the map in Figure 5.1. Why do you think the Black Death was able to spread so easily and quickly into Europe?

## The arrival of the Black Death

In the summer of 1348, a ship arrived at the busy port of Weymouth in Dorset. The crew were unaware that along with their goods the ship was carrying a deadly cargo: the Black Death. Within a few days, hundreds of men, women and children would be infected. Within a few months, around one-third of the population of England would be dead.

## What was the Black Death?

Most historians now think that the Black Death was a highly infectious disease known as bubonic plague, caused by bacteria – you will find out more about this in the next section.

## Where did the Black Death come from?

The first recorded outbreak of the Black Death was in central Asia in 1338–39. From there, the disease seems to have travelled along the trade route known as the Silk Road, reaching Kaffa in the Crimea on the Black Sea in 1343.

The disease then seems to have spread by ship into central Europe, arriving in Italy in around 1347 before spreading overland into France and Germany, and eventually by ship to England.

Once the Black Death arrived in Weymouth in May 1348, it spread quickly through England. The disease seemed to spread randomly, jumping from place to place and appearing in new locations without warning. This is probably because it was being spread across the land by the movement of rats and also by ships visiting trading ports along the coast. Source A describes the impact of the disease on England.

England was in a state of panic. All of the combined medical knowledge and wisdom of medieval doctors and the Church seemed to have no effect at all on the disease. Many people must have felt that the end of the world had come. One monk in Ireland tried to record the calamity of what had happened (see Source B). At the end of the account, someone else added the following words: 'Here, it seems, the author died'.

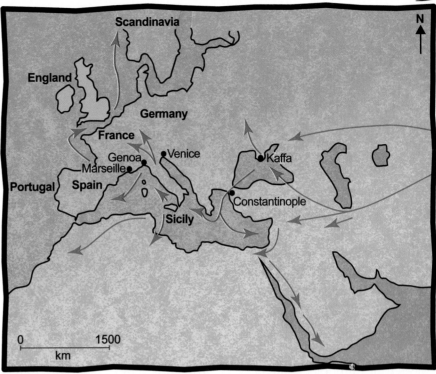

**Figure 5.1:** Map showing how the Black Death spread throughout Europe.

**Source A:** Written by Geoffrey the Baker, an English chronicler, in around 1350.

… it came to England and first began in the towns and ports joining on the seacoasts, in Dorsetshire, where, as in other counties, it made the country quite void of inhabitants so that there were almost none left alive. From there it passed into Devonshire and Somersetshire, even unto Bristol, [and was so terrible the people of Gloucestershire avoided those from Bristol at all costs]. But at length it came to Gloucester, yea even to Oxford and to London, and finally it spread over all England and so wasted the people that scarce the tenth person of any sort was left alive.

**Source B:** Written by Brother John Clyn of Kilkenney in around 1349. He seems to have been trying to record what was happening for future generations.

… so that the writing does not perish with the writer. … I leave parchment for continuing the work, in case anyone should still be alive in the future and any son of Adam can escape this pestilence and continue the work thus begun.

This is the last sentence written by Brother Clyn. After is written '*Here, it seems, the author died.*'

## Your turn!

**1** Read Source A. Write two things you learn from this source about the impact of the Black Death.

**2** Sources A and B are both written by monks. Give one reason why monks are a useful source of information from this time period.

**3** Read Sources A and B. What evidence is there that the authors of these sources may have thought the world was ending? Explain in a paragraph.

**4** As a class, imagine you are villagers living at the time of the Black Death. Think of as many questions as you can about the disease and note them down – for example: Why are so many people falling sick? Then discuss how medieval people might have tried to answer your questions.

# How did medieval people explain the Black Death?

## Key term

**Four Humours\*:** A theory about the causes of illness first developed by the Greek doctor Hippocrates (460–375 BC). He proposed that the body was composed of four 'humours' – phlegm, yellow bile, black bile and blood. The theory argued that people in good health had a balance of all four humours, while ill health was caused by one or more of the humours becoming out of balance.

As you have already learned in Chapter 2, medieval people were extremely religious. The Church was very powerful and controlled who was educated and what they were taught. It enforced its teachings strictly and people could be horribly punished for criticising the teachings of the Church. Medieval people believed that their time on Earth was only the blink of an eye, and that after death they could be punished if they had not confessed their sins. Therefore, it is no surprise that most of the explanations offered for the Black Death were religious ones.

Medical and scientific knowledge was very limited at this time. It would be hundreds of years before scientists understood that bacteria cause many diseases. Medical students were taught that the Four Humours\* explained illness. Unfortunately, as this theory argued that a disease was caused by internal factors, it couldn't explain why thousands of people were dying of the same disease with the same symptoms.

Therefore, medieval people turned to religion and superstition to explain the illness. Some argued that the disease was caused by an unusual alignment of the planets, others that it was caused by foul air. However, the most widespread explanation was that it was a punishment from God.

**Source C:** Written by an English monk at the time of the Black Death.

If I am asked what is the cause of [the disease], what is its physical cause and by what means can someone save himself from it, I answer to the first question that sin is the cause. To the second question, I say that it arises from the sea. ... For the devil, by the power committed to him when the seas rise up high, is [sending] his poison, sending it forth to be added to the poison in the air, and that air spreads gradually from place to place and enters man through the ears, eyes, nose, mouth, pores and other [entrances].

## Your turn!

5th **1** Read Source C. What does this source suggest about what people thought was causing the Black Death? Try to give two examples.

6th **2** Write a couple of sentences to explain why the writer of Source C thought in this way. Clue: look at who wrote the source. Think about what you have already learned about medieval religion.

**3** What do you think this monk would recommend people should do to avoid the Black Death?

**Figure 5.2:** A monk and a scientist arguing the causes of the Black Death.

## Did you know?

Due to strict laws against cutting up dead bodies, few medical students had the chance to see the inner workings of the human body. Instead, students were taught to accept the theories of ancient physicians* such as Hippocrates, who had died over a thousand years before.

## Key term

**Physician*:** Another term for a doctor.

## Your turn!

Consider the information about what people thought was causing the Black Death.

1   Make a mind map summing up some of the main theories about the cause of the Black Death. Try to use symbols to represent causes – for example, a cross to represent a punishment from God.

2   Explain in a paragraph why it was so difficult for medieval people to understand what was causing the Black Death. Try to include details on medical beliefs at the time – for example, the Four Humours.

## Checkpoint

1   Where did the Black Death come from?

2   What was actually causing the disease?

3   What did medieval people think was causing the disease?

4   What was the theory of the Four Humours?

# What were the causes, symptoms and responses to the Black Death?

## Learning objectives

- Know what the causes and symptoms of the Black Death were.
- Know what medieval people did to prevent, avoid and treat the Black Death.
- Understand why they thought these measures would work.

By carefully examining the evidence, historians and scientists now think that most victims of the Black Death were suffering from a disease known as bubonic plague.

**1.** The plague bacteria live in the guts of fleas. The fleas live on rats.

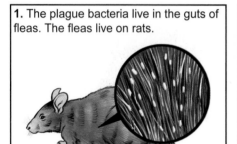

**2.** When the rat dies, the fleas have to look for a new host – for example, the nearest human!

Ow! I think something just bit me!

**3.** The fleas bite the human and vomit into their blood, infecting them with the plague bacteria.

Bleurgh!

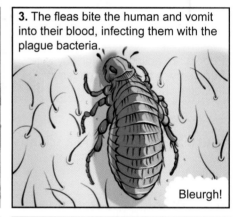

**4.** The infection causes lumps, which may occur in the groin, thigh, armpit and neck, known as 'buboes'. This is why it is called 'bubonic plague'. Fever sets in.

**5.** In some cases, the disease moves into the lungs. The victim then has pneumonic plague, which can be spread by coughing and sneezing, like a cold.

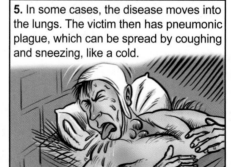

**6.** After 3–5 days, 80 per cent of those who are infected die.

God has taken him. Now you must pray for his soul.

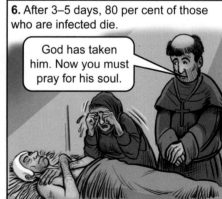

**Figure 5.3:** Causes and symptoms of the Black Death.

## Your turn!

1. Explain in a couple of sentences the difference between bubonic and pneumonic plague.
2. Modern organisations, like the Centers for Disease Control and Prevention in the USA, keep a record of all of the most dangerous diseases in the world, including bubonic plague. Design a fact file for their records, including details on what causes bubonic plague, how it is spread, and the symptoms.

## What happened to you if you caught the Black Death?

The Black Death was a deadly disease. Once someone had caught the Black Death, their chances of dying were as high as 80 per cent. As you have already learned, medieval medicine was virtually useless in treating people with the disease. Although they didn't understand what was causing the disease, many medieval records of the symptoms are accurate and can give modern historians an insight into the disease that killed so many people.

**Did you know?**

Although the Black Death disappeared from Europe hundreds of years ago, the disease still occasionally reappears in remote parts of the world. Don't worry, though – it can be cured with modern antibiotics.

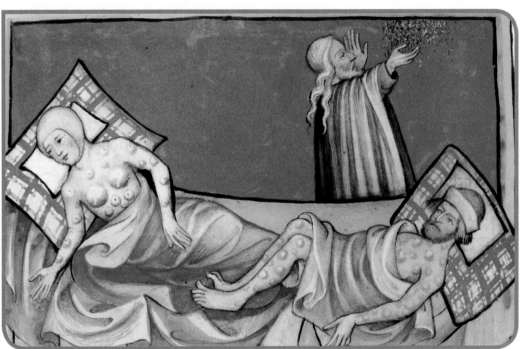

**Source A:** Image from the Toggenburg Bible, 1411, showing two people suffering from the plague. Look closely at their bodies.

**Source B:** Written by a French monk, Jean de Venette, at the time of the Black Death.

People lay ill little more than two or three days and died suddenly, as it were in full health. He who was well one day was dead the next and being carried to his grave. Swellings appeared suddenly in the armpit or in the groin – in many cases both – and they were infallible signs of death. This sickness or pestilence was called an epidemic by the doctors. Nothing like the great numbers who died in the years 1348 and 1349 has been heard of or seen of in times past.

**Your turn!**

1   Look at Sources A and B. List the symptoms shown or described in the sources.

5th 2   Why are Sources A and B useful evidence for what was causing the Black Death? Write one reason for each source. Remember to think about not just what the sources say, but who made them, and when.

6th 3   Using Sources A and B together, explain how you know these people were probably suffering from bubonic plague.

# Prevent, cure or run away?

Medical knowledge was extremely limited at the time of the Black Death, so the way that medieval people reacted to the disease can seem very strange to us.

## Treatment

It was very difficult for medieval physicians to treat the Black Death. Patients tended to die very quickly, which gave little time for treatment. Physicians were taught to believe in the Four Humours and that patients became sick when one or more of the 'humours' became out of balance – for example, if they had too much blood. Therefore, they tried to treat victims of the Black Death by 'rebalancing' the humours. For instance, as one of the symptoms of the Black Death was a fever, victims were given cold baths or told to eat cold foods to cool them down. Excess blood was thought to cause disease, so physicians tried draining blood from the patient into a bowl, a practice known as 'bleeding'.

**Source C:** Instructions issued by King Edward III to the Lord Mayor of London, 1349.

You are to make sure that all the human excrement and other filth lying in the streets of the city is removed. You are to make sure that there are no more bad smells for people to die from.

**Source D:** From a letter about the Black Death written by Ralph of Shrewsbury, the Bishop of Bath, to all the priests in his diocese in January 1349.

The plague... has left many parish churches... without parson or priest to care for their parishioners... Therefore, to provide for the salvation of souls... you should at once publicly command and persuade all men that, if they are on the point of death and cannot secure the services of a priest, then they should make confession to each other... if no man is present, then even to a woman.

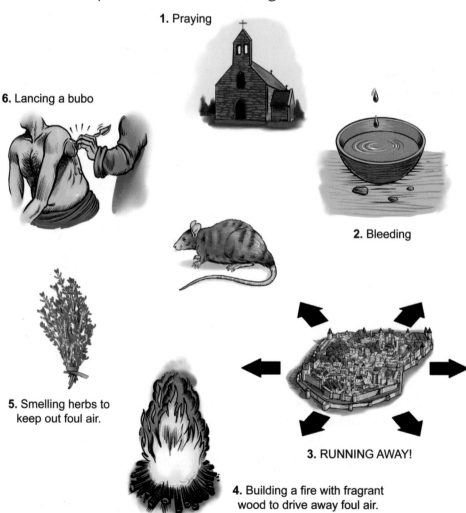

1. Praying

2. Bleeding

3. RUNNING AWAY!

4. Building a fire with fragrant wood to drive away foul air.

5. Smelling herbs to keep out foul air.

6. Lancing a bubo

**Figure 5.4:** What did medieval people do about the Black Death?

Physicians also tried to drain the pus from the buboes by lancing* them and then applying a poultice* to heal the wound. However, sometimes these poultices contained animal, or even human, excrement!

At best, these treatments made no difference to the patient other than making them feel that someone was helping them. At worst, they could make them weaker and even kill them.

## Avoiding the Black Death

As most treatments did not work, people tried to avoid catching the disease in the first place.

**Source E:** A procession of people in the Netherlands whipping themselves to show they are sorry for their sins, c. 1350.

- Many believed foul air was causing the disease, and so used herbs and fires to drive away bad smells.

- Others simply ran away from areas where the disease had taken hold – however, this just helped to spread the disease further.

As medieval people were very religious, the most common reaction was to pray. People believed that the plague must be a punishment from God, and so they looked for ways to gain God's favour. This could include going on a pilgrimage, or even whipping themselves (known as 'self-flagellation') to prove to God how sorry they were for their sins.

### Your turn!

1 Copy the table below. Using the information on these pages fill in as many examples as you can of ways people tried to avoid, prevent or treat the Black Death.

| Ways to avoid or prevent the Black Death | Ways to treat the Black Death |
|---|---|
|  |  |

**5th** 2 Look at Sources D and E. What can they tell you about how important religion was as an explanation for the Black Death?

**6th** 3 Look at Sources C, D and E. Explain why they show such different methods of dealing with the Black Death.

4 Imagine you are a medieval physician. Write a letter to a friend describing your work during the Black Death. Try to include information on what you think is causing the disease, and what you have done to try to help and advise people.

### Key terms

**Lancing*:** Using a sharp tool to 'pop' a boil or bubo.

**Poultice*:** A mixture designed to heal a wound – for example, butter, onions and garlic – pressed onto a wound with a bandage.

### Checkpoint

1 Why was it so difficult for medieval physicians to treat the Black Death?

2 What did people do to avoid catching the Black Death?

3 What did people do to try and gain favour with God?

# How terrible was the Black Death?

- Understand the short-term consequences of the Black Death.
- Understand the effect on towns and villages.

| Year | Population (millions) |
|------|----------------------|
| 1086 | 1.71 |
| 1190 | 3.10 |
| 1290 | 4.75 |
| 1348 | 4.81 |
| 1351 | 2.60 |
| 1400 | 2.08 |
| 1522 | 2.35 |

**Table 5.1:** Estimates of population in England over time, compiled by historians in 2010.

It can be difficult for historians to estimate precisely how many people in England died as a result of the disease. There are no accurate records, and no census was conducted in medieval times. However, from looking at evidence such as manorial records*, historians have been able to make estimates.

Accounts by people such as Henry Knighton (see Source A) can also give us an insight into the consequences of the huge loss of population.

**Source A:** From *Knighton's Chronicon* by Henry Knighton, an English monk. Knighton died in 1396 and probably had first-hand experience of the things he describes.

… there were small prices for everything on account of the fear of death. For there were very few who cared about riches or anything else. … Sheep and cattle went wandering over fields and through crops, and there was no one to go and drive or gather them for there was such a lack of servants that no one knew what he ought to do. Wherefore many crops perished in the fields for want of someone to gather them…

After the [disease], many buildings, great and small, fell into ruins in every city for lack of inhabitants, likewise many villages and hamlets became desolate, not a house being left in them, all having died who dwelt there; and it was probable that many such villages would never be inhabited. In the winter following there was such a want of servants in work of all kinds, that one would scarcely believe that in times past there had been such a lack. And so all necessities became so much dearer.

## Your turn!

**1** Using the figures in Table 5.1, draw a line graph to show the population changes over time. Label the graph to show when the Black Death happened.

**2** Explain in a paragraph what your graph suggests about:
   **a** how many people were killed by the Black Death
   **b** the impact on England's population.

**3** Why do historians have such accurate records for the year 1086? Look back at your work on the Norman Conquest to find out.

**4** Read Source A and look at Figure 5.5. In pairs, list as many changes as you can that occurred as a result of the Black Death.

## How were different parts of the British Isles affected by the Black Death?

**Key term**

**Manorial records*:** These are the records compiled within a manor – an area controlled by a lord – during medieval times.

N
Selkirk Forest, Scotland – Some accounts suggest that a Scottish army, seeing the weakened state of the English, prepared to invade. Instead, 5000 soldiers who had gathered in the forest of Selkirk died due to the Black Death, and the rest fled, spreading the disease into Scotland.
Ashwell, Hertfordshire – Message scratched on the wall of St Mary's Church says '1349 – Wretched, terrible, destructive year, the remnants of the people alone remain.'
Bristol – So few were left alive in the city that 'the grass grew several inches high in the High St and in Broad St' (Geoffrey the Baker, Chronicon Angliae).
Winchester – So many die that the local population attack a monk conducting the burial service, as they are worried the bodies are causing the foul air that is spreading the disease.
Weymouth – Thought to be where the plague arrived on 8 May 1348.
Durham – The bishop's records say that 'No tenant came from West Thickley [to pay their tithes] because they are all dead.'
Norwich – Population in 1330 = 25,000; in the 1370s = fewer than 9000
London – An estimated 40,000 out of a population of about 70,000 die.
Selkirk Forest
Durham
York
Lincoln
Norwich
Oxford
Ashwell
London
Bristol
Winchester
Weymouth
0
150
km

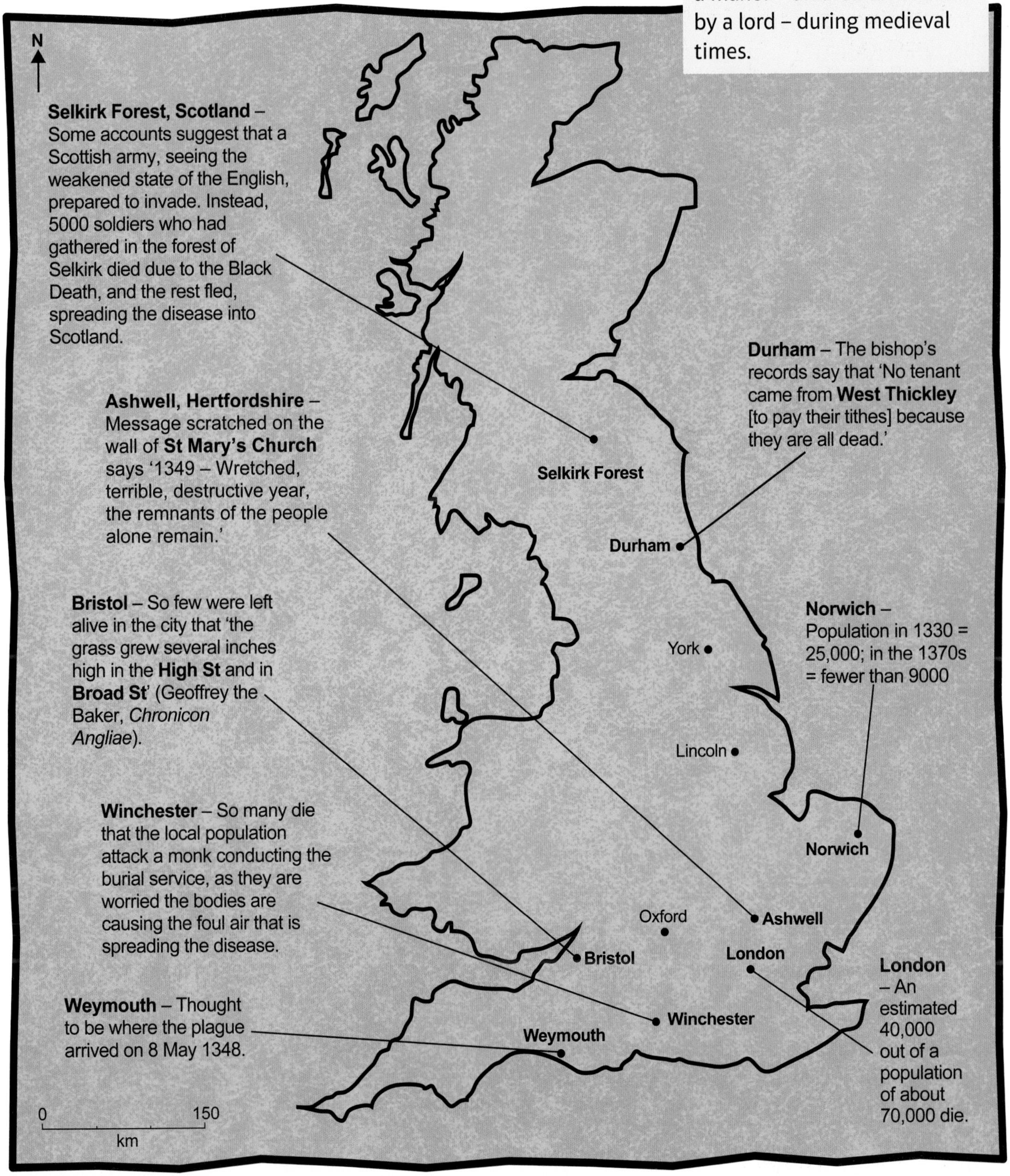

**Figure 5.5:** Map of the British Isles showing the impact of the Black Death on some areas.

## Key terms

**DNA analysis*:** A method used by scientists, which can identify individual people and other organisms such as bacteria.

**Last rites*:** A final blessing given by a priest to someone who is about to die, that is thought to prepare their soul for the afterlife.

## What happened to the victims of the Black Death?

In 2016, archaeologists excavating the site of Thornton Abbey in Lincolnshire found a mass burial site from the mid-14th century, containing 48 skeletons, 27 of which were of children. DNA analysis* of the teeth revealed the presence of the bacteria known as *Yersinia pestis* – which causes bubonic plague. It was clearly a Black Death plague pit. Archaeologists now think there was probably a hospital on the site. Family members would have brought their loved ones to the hospital in a last desperate attempt to find some treatment for them, and so that they could receive the last rites* from the priest before they died.

Archaeologists have found several plague pits around the country. They show how local systems for burying the dead were overwhelmed by the number of people who had died. However, this doesn't necessarily mean that people were thrown into the graves without respect.

## Abandoned villages

Historians have also collected information on settlements that were abandoned during the medieval period. The process was helped by the arrival of aerial photography in the early years of the 20th century. Aerial photographs reveal features that are invisible from the ground, such as the outlines of houses, streets and farms abandoned during the medieval period. One of the most famous examples is Wharram Percy in North Yorkshire, shown in Source D.

**Source B:** A small mass burial pit from the Black Death cemetery, East Smithfield, London.

## Your turn!

Look at Source B showing the plague pit at Smithfield in London. Archaeologists have noted that the bodies of children and adults were laid out carefully, and sometimes overlapped each other. Discuss with a partner why they may have been buried like this, and what this can tell us about medieval people.

**Source C:** An archaeologist excavating the mass grave at the site of Thornton Abbey, Lincolnshire.

The Black Death had a severe impact on villages like Wharram Percy, where the population was reduced from 67 to 45 by the Black Death, and the landowner himself died. However, it is unlikely that the Black Death alone was responsible for so many villages (over 3000) being abandoned. Records suggest that most of them were not deserted until many years later.

Other evidence suggests that the smaller number of people meant that harvests could not be collected and animals could not be looked after. This in turn led to food shortages and rising food prices, making life even more difficult for the survivors.

**Source D:** Aerial photograph of Wharram Percy, a deserted medieval village in North Yorkshire.

## Checkpoint

1 How was the population changed by the Black Death?

2 What problems were caused for landowners?

3 How did people cope with the number of dead to bury?

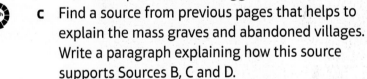

## Your turn!

1 Look at Sources B, C and D and answer the following questions.

    **a** What does each source show? Bullet point what you can learn from each source.

    **b** What could each source **suggest** about the impact of the Black Death? Explain each source separately – for example, 'Source B suggests that…'.

    **c** Find a source from previous pages that helps to explain the mass graves and abandoned villages. Write a paragraph explaining how this source supports Sources B, C and D.

    **d** What other factors may have been responsible for these villages being abandoned?

# Was 1348 the end of the world?

Working in groups, imagine that you are survivors of the Black Death. Taking a different role each (for example, a mother and father, child, farmer, travelling actor, priest, landlord, pedlar). Discuss how they might each answer the following questions.

**a** How have you and your family been affected by the Black Death?

**b** How has your local area been affected?

**c** What difficulties has the Black Death created for you and your village?

**d** What are your fears and hopes for the future?

Can you think of any other questions?

When you are prepared, perform your role play for the rest of the class.

# What have you learned?

In this section, you have learned:

- how to use evidence to examine the impact of the Black Death.

## Was 1348 the end of the world?

For some in 1348, it may have felt like the end of the world. Certainly it was for the one-third of the population who died! However, there are often two sides to a story, and the Black Death is no exception. Figure 5.6 shows some of the different arguments about the Black Death.

People thought the world was ending

Many thought God was punishing them

Physicians couldn't prevent or cure the disease

Hundreds of thousands died horrible and painful deaths

Two-thirds of the population survived

The population didn't recover for hundreds of years

One-third of the population died

Crops rotted in the fields

Some people may have had a natural immunity to the disease

Towns were left deserted

Some measures the government took, such as cleaning the streets, may have helped

Some people caught the disease and recovered

For some survivors, life was better after the Black Death – there was more work available

**Figure 5.6:** What was the impact of the Black Death?

### Your turn!

1. Look at some of the factors shown in Figure 5.6. What is the strongest evidence that the Black Death was devastating to England?

2. How do you think the survivors of the Black Death might have felt? How would their lives have been shaped by the experience?

# Writing historically

When writing an answer, it is really important to support your points with evidence. Police officers have to gather evidence to be able to arrest someone and send them to trial. Imagine what a judge would think if a prosecutor tried to argue someone was guilty but had no evidence to prove it – the trial wouldn't last very long! History is the same.

Let's look at an example question:

'Explain why medieval physicians were unable to prevent or cure the Black Death.'

Your answer will consist of claims which you will need to back up with evidence. For example, you might claim that the reasons why physicians couldn't prevent the Black Death included:

- lack of medical knowledge and training

- the nature of the disease

- the Church.

For each of these, jot down what evidence you would need to use. For example, for the first bullet point, you could mention that physicians still believed the theory of the Four Humours.

## Writing up your answer

Here are some examples of how students might approach answering this question.

**Your turn!**

Now try to answer the question yourself. You can use the reasons suggested here to help. Remember to back up all your claims with evidence.

### Student 1

Medieval physicians were unable to prevent or cure the Black Death because they didn't know anything about it.

There's an element of truth in this answer, but it doesn't provide any evidence to back up the statement.

### Student 2

Medieval physicians were unable to prevent or cure the Black Death because medical knowledge at the time was so basic. For example, physicians lacked knowledge because they were not allowed to dissect dead bodies.

This is better, as the student has provided a fact to support their claim. However, they don't explain how the fact supports the claim. Sometimes it is useful after giving some evidence to ask yourself 'So what?' If you haven't explained the evidence, you aren't answering the question.

### Student 3

Medieval physicians were unable to prevent or cure the Black Death because medical knowledge at the time was so basic. For example, physicians lacked knowledge because they were not allowed to dissect dead bodies. This meant that they had very little understanding of how the body worked, and had to rely on outdated and incorrect theories such as the Four Humours.

This is a much better answer – not only has the student provided some valid evidence by talking about dissection and the Four Humours, but they have linked this back to the question by explaining how this stopped physicians from preventing or curing the Black Death.

# What was it like to live in the shadow of the Black Death?

The Black Death was one of the deadliest epidemics in history. It killed millions of people across the medieval world and caused widespread problems. However, the story doesn't end there. In this section, you will learn about:

- the impact of the Black Death on living standards and wages, and how some people's lives were actually improved

- what caused the Peasants' Revolt, and its main events

- the long-term impact of the Black Death and the Peasants' Revolt on medieval society.

**What do you think?**

Why might some people have been better off after the Black Death?

# Effects of the Black Death

## Learning objectives

- Know how the Black Death affected farms, wages and living standards.
- Understand the consequences of these changes.

### Key term

Rent*: Medieval peasants had to pay rent to their lord. As most peasants had no money, this was usually paid in labour and goods – for example, produce from the peasants' land.

Who do these peasants think they are? Someone needs to put them in their place!

**Figure 5.7:** Life was not so good for landowners after the Black Death.

For the survivors of the Black Death, life seemed to go as normal. The land needed ploughing, livestock needed to be fed and looked after, and the harvests needed to be collected. However, the Black Death had caused some fundamental changes that would cause major upheavals for many and lead to a violent uprising. To understand the changes, first you need to look back on what you have already learned about the feudal system (see page 42) in order to understand how the structure of society changed.

## How were the lives of the peasants changed?

As there was such a demand for workers after the Black Death, peasants were in a much more powerful position. They could now demand pay for the work they did and could choose who they worked for. This meant they could pay their rent* in cash, instead of having to provide produce from their own land.

## The reaction of the landowners

As you can imagine, landowners were not pleased about these changes. Feudalism had helped to keep landowners wealthy and peasants in their place since the Norman Conquest, but now it seemed that the system was starting to break down.

**Figure 5.8:** How a peasant's life might have improved after the Black Death.

For landowners, living in the shadow of the Black Death meant:

- peasants could now demand wages and pay their rent in cash

- landowners could no longer expect free labour from peasants

- as workers would obviously work for whoever paid the best wages, neighbouring landlords could raise wages to try and attract each other's workers

- as there were fewer peasants around due to the Black Death, landowners received less rent

- there were higher prices for some goods, for example wheat, as crops rotted in fields due to lack of labour.

Soon landlords began to demand that these changes had to stop. The king agreed, and the stage was set for a confrontation between the peasants and those above them in society.

**Your turn!**

**5th 1** Look at Adam's story (Figure 5.8). Write a paragraph describing what has **changed** to make Adam happy.

**6th 2** Make an 'And so…' chain to explain why Adam's life has improved. Copy and complete the example below.

The Black Death happened And so …

One in three of the population died And so …

**6th 3** In small groups, imagine you are landowners after the Black Death. Discuss the following points.
 a What changes have happened.
 b What impact these changes have had on you.
 c How you feel about the changes.
 d What you would like to see happen to stop the changes.

**4** Write a letter to the king explaining the points above, and what you as a landowner would like to see happen.

151

# How were the peasants put in their place?

## Your turn!

1 Look at Figure 5.9. Note down two points that were in the Statute of Labourers.

5th 2 For each point, make a list of changes that it would cause for peasants and for landowners.

The rich and powerful in England were determined to bring an end to the peasants' demands for better pay and treatment.

In 1351, the government passed a new law – the Statute of Labourers – to control wages (see Figure 5.9). The law even went as far as to say that people who travelled the country looking for higher wages should be branded with a red-hot iron.

As you can imagine, many peasants were very angry about the changes brought about by the new law.

Wages must be the same as they were in 1346, before the plague.

Peasants are not allowed to move away to find better work.

Anyone refusing to work for these wages will be sent to jail.

It is forbidden to give charity to those who could work but choose not to do so.

Everyone under the age of 60 must work for the same wages as before the plague.

Anyone who breaks the law will be sent to prison.

It is forbidden for anyone to leave their place of employment without permission.

**Figure 5.9:** Peasants learning about the Statute of Labourers.

## Tax – the final straw

In 1377, Richard II became king. Richard was only 10 years old, so England was actually run by his uncle, John of Gaunt. As England was once again at war with France, the king's advisers desperately wanted to raise money to fight the French. Therefore, a new tax was introduced known as the 'Poll Tax', which everyone had to pay. The Poll Tax was collected in 1377, 1380 and 1381. In the first two years, the tax took account of the person's ability to pay. However, the third Poll Tax stated that everyone had to pay the same amount: one shilling (12 pence) per person (one penny bought two dozen eggs). Many felt that this was deeply unfair, as the tax was much harder for poor people to pay than the rich.

Many felt that the king was being badly advised by John of Gaunt. Some even questioned whether the feudal structure itself was fair. One such man was a priest called John Ball, who had been sent to prison on several occasions because of his speeches. See Source A for an example.

By 1381, a serious rebellion was brewing in England.

### Did you know?

History sometimes has a strange habit of repeating itself. In 1990, the British prime minister, Margaret Thatcher, introduced a new tax that everyone had to pay, regardless of how wealthy they were. It caused huge protests and many refused to pay it. It was known as the 'Poll Tax'. After some of the biggest riots in English history, it was abandoned in 1991.

**Source A:** From a speech by John Ball in 1381, reported in *The Chronicles of Froissart*. Jean Froissart was a French historian who lived and wrote at the same time as the Peasants' Revolt. He travelled widely and based his account on his own experiences, but also those of other writers.

My friends, the state of England cannot be right until everything is owned by all the people together and there is no difference between nobleman and peasant. We are all descended from our first parents, Adam and Eve, so how can they be better than us? Let us go to the king, for he is young, and show him how badly we are treated.

### Your turn!

1 Read Source A and discuss the questions below.
   a What kind of society did John Ball want to see?
   b How do you think others such as the lords and tenants-in-chief would have felt about what he was saying?
   c Do you agree with what he is saying? Should society be like this?

2 Make a flowchart summing up why the peasants were angry in 1381. Include a picture or description of each of these factors: The Black Death, demands for higher wages after the Black Death, the Statute of Labourers, the Poll Tax, plus any other factors you can think of.

3 In pairs, write five questions each to test your partner on the order in which events happened – for example, 'What came first: the Statute of Labourers or the Black Death?'

### Checkpoint

1 Give two ways in which peasants' lives improved after the Black Death.

2 Why were landlords unhappy about the changes?

3 What was the Statute of Labourers?

4 Why was the Poll Tax introduced?

5 What happened in 1381 to spark a rebellion?

# How and why did the peasants revolt?

**Learning objectives**

• Know about the main events of the Peasants' Revolt.
• Understand why the revolt came to an end.

**Did you know?**

Although Wat Tyler is an important person in English history, historians know very little about him and how he became involved in the rebellion. However, he must have been an impressive leader to command such a large force. Why do you think it is often difficult for historians to research the lives of 'ordinary' people like Wat Tyler?

The Black Death had killed millions across the world, but also improved the lives of many of those peasants who had survived. How did the peasants react when it seemed that many of those improvements were being taken away?

At first, people simply tried to avoid paying the Poll Tax. However, the investigations into why so few had paid made the problems worse. In May 1381, tax collectors in the town of Fobbing in Essex were attacked. Soon, the violence had spread across much of East Anglia and the surrounding counties. Two key groups of rebels began to emerge in the counties of Essex and Kent. The rebels selected a man called Wat Tyler as their leader. The rebels also managed to release the preacher John Ball from prison.

The rebels felt that if only they could explain their grievances to the king, he would understand. Therefore, both groups of rebels set out for London to plead their case. As the groups neared London, they sought out and destroyed records about the hated Poll Tax.

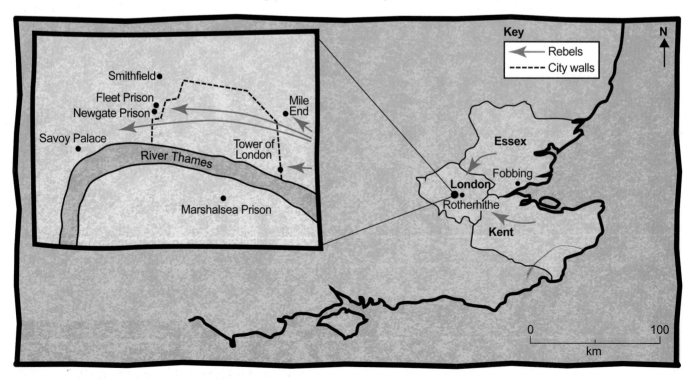

**Figure 5.10:** Map of the Peasants' Revolt.

**Source A:** From a speech given by the radical preacher John Ball in June 1381 at Blackheath during the Peasants' Revolt.

When Adam delved and Eve span, Who was then the gentleman? From the beginning all men by nature were created alike, and our bondage* or servitude* came in by the unjust oppression of naughty men… I exhort you to consider that now the time is come, appointed to us by God, in which ye may (if ye will) cast off the yoke of bondage, and recover liberty.

**Source B:** From an illustration in *The Chronicles of Froissart*, drawn in the 14th century. John Ball is on horseback, Wat Tyler is front left in the red tunic. The rebels are carrying the flags of the king and St George.

By 12 June, the groups had reached the London suburbs. Their numbers are hard to estimate, but are thought to have been around 50,000 – larger than most armies of the time.

The rebels demanded an audience with the king at Rotherhithe. The king travelled to the meeting place on the Thames in his royal barge, but after seeing the huge crowd he turned around and returned to the Tower of London.

The rebels, frustrated and angry, managed to enter the gates of the City of London. They broke into the Fleet prison, freed the prisoners, and burned down the Savoy Palace, home of John of Gaunt, Richard II's unpopular adviser.

On 14 June, the king again agreed to meet with the rebels at Mile End, just outside the City of London. The peasants presented their demands, and the king agreed to them. They included an end to feudalism, a pardon for the rebels and death for the king's unpopular advisers. Many of the rebels were satisfied and went home. However, that same afternoon some 400 rebels forced their way into the Tower of London. They dragged out Simon Sudbury (the Archbishop of Canterbury) and Robert Hales (the king's treasurer), and hacked off their heads.

Had the peasants won?

## Key term

**Bondage/servitude*:** To be an unfree peasant.

## Your turn!

A lot happened during the Peasants' Revolt. One of the skills you need to learn as a historian is to reduce the amount of detail to a few key points.

1   Read this section again, and aim to pick out six key moments. Make a list of them.

2   Using your six points, make a storyboard telling the story of the Peasants' Revolt in chronological order. Each box should include a picture and a brief description of what happened, with any key terms highlighted.

3   In pairs, pretend that one of you was present at the events described in this section, while the other was not but is very interested to find out what happened. Using your storyboard as a guide, practise talking through the events. Make sure you understand them and get them in the right order.

# How did the Peasants' Revolt end?

On 14 June, many of the rebels had already gone home. Several of the king's closest advisers including the Archbishop of Canterbury had been brutally murdered. Wat Tyler, along with the 30,000 rebels who had stayed, demanded another audience with the king.

On 15 June, at Smithfield, just outside London's city walls, the two sides met once more. On one side were Wat Tyler, John Ball and 30,000 rebels, confident after extracting promises from the king the day before. On the other side were the 14-year-old king, Richard II, the Lord Mayor of London, William Walworth and a few hundred soldiers loyal to the king.

What happened next is unclear. Many sources give different accounts of what may have occurred. What all sources agree on is that Wat Tyler was killed.

After Tyler's death, Richard II addressed the crowd. He promised them their freedom if they would return home. The crowd dispersed and the Peasants' Revolt was over.

## How and why did Wat Tyler die?

**Source C:** From *The Anonimalle Chronicle* (1381). This account contains a very detailed description of the uprising, but it is unknown who wrote it ('anonimalle' means 'anonymous'). It appears to have been pieced together by monks in York, hundreds of miles away from the events described.

At that time a certain valet from Kent... said aloud that Wat Tyler was the greatest thief and robber in all Kent... For these words Wat wanted to strike the valet with his dagger... but because he tried to do so, the Mayor of London, William of Walworth... arrested him... Wat stabbed the mayor with his dagger in the body in great anger. But, as it pleased God, the mayor was wearing armour and took no harm... he struck back at... Wat, giving him a deep cut in the neck, and then a great blow on the head. And during the scuffle a valet of the king's household drew his sword, and ran Wat two or three times through the body...

**Source D:** From Thomas Walsingham's *The History of England* (c. 1420). Walsingham was a monk at the Abbey of St Albans. He spent most of his life as a monk so it likely his information came from others.

Sir John Newton came up to him... to hear what he (Wat Tyler) proposed to say. Tyler grew angry because the knight had approached him on horseback and not on foot... Newton. ... replied, 'As you are sitting on a horse it is not insulting for me to approach you on a horse.' At this the ruffian brought out his knife and threatened to strike the knight and called him a traitor...

On this the king... ordered the mayor of London to arrest Tyler. The mayor, a man of spirit and bravery, arrested Tyler and struck him a blow on the head which hurt him badly. Tyler was soon surrounded by the other servants of the king and pierced by sword thrusts in several parts of his body. His death... was the first incident to restore to the English knighthood their almost extinct hope that they could resist the commons.

**Source E:** Illustration from *The Chronicles of Froissart*, around 1480. Wat Tyler is riding the small grey horse on the left.

## Your turn!

Sometimes it can be difficult to be 100 per cent clear on what happened at certain crucial moments in history. Wat Tyler's death is a good example of that.

1 Read Sources C and D. As a class, discuss:

    a who the sources suggest was responsible for the death of Wat Tyler

    b the differences between the sources.

2 Look at the background, or provenance, of the sources. Suggest two reasons why they give such different versions of what happened.

3 As a class, decide what you think really happened, based on the sources.

4 Explore the reasons why the Peasants' Revolt failed. To answer this question, you will need to focus on a small number of key events and not get bogged down in detail. Use your work from previous lessons to help you. Below are some suggestions of what you could include.

- Who was involved in the revolt, and why might this have been a weakness?
- What aims did the rebels have, and why might these have been unrealistic?
- What happened in London, and how might this have led to the failure of the rebellion?
- How did Wat Tyler die, and what effect would this have had on the rebellion?

## Checkpoint

1 What caused the Peasants' Revolt?

2 Why did the rebels want to meet with the king?

3 What violent acts were committed by some of the rebels while they were in London?

4 What had the king agreed to at Mile End on 14 June 1381?

5 What happened when Wat Tyler met the king at Smithfield on 15 June 1381?

# What were the consequences of the Peasants' Revolt?

## Learning objectives

- Understand how the king regained control after the Peasants' Revolt.
- Assess the long-term consequences of the Black Death and the Peasants' Revolt.

### Key terms

**Rustic\*:** An insulting word for a peasant.

**Posterity\*:** Future generations of people.

The events that followed Wat Tyler's death were brutal, but perhaps unsurprising. Loyal followers of the king travelled to the areas of revolt and crushed all resistance. Henry le Despenser, Bishop of Norwich, led an army through East Anglia, executing any rebels he found, before defeating the rebels at the Battle of North Walsham in Norfolk. The king had broken all the promises he had made to the rebels. This was to be the last major example of resistance against the king.

The king's men rode to Billericay in Essex, where there was still a major encampment of rebels. Violence followed, despite the protests of the rebels who showed the charters the king had so recently signed, granting them their freedom and a pardon. Later, the king is alleged to have made a speech to a representative of the rebels, shown in Source B.

> **Source B:** From an account written by Thomas Walsingham around 1420. He is reporting what the king is supposed to have said to a representative of the rebels.
>
> Rustics\* you were and rustics you are still… You will remain in bondage, not as before but… harsher. For as long as we live… we will strive with mind, strength and goods to suppress you… [as an] example to posterity\*.

**Source A:** A painting of the young Richard II, from around the 1390s.

### Your turn!

1 Read Source B and discuss the points below.
   a What do you think the king meant by his speech?
   b Why do you think the king might have told the rebels he would give them their freedom, only to take it away again a few days later?
   c Why do you think the king was so angry with the rebels?

The king's forces toured the areas that had rebelled, and put to death any rebels they found. In Hertfordshire and Essex, 500 were executed, while in Kent, up to 1500 people were hanged.

The worst punishment was reserved for those who had led the revolt. John Ball, the radical preacher who had questioned the whole feudal system, was captured. On 15 July, in front of a crowd in the marketplace in St Albans, he was hanged, drawn and quartered*. Wat Tyler's head was cut from his body, mounted on a pole and paraded through the streets of London, before being put on a spike on London Bridge. A clear warning was being sent out to those who had resisted the king and dared to question their place in society.

By the end of 1381, the revolt had been utterly crushed. The charters that the king had granted to the rebels were cancelled. Possession of one became evidence that that you were a rebel and a traitor.

Was the Peasants' Revolt a total failure?

**Figure 5.11:** A modern memorial to the Peasants' Revolt, in Wat Tyler Country Park, Pitsea, Essex.

## Key term

**Hanged, drawn and quartered\*:** This was a punishment for treason. Victims were hanged until they were almost dead, then they were cut down and cut open while they were still alive. Finally, the head was chopped off and the body was cut into pieces and sent to different edges of the kingdom, normally to be put on display as a warning to others.

## Your turn!

1 Why do you think those who had taken part in the revolt were given such harsh punishments? Give two reasons.

2 In small groups, role play a trial of someone who had taken part in the revolt. Divide each group into two teams – a team of rebels awaiting trial and a team of representatives of the king. Prepare the following:

a a speech from the rebels explaining why they rebelled and their justification for doing so

b a speech from the king's court, explaining why the rebels had no right to rebel, and why they should be punished.

You should also allow time for each team to ask the other questions. At the end, decide as a class who you agree with more – the rebels or the king.

3 Look at Figure 5.11, a modern memorial to the leaders of the Peasants' Revolt. Think about how the rebels were treated in 1381. There are now several memorials to the rebels. What does this tell you about how attitudes to the rebels have changed since 1381?

4 Design your own memorial to the revolt. Think about how you would like the revolt to be remembered.

# Did the Peasants' Revolt achieve anything?

## Key term

**Deposed\*:** Replaced in their role by someone else.

The Peasants' Revolt itself had failed. Its leaders were dead, the promises made to them had been shown to be worthless, and the king was back in control. Did this mean that the revolt changed nothing?

## What did the Peasants' Revolt change?

In the short term, the Peasants' Revolt failed. But in the long term, there were some changes that suggest the revolt was not totally pointless after all.

## What were the consequences of the Peasants' Revolt?

The leaders of the revolt were executed.

The government stopped trying to enforce the Statute of Labourers.

The king and the barons regained control.

There was no serious attempt to challenge the power of the king and the barons for hundreds of years.

It took another 500 years for working people to gain the same rights as the rich and powerful – for example, the right to vote.

The government gave up trying to collect the Poll Tax, and it was never introduced again.

Richard II upset the barons by trying to rule the country on his own. He was deposed\* by John of Gaunt's son, Henry of Bolingbroke, and died in prison. It is thought he probably starved to death.

As there was still a high demand for labour, the peasants continued to bargain for higher wages and for a change in their status. The landowners were powerless to stop this.

By 1500, feudalism had almost entirely disappeared.

In 1574, Elizabeth I formally freed the last remaining unfree peasants.

## Your turn!

1 Copy the following table and complete the activities below.

| Change (how life changed after the Peasants' Revolt) | Continuity (how life continued as before, after the Peasants' Revolt) |
|---|---|
|  |  |

2 Look at the different consequences of the revolt. Decide whether each is an example of change or continuity, and summarise it in your copy of the table.

3 Which do you think were the most important changes? Pick two and explain why.

4 What caused the changes? Was it an individual, an event or other factors? Try and pick an example and explain what caused it.

5 Could it be argued that the Peasants' Revolt achieved nothing? What would be the most important argument in support of this statement?

**Figure 5.12:** How far did the Peasants' Revolt lead to change?

## Checkpoint

1 Give two ways in which the king regained control after the Peasants' Revolt.

2 What happened to John Ball and Wat Tyler?

3 What were the main examples of change after 1381?

4 What were the main examples of continuity?

# What was it like to live in the shadow of the Black Death?

Draw a flowchart summing up the key events from 1348 to the formal end of feudalism in 1574. Use pictures and text to sum up the main changes and turning points along the way. You could even indicate turning points by taking your flowchart in a different direction.

# What have you learned?

In this section, you have learned:

- how the Black Death and the Peasants' Revolt changed England.

Change questions

History can sometimes seem like long stretches of continuity where little changes. However, sudden changes such as the Black Death can move people and society onto an entirely new course.

## What makes a change important?

How big were the changes caused by the Black Death? First we need to think about what change looks like and how we decide the scale of a change. Here are a few examples that suggest a change is important – can you think of any more?

- A lot of people are affected by the change.
- Life is very different after the change compared with before.
- The change is long-lasting.
- The change is sudden.

Conversely, we can consider what might make a change less important.

- The change affects only certain people.
- Life goes on as normal.
- The change does not last long.
- The change is gradual, and as a result people may not have noticed it.

Small changes are happening all the time. You might decide, however, that they are not that important. When no important changes happen, this is called 'continuity'.

### Quick quiz

1. Name two symptoms of the Black Death.

2. Name two ways medieval people tried to avoid, prevent or treat the Black Death.

3. List two ways people's lives were changed after the Black Death.

4. Name two causes of the Peasants' Revolt.

5. Who were the leaders of the Peasants' Revolt, and what happened to them?

6. Name one change after the Peasants' Revolt.

7. Name one example of continuity after the Peasants' Revolt.

### Your turn!

1. Draw a table with two columns and the headings 'Change' and 'Continuity'. Look at the following factors in relation to this period and decide under which heading they belong: family life, medical knowledge, the economy, the feudal system. Try to add some more examples to each column.

2. Look at your completed table. What changed most because of the Black Death? Was there anything that didn't change at all?

# Writing historically

Identifying change and continuity is a key part of the job of the historian – however, this is not always straightforward. It may help to think of change and continuity as being on a scale, rather than being one or the other.

'How far did England change after the Black Death?' This question requires you not only to look at change and continuity, but also to consider the extent to which England changed. To plan for this answer, copy Figure 5.13 and look back through this book to find relevant facts: for example, 'One-third of the population died'. Add these to your diagram, at different points on the scale to show whether they are examples of change or continuity.

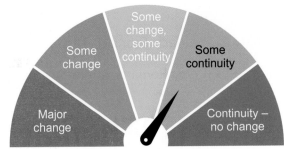

**Figure 5.13:** What does change and continuity look like?

## Structuring your answer

When you have completed your plan, you should have a lot of examples of change and continuity as a result of the Black Death. Remember to start your answer with an introduction in which you show you understand the question, and set out your argument. You should then write some paragraphs that evaluate the different sides of the argument – in what ways did England change and in what ways did it stay the same? Then, write your conclusion, in which you offer your final judgement.

## Writing up your answer

Here are some extracts from typical student answers, which will show you what you need to aim for.

### Student 1

England changed after the Black Death. Everyone died and there was no one left to do the work.

This answer is exaggerating a little! Remember, it is better to talk about degrees of change, rather than simply stating that everything changed, which is rarely true.

### Student 2

England changed significantly after the Black Death. One of the main changes was the loss of one-third of the population. This led to change as it meant fewer peasants were available to work for their lords. In the long term, this meant that peasants were in a more powerful position and could ask for wages.

This is a much better answer – the student has talked about degrees of change ('changed significantly'). The student has also used accurate facts, such as the loss of population, and explained how this led to change. They have signalled this by using phrases like 'This led to…' and 'In the long term, this meant…'.

**Your turn!**

Now, using your plan, write up your answer to the question.

# Who were the first English people?

It's hard to imagine now, but there was a time when the British Isles were completely empty of people. Over the last few thousand years, waves of people have come to our islands, for many different reasons. Some came for violence and plunder, others to invade, while many hoped to find a better quality of life.

In this chapter, you will learn about some of these different groups of people, but first of all you will find out:

- how to approach Thematic History
- who the Celts, Romans, Anglo-Saxons and Vikings were, and why they came to the British Isles.

# What is 'Thematic History'?

## Learning objectives

- Understand how to learn about the past through themes.
- Know the key chronology for this topic.

## What do you think?

What has attracted people to migrate to the British Isles over time?

History is a fascinating topic, but so much has happened in the past, and so much evidence has been left, that it can sometimes be difficult to make sense of it. One of the best ways to do this is by looking at themes in history. This means focusing on one aspect of the past and following it over the course of hundreds or thousands of years, rather than looking at everything that happened to everyone in the same time period, which would be completely overwhelming. Figure 6.1 shows some examples of the kinds of themes that historians look at.

**Theme 1: Political History**
I focus on how countries are governed – from emperors and kings to prime ministers and presidents. I focus on how countries are ruled, and laws that are passed, rather than people's lives.

**Theme 2: Social History**
I look at the lives of everyday people: how they lived, worked and died. I look at the effect that governments have on people's lives, but I don't look at the personalities running the country.

**Theme 3: Military History**
I study war over time, and the history of fighting: how battles were fought, the types of weapons and tactics used, and how these have changed over time. I learn about different wars.

**Theme 4: Economic History**
My expertise is to do with money and trade over time. I look at how governments and people have traded with each other, from the Silk Road to the internet. I look at factors such as unemployment, taxes and the reason why economies sometimes collapse.

**Figure 6.1:** Historians discussing different types of history.

## Your turn!

1 Make a concept map showing the four different themes of history in Figure 6.1 – political, social, military and economic. Explain what each of them is and include a symbol for each – for example, coins for economic history.

2 In this section, you will be learning about the history of migration over time. You will look at how and why people have travelled to Britain, and what their lives were like once they reached Britain. What theme, or themes, do you think this topic belongs in? Explain your answer in a paragraph.

# Migration to Britain over time – an overview

Studying thematic history involves covering a much wider time span than in non-thematic topics. For example, the topics you have covered on the Norman Conquest and the Black Death spanned only a few decades, while in this topic you will be looking at changes over thousands of years. Therefore, it's important to have a good grasp of the chronology.

## Invaders or settlers?

**800,000 BC**
**First humans** arrive in the British Isles.

**500 BC**
Arrival of the **Celts** from Europe.

**AD 43–410**
**Romans** arrive and rule for hundreds of years.

**AD 450**
Arrival of **Angles** and **Saxons** from Denmark and Northern Germany.

**AD 800**
First **Viking raids** begin. In 1016, a Viking, Canute, becomes king of England.

## Migration to escape religious persecution

**1620**
*Mayflower* **arrives in the 'New World'** (modern-day USA), with Puritan settlers from England.

**1572**
St Bartholomew's Day massacre in France – leads to **Huguenots** arriving.

**1290**
After decades of discrimination, the **Jews are expelled**. They are not permitted to return until 1656.

**1066**
**Normans** conquer England. First **Jews arrive from Europe**.

## Economic migration

**1845–52**
**Irish potato famine** leads to widespread migration of Irish families into the UK.

**1948**
*SS Empire Windrush* arrives from the West Indies. This is seen as the start of modern-day mass migration into the UK.

**1968**
**'Rivers of Blood'** speech. Enoch Powell, a Conservative politician, makes a very controversial speech about immigration.

## More recently

**2016**
**The UK votes to leave the European Union.** Many state that immigration was a main reason for wanting to leave.

**2012**
**London Olympics.** Immigrants such as Mohamed Farah win medals for Great Britain. The opening ceremony celebrates the arrival of immigrants. Has Britain learned to accept immigrants?

**Figure 6.2:** Key dates in the history of migration to the British Isles.

## Your turn!

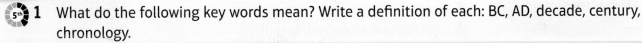

5th **1** What do the following key words mean? Write a definition of each: BC, AD, decade, century, chronology.

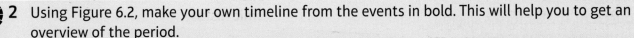

5th **2** Using Figure 6.2, make your own timeline from the events in bold. This will help you to get an overview of the period.

5th **3** Name the centuries in which each event on your timeline happened (for example, 1066 was in the 11th century).

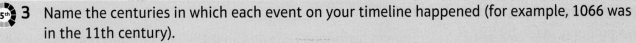

6th **4** Look back through the book and some of the other topics you have studied – for example, the Norman Conquest or the Black Death. Using different colours, add any key events that you think might be relevant onto your timeline.

# Where did early migrants and settlers come from?

## Learning objectives

- Understand which groups first settled in the British Isles, and why.
- Learn about the key features of Celtic and Roman Britain.

## Key term

**Hunter-gatherers\*:** People who survive by hunting, fishing and gathering wild food rather than farming.

**Source A:** The Battersea shield, which was found in the River Thames near Battersea in 1857. It was probably made by the Celts in around 350–50 BC. It is thought the shield was thrown into the River Thames as an offering to their gods.

Until around 8000 years ago, the country we now call Britain was not an island. Instead, it was a cold and inhospitable corner of the European landmass. Early humans could walk to Britain from Europe across a stretch of dry land; a 'land bridge', known as 'Doggerland', until rising sea levels at the end of the last Ice Age submerged the land bridge and created the islands we live on today. These early humans were probably hunter-gatherers\* who wandered from place to place to survive. However, by around 3000 BC, they had discovered agriculture and began to grow their own food, showing that some settled permanently in these isles.

## The arrival of the Celts

Around the year 500 BC, the Celts began to cross the sea to settle in the British Isles. The Celts were a collection of different warring tribes that lived in central Europe. They were probably attracted to Britain by the promise of rich and fertile farmland.

Over the next few hundred years, the Celts prospered and left their mark on Britain. Although they lived simple lives, they also introduced some important new innovations to Britain. For example, they were the first to introduce iron working and the first to use the iron plough. They also built or expanded defensive forts around Britain, many of which, such as Maiden Castle in Dorset, can still be seen today.

Archaeologists have made discoveries that suggest some Celts were highly skilled – for example, the Battersea shield (Source A) displays intricate metalworking skills.

## Did you know?

Roman historians recorded that the Celts fought battles stripped naked and covered in blue paint to terrify their enemies. There is also some evidence that they severed the heads of their enemies and kept them as trophies.

## The arrival of the Romans

At the same time as the Celts were settling in the British Isles, the Romans were building up the greatest empire the world had ever seen. It stretched from the shores of the Atlantic in modern-day Portugal to the modern-day Middle East. In AD 43, Roman legions landed on the south coast of England and claimed the British Isles for Rome. Source B gives an idea of why the Romans were attracted to Britain.

The invading Roman legions are said to have fought a battle against the native Celts near the River Thames, before attacking the Celtic capital at Camulodunum (Colchester). The Romans then turned their attention to the south-west of Britain, besieging and destroying the hill forts built by the Celts.

Soon, most of what is now England had been conquered by the Romans, who then focused on trying to subdue the rebellious tribes in Wales. However, the Romans were about to face a serious rebellion in East Anglia.

**Source B:** Written by the Roman historian, Tacitus, c. AD 98. Here Tacitus describes the British Isles.

With the exception of the olive and vine, and plants which usually grow in warmer climates, the soil will [grow] all ordinary [crops]… [due to] the excessive moisture of the soil and of the atmosphere. Britain contains gold and silver and other metals, as the prize of conquest. The ocean, too, produces pearls, but of a dusky and bluish hue.

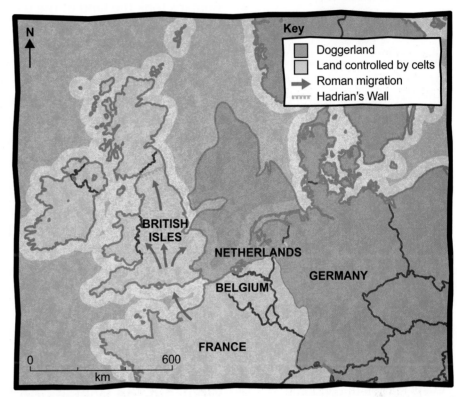

**Figure 6.3:** A map showing the location of the 'land bridge', as well as Roman migration to Britain.

### Your turn!

1. Look at Source A. What can you learn from this source about what the Celts were like? Write down at least two inferences.

2. Read Source B. What can you learn from this source about why the British Isles were attractive to the Romans? Write down three reasons they might want to invade.

3. In pairs, think of some questions that historians might want to ask about Source A to find out more about it. Try to also consider what the answers might be.

# Resistance to Roman rule

**Source C:** The head of a bronze Roman statue of Emperor Claudius. It was probably part of a much bigger statue, possibly one situated in the temple in Colchester. It was found in 1907 in the River Alde in Suffolk.

### Did you know?

Historians don't know where the final battle against Boudicca was fought, or where she is now buried. Suggestions range from Birmingham to beneath King's Cross station in London!

By the middle of the 1st century AD, resistance to the Romans in the land they named Britannia had dwindled. The Romans told the tribal leaders of the Celts that they could keep their power, as long as they accepted the authority of Rome. One such tribe were the Iceni in East Anglia, whose leaders, Prasutagus and his wife Boudicca, submitted to Rome. However, when Prasutagus died, the Romans took the land of the Iceni. When Boudicca objected, the Romans whipped her and raped her daughters. The Romans may have regretted this, for by AD 61 Boudicca had become the leader of a violent revolt against them.

At first, the revolt achieved success. The Roman legions were distracted dealing with trouble in Wales, allowing Boudicca and her armies to destroy the Roman towns of Colchester, London and St Albans. It is said her armies killed over 80,000 people.

In AD 61, Boudicca prepared for a battle with a much smaller Roman army in the 'Battle of Watling Street'. The rebellious Britons were so confident of victory that the Roman historian Tacitus claims that warriors brought their wives with them to see the victory. Unfortunately, Boudicca's army was lured into a trap and disciplined Roman legions cut the rebel army to pieces. Seeing that she had been defeated, some sources claim Boudicca poisoned herself and her daughters rather than face capture.

With Boudicca's death, serious resistance against the Romans ended.

## What did the Romans do for us?

The Romans introduced many of the most impressive aspects of their civilisation to Britain (see Figure 6.4).

Recent research has also revealed some surprising facts about Roman Britain. In 1901, a coffin was found in York, dated to the Roman period. The coffin contained the skeleton of a woman. She appears to have been of high standing due to the items included in her coffin, such as expensive jewellery and a glass mirror.

**Interpretation 1:** Boudicca and the Iceni fighting against the Romans.

Recent DNA analysis of the skeleton has revealed that she was a black woman of North African descent. Other Roman cemeteries in Britain have revealed similar finds; in one cemetery, up to 51 per cent of the bodies are thought to be of African descent. Therefore, some cities in Roman Britain may have included many different people from across the Empire.

However, other scientific studies have suggested that there is little evidence of Roman DNA among the population of Britain today. This may suggest that the native Celts and Romans lived quite separate lives and did not intermarry.

Roman law heavily influenced the British legal system

The first towns and cities

The first proper roads

Vegetables, such as cabbages, peas, turnips and carrots

**Figure 6.4:** Some of the contributions the Romans made to Britain.

## Your turn!

 **1**  Make a timeline showing the key events from the arrival of the Celts to Boudicca's defeat.

 **2**  Design a memorial to Boudicca. Explain why you think she was significant and why she might deserve to be remembered.

**3**  Look at Source C. Historians can't be sure where this head came from, or why it ended up in a river. However, some think that it was taken from a statue in Colchester during Boudicca's rebellion. Sources like this can give us a fascinating glimpse into the past, but we will never be able to be sure what happened to the statue. Write a piece of historical fiction in which you imagine the story behind the head.

## Checkpoint

**1**  When did the first settlers arrive in the British Isles?

**2**  What probably attracted the Celts and the Romans to Britain?

**3**  Who was Boudicca, and why did she rebel against the Romans?

**4**  What happened to Boudicca and her revolt?

**5**  What did the Celts and the Romans introduce to Britain?

# The arrival of the Anglo-Saxons

## Did you know?

The Roman roads remained the main method of transport in Britain for well over a thousand years. It would take until the 18th century before roads of such quality were built again.

By AD 410, the Roman Empire was in deep trouble and the Roman legions were withdrawn from Britain to help to defend the Empire from its enemies. Within a few generations, the Roman Empire had collapsed, and with it went the Roman way of life in Britain. The fine buildings and structures that the Romans brought to Britain fell into ruins, as the knowledge of how to maintain them was lost. Some historians call this era the 'Dark Ages'*, due to the collapse of Roman civilisation in Britain.

However, the Roman withdrawal meant tempting new opportunities for other tribes who were keen to benefit from Britain's fertile lands. Among these were the Angles and Saxons.

## The Angles and Saxons invade

From about the year AD 450, the British Isles began to be invaded by tribes from Northern Europe. These included the Angles and Jutes (from modern-day Denmark), and the Saxons (from modern-day Germany).

## Key term

**Dark Ages*:** A term for the period between the Roman withdrawal in AD 410 and the arrival of the Normans in 1066. Not all historians like this term, as it has been used to suggest that there was no culture or civilisation in this period.

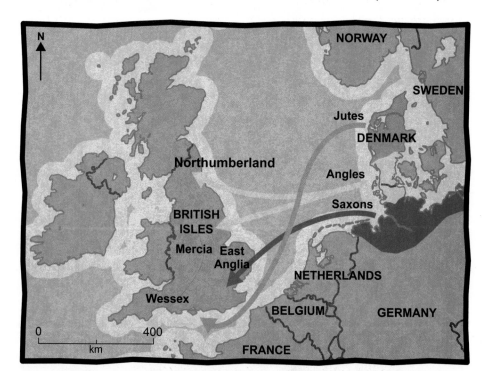

**Figure 6.5:** A map of invasions by the Angles, Saxons and Jutes.

## Impact of the Anglo-Saxons

Initially, the Anglo-Saxons were more like a hostile invasion than a migration. In Source A, the English monk, the Venerable Bede, talks about the arrival of the Angles, Saxons and Jutes. He was writing several hundred years after the events.

Although some sources suggest a violent invasion, the reality may have been somewhat different. For many years it was thought that these tribes killed off the native 'Celtic' British people and drove them away from their lands. There is some evidence to support this, as DNA evidence shows that those with Celtic ancestry now live on the fringes of the British Isles, while the majority of English people are of Anglo-Saxon descent. However, others argue it means that the Anglo-Saxons settled and married into the local population, rather than killing them. Whatever happened, within a few generations, the Anglo-Saxons were firmly in control of England. Indeed, we might even see them as being the first 'English' people.

> **Source A:** From the *Ecclesiastical History of the English Speaking Peoples* by the Venerable Bede, c. 731.
>
> In the year of our Lord 449… the Angles, or Saxons, [who had been invited by the king to defend Britain] arrived… with three long ships, and had a place assigned them to reside in by the same king, in the eastern part of the island, that they might thus appear to be fighting for their country, whilst their real intentions were to enslave it. [After finding out about] the fertility of the country, and the cowardice of the Britons, a more considerable fleet was quickly sent over, bringing a still greater number of men, which, being added to the former, made up an invincible army. The newcomers received of the Britons a place to inhabit, upon condition that they should wage war against their enemies for the peace and security of the country, whilst the Britons agreed to furnish them with pay.

**Did you know?**

The Venerable Bede is considered by some to be the 'Father of English History', as he was the first English person we know of to attempt to record what had happened before and during the time of the Anglo-Saxons.

**Source B:** Image of the Venerable Bede from the *Nuremberg Chronicle*, created in 1440.

**Your turn!**

1 According to Source A, why did the Angles and Saxons come to England? Give two reasons.

2 What does Source A suggest about how these tribes took over England? Pick a quote and explain it.

3 What does Bede think of the Angles and Saxons? Pick a quote that gives an idea of his opinion.

4 What are the strengths and weaknesses of Bede's account of what happened? Give an example of each.

# Were the Anglo-Saxons invaders or the founders of England?

**Source C:** Greensted Church in Essex, the oldest surviving wooden church in the world. It was originally built by the Anglo-Saxons.

How should we see the Anglo-Saxons? Were they invaders, or the first people we might class as being English, even though they came from modern-day Germany and Denmark? When they first appeared, the Anglo-Saxons probably were seen as violent invaders. However, within a few generations, the Anglo-Saxons had settled, married into the local population and become part of the fabric of the country. The Anglo-Saxons have had a huge impact on England, as can be seen by place names such as 'East Anglia'. The word 'England' itself comes from the term 'Land of the Angles'. In many other ways, our country still bears the imprint of the Anglo-Saxons.

## Religion and language

As well as settling the land, the Anglo-Saxons also replaced the Celtic gods with their own pagan gods. Although virtually no one believes in these gods any more, we still use their names frequently, centuries later, as some of our days of the week are named after them!

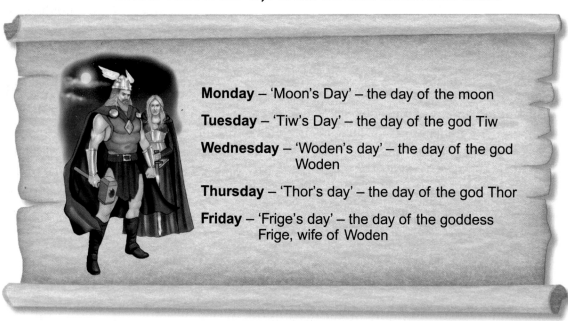

**Monday** – 'Moon's Day' – the day of the moon

**Tuesday** – 'Tiw's Day' – the day of the god Tiw

**Wednesday** – 'Woden's day' – the day of the god Woden

**Thursday** – 'Thor's day' – the day of the god Thor

**Friday** – 'Frige's day' – the day of the goddess Frige, wife of Woden

**Figure 6.6:** The Anglo-Saxon influence on our days of the week.

However, in AD 597, the pope sent a monk named Augustine to introduce England to Christianity. He converted the Anglo-Saxon king, Ethelbert, to the new religion and founded some of the first Christian churches in England. Within a few generations, the old gods had been largely forgotten and replaced by the one Christian God. Christianity was to become one of the most powerful forces in English people's lives for the next thousand years and more.

## Beowulf

Another significant Anglo-Saxon contribution to our culture is the epic poem *Beowulf*. It was composed at some point in the Anglo-Saxon period, but its original author is unknown. It probably existed for several hundred years, being passed down by word of mouth from person to person, before finally being written down in the early 11th century. Only one copy of the manuscript survives; without this, historians would know nothing about the poem, which people continue to enjoy today.

The poem tells the story of Beowulf, a heroic warrior who has to defend his homeland against a terrifying monster called Grendel. Beowulf kills the monster, but is then forced to fight Grendel's mother, who is a dragon.

So, what do you think – were the Anglo-Saxons really living in the 'Dark Ages'?

**Source D:** An extract from a modern translation of the Anglo-Saxon poem *Beowulf*, in which Beowulf is fighting for his life to defeat the dragon in its cave.

Then Beowulf saw among weapons an invincible sword
… it was so huge that no man but Beowulf
could hope to handle it in the quick of combat.
Ferocious in battle, [he]
grasped the ringed hilt, swung the ornamented sword
despairing of his life – he struck such a savage blow
that the sharp blade slashed through her neck,
smashed the vertebrae; it severed her head
from the fated body; she fell at his feet.
The sword was bloodstained; Beowulf rejoiced.

**Figure 6.7:** A modern collage showing the original text of *Beowulf* with an illustration from a French medieval manuscript.

### Did you know?

*Beowulf* has been rewritten and retold many times over the centuries, and was even made into a film (and video game) in 2007. It was also a key influence on the author J.R.R. Tolkien, who was an expert on the Anglo-Saxons and drew on this to write *The Lord of the Rings*.

### Your turn!

1. What might a historian learn about the Anglo-Saxons if they only had *Beowulf* as evidence?

2. Look at Sources C and D. What two things can you learn from these about Anglo-Saxon England?

3. What are the strengths and weaknesses of *Beowulf* as evidence about Anglo-Saxon society?

4. Design a poster with the heading 'What have the Anglo-Saxons done for us?' to convince others that the term 'Dark Ages' is inaccurate. Include as many pictures/facts as possible.

### Checkpoint

1. When and why did the Romans leave Britain?

2. Where did the Anglo-Saxons come from?

3. What attracted them to England?

4. Name two ways in which the Anglo-Saxons changed England.

# The Vikings – murderous invaders or peaceful settlers?

## Learning objectives

- Learn who the Vikings were, and where they came from.
- Understand the impact the Vikings had on England.
- Learn how the Vikings explored and settled other countries.

## What do you think?

What do you already know about the Vikings?

## Key term

**Danelaw\*:** The areas of Anglo-Saxon England that were populated by the descendants of Vikings. These areas followed Viking laws and customs.

In AD 793, monks working peacefully at their monastery in Lindisfarne, Northumbria, were surprised by the appearance of sails on the horizon. The ships drew closer and hordes of warriors came ashore. They ransacked the monastery, stole its gold and jewels, and killed its inhabitants. The monks, who carried no weapons, were defenceless.

Some at the time described the invaders as 'pagans', or people without religion. Others called them 'Danes' or the 'Northmen'. It wasn't until the 11th century that they received the name 'Vikings', which means 'pirate raiders'. The raid on Lindisfarne was only the first of many; soon, the Vikings attacked other targets, and in larger numbers. For the next 250 years, Britain faced repeated attacks from the Vikings.

## Who were the Vikings?

The Vikings were different groups of people who came from the modern-day countries of Denmark, Norway and Sweden. Life at home was probably very hard, with too many people and not enough land. It's possible that merchants who had traded with the Anglo-Saxons returned home to the Viking homelands and spoke of the fertile lands and riches to the west. It's not surprising that many chose to risk the journey across the sea to Britain.

**Figure 6.8:** Viking raiders.

## What made the Vikings such effective raiders?

The Vikings were highly effective sailors. Their ships used a combination of sails and oars, allowing them to travel long distances. They were also able to navigate rivers that were too shallow for most ships, allowing them to penetrate deep inland where people least expected it.

## The Viking invasion

In AD 865, the Vikings changed tactics. Instead of small hit-and-run raids that aimed to carry away loot and plunder, the Vikings launched a full-scale invasion. One by one, the Anglo-Saxon kingdoms were defeated, until only the kingdom of Wessex, ruled by Alfred, was left.

However, Alfred proved to be an impressive military leader and defeated the Viking army, forcing their leader to convert to Christianity. Because of his victory, Alfred gained the title by which he is commonly known – Alfred 'the Great'. However, he was unable to drive the Vikings completely from Britain. Instead, he divided the land into two kingdoms. The Anglo-Saxon kingdom covered most of southern England, while the Viking kingdom included much of northern England and East Anglia. This became known as the 'Danelaw'*. Many Vikings settled there and, over time, became part of the general population, until it would have been difficult to tell who was a Viking and who was 'English'.

In Britain, the Vikings have had a lasting impact. The Viking city of Jorvik (modern-day York) had 10,000 inhabitants at its peak and was a major trading centre. You can still see the impact of the Vikings on place names today. Places with the suffixes '-by' or '-thorpe' (e.g. Whitby, Derby, Scunthorpe) were probably founded by the Vikings.

**Figure 6.9:** A Viking longboat.

### Did you know?

One recent study suggested that one million people in Britain today are direct descendants of the Vikings. In some areas, such as the Shetland Islands, as many as 30 per cent of the population are descended from Vikings.

### Your turn!

1   Draw a 'push' and 'pull' diagram to show why the Vikings came to Britain. For 'push', include the reasons that made them want to leave their homeland. For 'pull', include what attracted them to Britain.

2   Read Source A. Suggest a reason why this source is useful to historians wanting to find out about the impact of the Vikings in Britain.

3   What else can you learn from Source A about:
    a   Alfred as a leader
    b   agreements Alfred made with the Vikings?

4   What evidence is there in Source A that the Vikings were not just raiders and plunderers, but instead settled in Britain? Pick a quote and explain it.

5   Explain how evidence such as place names and the remains of Jorvik also suggest that the Vikings eventually settled down.

**Source A:** An extract from the Peterborough Manuscript of the *Anglo-Saxon Chronicle*. This was written by monks from the ninth to the 12th centuries AD.

[Alfred]… made peace with the raiding-army, and they granted him as hostages the most distinguished men who were next to the king in the raiding-army, and they swore him oaths on the sacred ring, which earlier they would not do to any nation, that they would quickly go from his kingdom… And that year Halfdan divided up the land of Northumbria; and they were ploughing and were providing for themselves.

# The Vikings as empire-builders

**Did you know?**

Until recently, it was thought that Christopher Columbus was the first European to discover the Americas in 1492. However, the Vikings had arrived first, some 500 years earlier.

The reputation of the Vikings is of violent warriors who raided and pillaged the British Isles. However, the reality is more complicated; as you have already learned, many Vikings peacefully settled in Britain and became part of the general population over time.

Also, it's important to remember that England was just one of many places that the Vikings travelled to. They were fearless explorers and traders who managed to build a large empire. Below are some examples.

## The Vikings as explorers and state-builders

The Vikings colonised large parts of Scotland, the Orkney Islands and the Isle of Man, and founded the city of Dublin. They also took control of northern France. As they came from the north, they were known as the 'Nor(th)men', so this part of France became known as 'Normandy'. William the Conqueror was a descendant of Viking settlers. Therefore, in turn, the Norman invasion and conquest of England in 1066 can be seen as a further expansion of the Viking empire.

## The Vikings as traders and craftsmen

The Vikings did not just attack neighbouring settlements; they also traded with them. There is evidence of extensive trading networks, which exchanged goods such as silver, silks, spices, wine, jewellery, glass and pottery. Excavations have revealed that some Vikings were talented craftsmen, making sophisticated metalwork and wooden carvings.

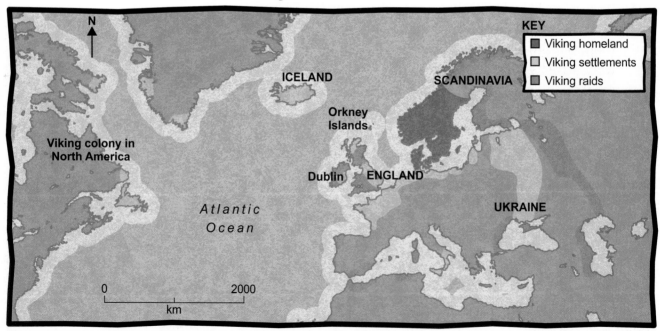

**Figure 6.10:** A map of Viking exploration.

## Your turn!

Read Interpretation 1 and answer these questions.

**5th** **1** Summarise in a few sentences what interpretation the historian gives about the Vikings.

**6th** **2** Using the information on these pages, and your notes, provide evidence both to support and to challenge the viewpoint of the historian.

**6th** **3** How convincing do you find Interpretation 1? Explain your view, giving evidence to support your opinion.

## Checkpoint

**1** Where did the Vikings come from?

**2** Who was Alfred, and how did he help to manage the Viking threat?

**3** What was the 'Danelaw'?

**4** Explain how you think the Vikings should be remembered – as ruthless warriors or as settlers and explorers.

**Interpretation 1:** From *The Age of the Vikings* by Anders Winroth, a historian who has aimed to change public perception of the Vikings.

The Vikings were violent, even ferociously so. They hunted slaves, killed, maimed and plundered over much of Europe... [but] the Middle Ages were a violent time overall... the Viking Age was also a moment of great cultural, religious and political achievement... Literature flourished... Scandinavians experienced a great boom in decorative art... trade and exchange, bought not only untold riches... but also all kinds of exotic trade goods. Chieftains impressed people by drinking [German] wine from Egyptian glasses, by [gaining] the strongest steel in the world for their swords from central Asia and India, by wearing Chinese silk and Indian gems, and by offering those they counted as friends a share in all that wealth.

# Who were the first English people?

As you can see, it's hard to establish who really were the first English people. Who do you think has the best claim to the title? Is it about who was there first, or who had the greatest impact?

In your class, divide into groups of four. Each person in the group should take on the role of one of the groups of people you have learned about – either the Celts, Romans, Anglo-Saxons or Vikings. Each person should think about the following.

- Why you came to the British Isles.

- What important contributions you have made to this part of the world.

- Why you deserve to be remembered as part of the story of England.

When you have prepared, discuss the points above in your groups. Can you come to an agreement on who deserves the title?

# What have you learned?

In this section, you have learned to:

• which different groups came to Britain before 1066

• some of the reasons that drove them to migrate.

As shown in Figure 6.11, it is very difficult to decide who the first 'English' people were. One explanation is that all of them were English. At one time, the land we call 'England' was empty of people, so it is only through waves of migration and invasion that these islands have become populated. These waves of migration tended to be seen at first as hostile invasions by whoever the native inhabitants were, until over time the invaders simply became part of England. It wasn't until the tenth century that England was formally united as a country, under one king.

**1** I was here first.

**2** We were the first to settle.

800,000–500 BC: Were the first English people the hunter-gatherers who walked to England when it was joined by a land bridge to Europe?

If so, what does that make the Celtic tribes who arrived from about 500 BC onwards? Were they 'English', or did they conquer the true English people?

**3** But we brought civilisation.

**4** We invented the word 'England'.

**5** We named many of England's towns.

The Romans arrived in AD 43. They brought roads, towns and new foods to Britain, and had a big influence on England.

After the Romans left, from about AD 450 England was settled by waves of Germanic tribes – the Angles, Saxons and Jutes. They had a huge influence on the English language.

From about AD 793 onwards, the British Isles experienced waves of attacks from Vikings. Eventually, the Vikings settled and blended into the local population, founding many towns and cities that still exist today.

**Figure 6.11:** Different groups who might claim to be the first 'English' people.

# Writing historically

One of the skills that you have been working on throughout this section is chronology. This is really important in a thematic section such as this, where in a few pages you have covered events that stretched over hundreds, or even thousands, of years.

## Describing the historical context of an event

Being able to locate an event within its historical context is an important skill. Some questions will demand more or less detail, depending on what is being asked.

For example, consider the question 'When was the Battle of Edington?'

**Student 1**

During the Dark Ages.

> Student 1 is too vague – The Dark Ages lasted for around 600 years. Also, not all historians agree on when this period began or ended.

**Student 2**

In AD 878.

> Student 2 is correct, but simply stating a date on its own doesn't give any historical context.

**Student 3**

In AD 878, during the reign of King Alfred.

> Student 3 gives the best answer, a specific date and a some context to locate the event in time. The reigns of monarchs are useful references to locate points in time.

Now consider the question 'When was Roman Britain?'

**Student 1**

AD 43.

> Student 1's answer is too short. This question is asking for the rough time span of a historical era, rather than a one-off event.

**Student 2**

Roman Britain began in the first century AD with the Roman invasion in AD 43. It ended in the fifth century AD with the withdrawal of Roman troops in AD 410, at a time when Rome itself was under threat.

> Student 2's answer is better, as not only does it give the commonly accepted start and end dates for the era, but also provides the century for each date and some wider context.

### Your turn!

Use the examples above as a guide to answer the following questions.

1 When did the Vikings attack Lindisfarne?
2 When was the Anglo-Saxon period?
3 When did Boudicca's revolt take place?
4 When did Christianity first arrive in England?
5 Approximately when was *Beowulf* composed?

# What drove people to migrate?

The Norman Conquest of 1066 ended 1000 years of invasion from other countries. From then on, people came to England not to conquer, but to seek a better life for themselves. Others, such as the Puritans, migrated away from England for the same reasons. How important was religion as a motivating factor for these groups?

In this section, you will learn about:

- why the Jews, the Huguenots and the Puritans migrated

- what caused migration from Ireland and the West Indies, and how migrants were treated.

# The role of religion

## Learning objectives

- Understand why different groups, such as the Jews, Huguenots and Puritans, migrated.
- Assess the role of religion in their migration.

## What do you think?

What do you think motivates people to migrate? Do you think these reasons have changed much over time?

## Key terms

**Old Testament\*:** The first part of the Bible, believed by both Christians and Jews to be the word of God.

**Diaspora\*:** A population that once lived in one place, but has been scattered.

A common reason why people wanted to migrate in the past was religious persecution. This means people being discriminated against, and sometimes physically attacked and killed, because of their religious beliefs. This was particularly true of Jewish migration.

## Case study 1 – Jews in England

Jews share common beliefs with Christians. Both religions believe that there is only one God, and both believe in the teachings of the Old Testament\*. However, whereas Christians believe that Jesus (who was a Jew) was the son of God, Jews believe that Jesus was simply an important prophet. There are also other important differences in rituals and traditions.

Discrimination against the Jews meant they were pushed out from their original homeland in the Middle East in the second century AD. As a result, the Jewish population settled in many different countries around the world. This is known as the Jewish diaspora\*. Jews have faced discrimination and persecution in many countries, largely due to their religious and cultural differences.

**Source A:** The 'Jew's House' in Lincoln. It is one of the oldest houses in England and before 1120 it belonged to a prosperous Jewish family. The doorway was probably the entrance to a synagogue, which stood behind the house.

## The arrival of the Jews in England

Before 1066, there were no Jews living in England. The nation was exclusively Christian. However, William the Conqueror needed to raise money quickly to build castles and cathedrals to strengthen his hold on England. It was considered a sin (known as usury) for Christians to become rich by lending money to other Christians. As the Jews were not Christian, William invited them into England to become money lenders. Initially, the Jews prospered.

## Hostility and persecution

However, some people resented having to borrow money from the Jewish community and paying interest. Jews were also regarded with suspicion as the only major non-Christian minority in England. The Crusades, which started in 1095, preached that anyone who didn't believe in Christianity was an 'unbeliever'. Therefore, Jews in England – and elsewhere in Europe – were subjected to hostility and violence.

## Persecution, violence and expulsion

Violence against the Jews in England continued to increase. In 1190, hundreds of Jews were murdered by the inhabitants of York. Conditions continued to worsen over the next 100 years. In 1290, King Edward I, responding to an increasingly hostile attitude towards the Jews, ordered them to leave England or face execution. The Jews were not allowed to return for almost 400 years.

In 1656, Oliver Cromwell finally allowed Jews to return to England. Since then, they have played an important role in British society. Britain now has one of the largest Jewish populations in the world.

**Source B:** An anti-Semitic picture from a 13th-century manuscript, showing Jews lending money. The image of a greedy, hooked-nose Jew was a common racist stereotype.

**Interpretation 1:** From remember.org, a website that examines Jewish history.

```
Jewish life in the Middle Ages was
for the most part a story of social
and economic isolation, persecution
and massacres. Jews were isolated
both physically and socially from the
fabric of life in the Middle Ages and
the period following the Middle Ages.
Yet they filled an important niche.
Christianity outlawed usury, the
lending of money. Jews were permitted
to fill this vacuum by acting as
moneylenders and financiers.
```

### Your turn!

1 Draw a 'push' and 'pull' diagram explaining why Jews migrated to England.

2 What do Sources A and B suggest about what it was like to be a Jew in medieval England?

3 Read Interpretation 1. Explain in a couple of sentences what the author is arguing about:
   **a** the treatment of Jews in the Middle Ages
   **b** the role Jews performed within society.

4 Explain in a paragraph why the author has arrived at this interpretation. Use your knowledge from this section.

# The religious Reformation

## Key terms

**Protestants\*:** Christians who broke away from the Catholic Church to form their own religious groups.

**Reformation\*:** Refers to the rise of Protestantism in the 16th century and the end of the dominance of the Catholic Church in some countries, for example England.

**Low Countries\*:** Refers to the geographical area including modern-day Belgium and the Netherlands.

## Did you know?

One study suggested that one in every six Britons is related to a Huguenot refugee.

At the start of the 16th century, the Catholic Church still dominated Europe, as it had for centuries. However, some people began to criticise the Catholic Church and call for change. They became known as Protestants\*. Countries in Europe descended into violence and civil war over who was right – Catholics or Protestants. This process is known as the Reformation\*.

## Case study 2 – the Huguenots

One group who became caught up in the religious struggles of the 16th century were the Huguenots. They were Protestants who lived in areas of France and the Low Countries\*. As they lived in strongly Catholic areas, they became targets for discrimination and persecution.

The first group of Huguenot refugees arrived in England in the 1560s, driven by discrimination from their Spanish–Catholic rulers. However, many more arrived from France after the St Bartholomew's Day massacre. In 1572, the French king ordered the execution of some of the leaders of the Huguenot movement. This led to an outpouring of violence and hatred throughout France against the Huguenots, in which angry mobs massacred innocent men, women and children. The massacre lasted several weeks and spread far into the French countryside. It is unknown precisely how many people died but estimates vary from 2000 to as high as 70,000.

## Huguenot migration to England

Protestant nations were horrified by the massacre and the English government welcomed large numbers of Huguenots to England. Charities and food kitchens were set up to help the refugees, who had often faced very dangerous journeys to reach England.

The refugees soon proved to be a valuable resource for England. Many were experienced cloth merchants and became an important part of the textile industry in England. Huguenots also helped to found Sheffield's cutlery industry, while the foundation of the Bank of England in 1694 was partly financed by Huguenot money.

**Source C:** Detail from the painting *The St Bartholomew's Day Massacre* by François Dubois, a French Huguenot, c. 1572.

## Case study 3 – the Puritans and the *Mayflower*

Like the Huguenots, the Puritans were a religious group who lived in a country that was hostile to their beliefs and were looking to migrate. However, in this case, the Puritans wanted to migrate *away* from England.

## Who were the Puritans?

In England, in the late 16th and early 17th centuries, a group of extreme Protestants known as the Puritans emerged. They argued that the religious Reformation that had happened in England under the Tudors had not gone far enough. They refused to swear allegiance to the new Church of England, believing it was as bad as the old Catholic Church.

**Interpretation 2:** The *Mayflower* in Plymouth harbour, painted in 1882 by William Halsall.

By the 1620s, the government in England responded to the criticisms of the Puritans by starting a campaign of religious persecution. Some Puritans received extreme punishments for refusing to renounce their ideas. In 1630, one Puritan was given a sentence of life imprisonment. He was also tortured, having his nose and ears cut off and the letters 'SS' branded onto his head (for 'Sower of Sedition' – a way of calling someone a troublemaker).

**Did you know?**

The colonists are now known as the 'Pilgrim Fathers', in recognition of their role in helping to found their country.

The Puritans wanted to relocate to a place in which they could practise their religion freely. They decided to start a new life, in the 'New World', now known as North America.

## The voyage of the *Mayflower*

In September 1620, a ship called the *Mayflower* set sail from Plymouth for the New World with about 100 Puritans on board. After a miserable journey lasting around two months, the Puritans landed at what is now known as Cape Cod. The Puritans named their colony 'New Plymouth'. They aimed to create a society in which they could practise their religion in peace.

Over time, many more colonies were started and, much later in 1776, the colonies declared independence from Britain to form a new country – the United States of America. One of the founding principles of the USA was that no one should be persecuted for practising their religion.

**Your turn!**

1   Complete 'push' and 'pull' diagrams for the Huguenots and the Puritans.

2   In groups of three, conduct a short role play. Imagine the migrants are being interviewed about their experiences. Each of you should play someone from one of the groups of migrants. Role play asking and answering questions on the following themes.
   a   Why did you migrate?
   b   Has migration improved your life? If so, how?

**Checkpoint**

1   Name one reason why each of these groups migrated – Jews, Huguenots and Puritans.

2   How were each group of migrants received in their new country? Try to give an example for each.

3   Discuss which groups you think had the most positive and the most negative experiences as migrants.

# Economic migration – the Irish and West Indians

## Learning objectives

- Understand what made Irish and West Indian people want to migrate to Britain.
- Assess how far migrants were accepted by British people.
- Understand the political reaction to migration, such as the 'Rivers of Blood' speech.

### Key term

**West Indians\*:** People from an area of the Caribbean, including many island nations that were formerly part of the British Empire, such as Jamaica.

**Source A:** From the *Illustrated London News*, published in 1846, this image shows starving Irish children scavenging for potatoes.

People often have economic reasons for wanting to migrate, such as wanting a better job and standard of living. For the Irish in the 19th century, and West Indians\* in the 20th century, this was certainly the case.

## What made so many Irish people want to leave their homeland?

In the 19th century, Ireland was not an independent country, like most of it is today. The entire island was a British colony, ruled by the British as part of their Empire. Many of Ireland's people in the 1800s were desperately poor. The Catholic population was growing, but there was not enough work to go around and the rents charged by Protestant landlords, who lived elsewhere, were high.

Many poor Irish families were reliant on potatoes for food, which grew easily in the wet, cold conditions of Ireland. However, in the 1840s, a disease destroyed many of the potatoes, leaving millions of poor Irish people with nothing to eat. This was known as the Great Famine. As a result, approximately one million Irish people starved to death. Another million emigrated, mainly to the USA, Canada and Great Britain\*.

Britain was an attractive destination for many, not least because it was so close. At the time, Britain was rapidly changing from an economy largely based on agriculture to one largely based on industry. There was a huge demand for labour, which Irish migrants were able to fill. Irish migrants did many different types of work, from hard manual labour in factories, mines and quarries, to professional jobs such as doctors and policemen. Thousands of so-called Irish 'navvies' helped to build many of the railway lines, tunnels and canals that we still see and use today.

## What was life like for Irish migrants?

Life for Irish migrants was often tough, and they were a target of discrimination in Britain. Unable to afford expensive lodgings in unfamiliar cities, Irish migrants would cluster together in certain cities, such as Glasgow, Manchester, Liverpool and London, where most of the jobs were available. Conditions in many industrial cities were terrible, and many were forced to live in overcrowded, cramped houses known as 'slums'* (see Source B).

As Irish migrants were forced into filthy houses out of desperation, this helped to fuel a stereotype in the media of Irish people as ignorant, unclean and violent. This can be seen in Source C. The author, Friedrich Engels, was a German socialist who wanted to highlight the poor condition of the English working class. He was very critical of the Irish people he encountered.

Irish people were also viewed with suspicion as they were different – most Irish migrants were devout Catholics, at a time when England was mostly Protestant. Migrants were accused of taking English people's jobs and being prepared to work for less. As a tiny minority of Irish people had planted bombs in Britain in protest at British rule in Ireland, they were also seen as potential terrorists, (although this word was not used at the time).

However, not all Irish migrants were poor. Some came from prosperous middle-class families and continued their professions. For example, there were many Irish doctors in 19th-century Britain. Others were able to improve their social position over time, becoming part of the middle class.

**Source B:** The 'Irish Rookery' in Kensington, London, c. 1865. Such places were seen as areas of criminal activity.

**Source C:** Extract from *The Condition of the Working Class in England* by Friedrich Engels, published in 1845.

The worst dwellings are good enough for [the Irish]; their clothing causes them little troubles, so long as it holds together by a single thread; shoes they know not; their food consists of potatoes and potatoes only; whatever they earn beyond their needs is usually spent upon drink. What does such a race want with high wages? The worst quarters of all the large towns are inhabited by Irishmen.

### Your turn!

1   Write down two headings: 'Push' and 'Pull'. Under each, note down the factors that made people want to leave Ireland ('push' factors) and want to come to Britain ('pull' factors).

2   Look at Source A. Explain what you can see in this source, and what this tells you about why people left Ireland.

3   Look at Sources B and C. What can you infer from these sources about the experiences of Irish migrants? Try to comment on living conditions and how other people felt about them. Aim to write a paragraph on each point.

### Key terms

**Great Britain*:** England, Wales and Scotland. They were united with Ireland in 1801 to become the United Kingdom of Great Britain and Ireland.

**Slums*:** Poorly built and overcrowded houses, often located in industrial cities.

# What was life like for West Indians in Britain?

**Source D:** The *SS Empire Windrush* arriving at Tilbury docks in 1948.

**Source E:** The kind of sign commonly seen in Britain before the 1965 Race Relations Act made such discrimination illegal.

Like the Irish, in the mid-20th century, many West Indians decided to move to Britain for economic reasons. Opportunities in West Indian countries were poor, with few jobs and high unemployment. In contrast, after the Second World War, Britain needed workers to staff the NHS, run public transport and help rebuild Britain's bombed cities. For many, a new life in Britain was very appealing. Many West Indians had also served in the British armed forces during the Second World War, had liked Britain and felt a responsibility to help her.

On 22 June 1948, a ship called the *SS Empire Windrush* arrived at Tilbury docks on the River Thames with 492 people on board, many of whom were from the West Indies. Although the ship was not the first to bring black migrants to Britain, it is commonly seen as being the symbolic start of mass migration after 1945, a change that has helped to make Britain the multicultural nation it is today.

Unfortunately, many migrants faced hostility, prejudice and violence. Work was plentiful, but was often low status and badly paid. Migrants seeking accommodation were met with doors slammed in their faces and signs such as that in Source E. Consequently, migrants were forced to take whatever accommodation they could get, which was often cramped, dirty and expensive.

Migrants also faced violence. In 1958, race riots erupted in Notting Hill in London and in Nottingham, after white youths attacked black youths. In 1967, a group called the National Front was founded. It sought to stop migration and return migrants to their country of origin.

## The 'Rivers of Blood' speech

Migrants also faced criticism from politicians. In 1968, Enoch Powell, a leading Conservative politician and someone who was tipped as a future prime minister, made a highly controversial speech, known as the 'Rivers of Blood' speech (see Source F).

Powell's speech caused a sensation in the media. He was sacked from his job by the Conservative leader Edward Heath. *The Times* newspaper described the speech as 'evil', and said that Powell had 'appealed to racial hatred'. However, 1000 dockworkers went on strike to protest at his dismissal, while Powell received tens of thousands of letters of support to his home address. The reaction to Powell's speech seemed to suggest a nation divided by the issue of migration.

**Source F:** Extract from the so-called 'Rivers of Blood' speech, made by Enoch Powell on 20 April 1968.

```
In 15 or 20 years, on present trends, there will be in this country
three and a half million Commonwealth immigrants and their descendants...
[by] the year 2000... it must be in the region of five to seven million...
The natural and rational first question... to ask [is]: "How can [the
numbers of immigrants] be reduced?"... [the answer]... by stopping, or
virtually stopping, further inflow, and by promoting the maximum outflow.

As I look ahead, I am filled with foreboding; like the Roman, I seem to
see "the River Tiber foaming with much blood".
```

Governments in Britain since have seemed torn over migration. On the one hand, employers such as the NHS need a certain level of migration. On the other, migration has been reported in a largely negative way in the media. In 1962 and 1968, the government sought to reduce migration by introducing two Commonwealth Immigrants Acts, which made it more difficult to gain entry to Britain.

## Your turn!

1 Draw a 'push' and 'pull' diagram, noting down the factors that made people want to leave the Caribbean ('push') and those that attracted them to Britain ('pull').

2 Look at Sources D–F and note down what type of source each is – for example, Source D is a photo of the *SS Empire Windrush*.

3 What do Sources D–F suggest about what it was like for Caribbean migrants coming to Britain? Write one inference for each.

4 What questions might you ask of Sources D–F to find out what it was really like for migrants? Try to write at least three examples.

## Checkpoint

1 What made so many Irish people migrate to Britain in the 19th century?

2 What made people from the West Indies want to migrate to Britain in the 20th century?

3 What similarities are there between the ways both groups were treated by British people?

4 Sum up your final answer to the question 'What drove people to migrate?' by explaining why Irish and West Indian people migrated to Britain. Write at least a paragraph on each.

# What drove people to migrate?

Look back over this section, and the different reasons that led people to migrate. Compare the 'push' and 'pull' diagrams you have made for each group, and answer the questions below.

- What were the main factors that made people want to migrate?

- What similarities are there between any of the reasons why people migrated?

- Did any groups migrate for completely different reasons from others?

# How have migrants changed Britain?

Many different groups have migrated to Britain over the last 2000 years. Each group has brought with them new technologies, new ideas, and different languages and culture. But what impact has migration had on modern Britain?

In this section, you will learn about:

- how migrants have changed Britain

- the short-term and long-term impacts of migration on Britain.

## What do you think?

In what ways has migration affected you? Try to think of some examples – for example, music or food.

## Learning objectives

- Understand how migrants have changed Britain.
- Assess the short-term and long-term impacts of migration on Britain.

## Migration through time

Below is a summary of some of the different groups of migrants you have read about. Read what each person says and complete the 'Your turn!' activities.

**West Indians**
We came to Britain as opportunities back home were so poor. Britain was our 'Mother Country' and some of us felt a duty to help her in her hour of need. Also, there were plenty of jobs and we hoped to get a better standard of living. We helped to staff the NHS, keep the transport system running, rebuild bombed houses and do many other jobs. Unfortunately, we also faced discrimination from people who felt we didn't belong in Britain.

**The Irish**
We had to migrate due to the Great Famine and the poor opportunities available at home. Britain offered us the chance of a new life, with jobs and decent pay for all. We helped to build the railways and canals that made Britain the 'workshop of the world'. Sadly, we were often discriminated against.

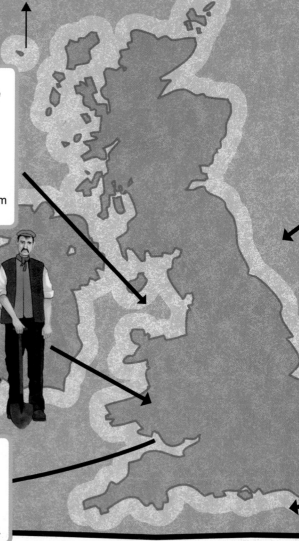

**The Puritans**
We had a different experience from some others. We had to leave England because of the religious persecution we suffered. We were lucky that we were able to start a new life in the New World, and our ideas still influence the United States of America today.

## Your turn!

1 Read the examples in Figure 6.12 and identify at least three reasons why people migrated. One might be 'economic' – for example, to secure a better job.

2 Explain one way in which the reason people migrated changed over time.

3 Then try to identify and explain some examples of continuity. Which groups had similar reasons for migrating over time?

4 On a concept map, note down some of the short-term changes caused by each group – for example, the West Indians helped to fill a labour shortage.

5 Which group do you think had the biggest impact on England? Explain your answer in a paragraph.

6 In which area do you think migrants have caused most change – political, economic or social, or a combination of one or more of them? Explain your answer.

**The Vikings**
Many of us came to England in search of plunder, but many also decided to stay and settle when we saw England's fertile lands. We helped to found many of England's major towns, not least Jorvik, and for many years ruled large parts of England – the 'Danelaw'.

**The Anglo-Saxons**
We took the place of the Romans and settled in the nice, fertile land. We united England as one country, invented the English language and the word 'England'. We also did our best to stop the Vikings from destroying our way of life.

**The Romans**
We came to add Britannia to the Roman Empire. We brought with us all the benefits of civilisation – roads, running water, even toilets. Many of your greatest cities were founded by us. When we left, you let everything fall apart!

**The Celts**
We came in search of fertile land and a better way of life. We introduced iron working and the iron plough to Britain, and religious festivals such as May Day and Halloween.

**The Jews**
We came because we were invited to be money lenders for medieval kings. Our money helped to finance some of the greatest buildings in England. We hoped England would be a safe haven after the religious persecution we had experienced. Sadly, we were persecuted in England too and told to leave in 1290. We were allowed to return in the 17th century and since then have prospered.

**The Huguenots**
We came to England because we were being persecuted for our religion in Europe. England offered us sanctuary. It probably helped that we followed the same religion! We have prospered over the centuries, and England has benefited from our expertise as merchants and craftsmen.

0                                    400
km

**Figure 6.12:** Migrants to (and from) Britain over the last 2000 years.

# What influence have migrants had in the long term?

So much of what we now see as being British has been defined by different waves of migration. Think of the different groups of migrants you have learned about. If they had never come to Britain, how different would our lives be? Here are some of the ways in which our nation has been defined by influences from abroad.

## Political influence

Britain is run by one of the world's oldest parliaments. The word 'parliament' itself is derived from the old French word *parlement*, meaning 'speaking'. This is because our political systems emerged after the Norman Conquest. Many of William's descendants spoke French and considered themselves to be French. Even Richard the Lionheart, often seen as the perfect example of Englishness, spoke no English and rarely visited England.

**Figure 6.13:** NHS staff.

**Figure 6.14:** The Houses of Parliament in London, in front of which stands a statue of Richard the Lionheart.

## Economic influence

In the 18th and 19th centuries, Britain experienced an industrial revolution, becoming the first country in the world to build factories on a large scale. The Huguenots, with their expertise in different fields such as textiles, played a significant role in helping Britain start to industrialise. Much of the canals and railways that drove industrialisation were built by 'navvies', many of whom were Irish migrants.

In more recent times, Britain has relied heavily on migration to help fill the labour shortages created by the Second World War. The NHS, set up in 1948, contains a large number of migrants working at all levels. One study showed that, in the years 2004–2007, 37.5 per cent of all doctors working in the NHS were foreign-born.

## Social influence

One of the biggest changes since the Second World War has been in the increased diversity of our country. The 2011 census revealed the number of people defining themselves as 'white' fell from 94.1 per cent in 1991 to 86 per cent in 2011. The same survey found that Muslims are now the second largest religious group in England after Christians, making up 4.8 per cent of the population. Most cities in England now include many different places of worship, from Christian churches to Jewish synagogues and Muslim mosques.

Of course, one of the other ways in which we all benefit from the impact of migrants is food. Most of us enjoy eating pizza, pasta, curry and Chinese, Thai and Mexican food, among others. It's hard to believe now that, only a few generations ago, it was virtually impossible to buy any of these meals in restaurants or even to buy the ingredients to cook them at home. Until relatively recently, olive oil could only be bought in chemists and was used as a treatment for earache!

In 2016, the United Kingdom held a referendum on membership of the European Union, in which 52 per cent of the country voted to leave. For many people, migration was a key reason for voting to leave. One poll suggested that 70 per cent of people polled wanted limits on EU migration. It seems likely that migration will continue to be a source of controversy.

**Source A:** Front page of the *Daily Express* newspaper in 2012.

### Your turn!

**1** Make a concept map noting down some of the main changes in the different influences.

**2** Pick what you think are three of the most important changes. Explain why they were so significant.

**3** Have migrants had more of a political, economic or social impact on Britain? Explain your answer in a paragraph.

**4** Look at Source A. Is this an example of change or continuity? Compare the headline to what you have learned about attitudes to migration in the past.

### Checkpoint

**1** List three ways in which migration has changed Britain.

**2** Give two reasons why migrants have come to Britain over time.

**3** Explain how migrants have been received in Britain over time.

**4** Explain whether you think there has been more change or continuity in the following areas over time:
**a** reasons for migration
**b** experiences of migrants.

# How have migrants changed Britain?

Individually or in pairs, pick a group of migrants from this chapter and make a poster summing up their impact on Britain. You could also include some of your own research.

Use your poster to create a classroom display on how migration has changed Britain.

# What have you learned?

In this section, you have learned to:

- understand some of the ways in which migration has changed Britain.

Analysing interpretations

Migrants were almost always viewed with suspicion by the groups already living in Britain.

Migrants often faced discrimination and even persecution due to religious, cultural and racial differences, among others.

Over time, migrants tend to become an accepted part of society. For example, almost everyone in Britain today is descended from one or more groups of migrants.

Each group of migrants changed Britain – whether it was a social, cultural, economic or political change. Many of these changes have become an important part of what it is to be British. For example, fish and chips was first introduced by Jewish immigrants in the 19th century.

**Figure 6.15:** A summary of migration over time.

To draw conclusions from what you have learned, let's look at two different interpretations of migration.

**Interpretation 1:** From an article in 2014 on the website of Migration Watch UK, a UK think-tank that campaigns for managed migration.

```
For nearly a thousand years migration was on
a very small scale compared to the size of
the population. In the decades between the
Second World War and the late 1990s, foreign
immigration grew steadily at a relatively
modest rate before declining in the late 1960s
and becoming fairly stable between 1971 and
1981. The massive increase in the level of
migration since the late 1990s is utterly
unprecedented in the country's history, dwarfing
the scale of anything that went before.
```

**Interpretation 2:** From an article in the *Independent* newspaper entitled 'Ten things that immigration has done for Britain', written in 2014.

```
... according to some, [immigrants] represent
a net drain on the economy, claiming benefits,
abusing public services, thieving and generally
loafing around in parks.

This does not accord with common sense or
experience, ... everyone who has ever used a
minicab, visited a hospital or called a plumber
will most likely have found themselves in the
company of a hard-working individual who has
travelled halfway around the world simply to make
a better life for themselves and their family.
```

## Your turn!

1 In pairs, read Interpretations 1 and 2 carefully and discuss the points below.
   a What are they saying about migration?
   b What is the purpose of each article?

# Writing historically

One of the skills that you will need to develop in History is understanding historical interpretations. Look back at pages 116–117 if you are not sure what historical interpretations are and how they are created.

## Identifying differences between historical interpretations

One of the most basic skills is identifying differences between historical interpretations. This involves reading the extracts carefully, understanding their argument and then trying to explain the difference in their arguments. Look at Interpretations 1 and 2, and answer the question 'What is the main difference between these views?'. Then look at the answers below.

### Student 1

One difference between the interpretations is that one was written in a newspaper, while the other comes from a website.

Student 1's answer is accurate, but it doesn't identify the differences in argument between the two interpretations.

### Student 2

The extracts are different. One talks about numbers of migrants, while the other talks about the kind of jobs migrants do.

Student 2's answer is accurate, but only picks out isolated details from the interpretations rather than explaining the differences.

### Student 3

The extracts are different. Interpretation 1 is concerned about the scale of recent migration, arguing that the levels of recent migration are 'unprecedented in the country's history'. In contrast, Interpretation 2 is positive about migration and argues that it helps Britain, as migrants fill vital jobs in the NHS.

Student 3's answer is much better. It identifies the essential differences in argument between the two interpretations, and uses some examples to support the points. It also contrasts the extracts, rather than describing them individually.

## Identifying differences in purpose

Identifying the purpose of interpretations can also help to explain the differences. For example, Interpretation 1 is from a think-tank that wishes to monitor the level of migration into the UK. Therefore, it follows that the article focuses on the scale of migration. Interpretation 2 is from an article entitled 'Ten things that migration has done for Britain'. The title suggests that the article is going to be supportive of migration and the content of the interpretation follows from that.

## Quick quiz

1  Which invaders first brought roads and functioning toilets to Britain?

2  Which group of invaders gave their name to England and to East Anglia?

3  Which group of migrants were invited into England in 1066 to lend William the Conqueror money?

4  What made the Huguenots come to England?

5  What happened in Ireland from 1845 to 1852 that killed millions and made thousands emigrate to Britain?

6  What was the *SS Empire Windrush* and why is it seen as being significant?

# Murder mystery: What happened to the princes in the Tower of London?

There are many historical mysteries. These are events that have puzzled people for years – sometimes hundreds of years. Historians have researched all kinds of sources, and have not come up with an answer with which everyone can agree. One of these mysteries concerns two princes in the Tower of London. In about 1483, they simply disappeared. No one knows for sure what happened to them. Many people believe they were murdered – and probably murdered by their uncle Richard, Duke of Gloucester, so that he could become king. Others believe the boys were murdered, but not by Richard – possibly by the Duke of Buckingham or even by King Henry VII. There are people, too, who say there is no evidence of a murder – only of a disappearance. They suggest that maybe the boys died as the result of an illness, or that they escaped and lived out their lives in anonymous safety.

# Investigating the mystery

## Learning objectives

- Understand the evidence provided by the sources about the disappearance of the princes.
- Evaluate the evidence provided by the sources.
- Reach a conclusion based on the evidence.

## What do you think?

Detectives always look for motives when there is a crime. Why would someone want to 'disappear' a member of the royal family?

**Source A:** A portrait of Richard III, painted in about 1520. It was copied from an earlier, lost portrait.

## Background: April–July 1483

In April 1483, King Edward IV died unexpectedly. He had two sons, Edward (aged 12) and Richard (aged 9). Edward was too young to rule by himself and so, just before the king died, he made his trusted brother, Richard, Duke of Gloucester, Protector* of the young princes. The two boys stayed in the Tower of London, which was a royal palace as well as a prison, while arrangements were made for Edward's coronation as King Edward V. However, in June 1483, it was announced that the dead king, Edward IV, had not been legally married to Elizabeth Woodville, the princes' mother. This meant that the boys were illegitimate* and so couldn't inherit the throne. In July 1483, Richard, Duke of Gloucester, was crowned King Richard III. The two princes were never seen again.

## Key terms

**Protector*:** An adult who rules in the name of a young monarch until that monarch is old enough to reign alone.

**Illegitimate*:** A child born to parents who are not legally married.

194

## Did Richard III kill the princes?

**Source B:** From *How Richard III Made Himself King*, written by Domenico Mancini in 1483. Mancini was an Italian writer who visited England between 1482 and 1483. His English was very poor and he didn't travel outside London.

After June 1483 all the young Prince Edward's servants were kept from him. He and his brother Richard were taken to rooms further inside the Tower. They were seen less and less often, behind bars and windows until finally they were seen no more. I have seen men burst into tears at the mention of his name, for already some people suspected that he had been done away with. So far I have not discovered if he had been killed, nor how he might have died.

**Source C:** From the anonymous author of *The Croyland Chronicle*, probably a monk, writing in 1486. Some historians think the author got his information from a member of the royal court; others that it was from John Morton or Margaret Beaufort, both of whom were enemies of Richard.

For a long time the two sons of King Edward remained under guard in the Tower. Finally in 1483 people in the South and West began to think of freeing them by force. The Duke of Buckingham, who deserted King Richard, was declared their leader. But then a rumour was spread that the princes had died a violent death, but no one knew how.

**Source D:** From *The History of King Richard*, written by Thomas More in 1513. He was five years old when Richard was crowned king. He got most of his information from John Morton, the Bishop of Ely, who hated Richard.

After his coronation in July 1483, King Richard decided that he must kill his nephews. This was because as long as they were alive, no one would believe him to be the true king. Sir James Tyrell agreed to plan the murder. He chose Miles Forest and John Dighton to do the deed. Forest was one of the princes' guards and had murdered others. The two men pressed feather beds and pillows hard on the children's faces until they stopped breathing. Tyrell had the princes buried at the foot of the stairs, deep down under a pile of stones. But King Richard wanted them to have a better burial so they were dug up and buried secretly in another place. The story is well known to be true because Sir James Tyrell confessed to it when he was imprisoned in the Tower in 1502.

### Your turn!

1 Look carefully at Source A. Write down three words to describe Richard III. Do you think this is the face of a murderer? How valuable do you think this portrait is as evidence of Richard's character?

2 Sources B and C are the earliest written sources we have about the disappearance of the princes.
   a On what points do they agree?
   b On what points do they disagree?

3 What does Thomas More (Source D) say was Richard's motive for murdering the princes? What evidence does he give for this?

4 List the authors of Sources B–D. On a scale of 1–5, where 1 = 'Do not trust at all' and 5 = 'Trust completely', rank the authors as to whether you think they are providing reliable evidence about the disappearance of the princes. For each author, write a sentence explaining your decision.

# Did someone else kill the princes?

## Background: 1485

In 1485, Henry Tudor, the son of Margaret Beaufort, invaded England. He challenged Richard III for the throne, and defeated him at the Battle of Bosworth on 22 August 1485. He was crowned Henry VII on 30 October 1485.

**Source E:** From *The Croyland Chronicle*, 1486.

In 1484 after strong persuasion from Richard, Queen Elizabeth Woodville sent all her daughters from sanctuary to Richard's court at Westminster. Christmas that year was celebrated with great splendour in the Great Hall at Westminster. There was far too much dancing and fun. King Richard presented Queen Anne [his wife] and Lady Elizabeth [the sister of the young princes] with a set of new and fashionable clothes each.

**Source F:** From *A History of England*, written by Polydore Vergil in 1517. He was an Italian writer who came to England 16 years after Richard's death.

Richard decided to try all he could to make his peace with Queen Elizabeth Woodville – and so he sent messengers to her in Sanctuary. After a time, she forgot her troubles and sent her daughters to stay with Richard at Court. After this she wrote secretly to the marquis of Dorset [her son by an earlier marriage] advising him to forget Henry Tudor and return quickly to England where he would be sure to be treated well by King Richard.

**Interpretation 1:** From *Richard III* by Professor Paul Kendall, published in 1955.

```
There is no proof that Richard murdered the
princes. On what is the accusation based? It
is based on rumours, on hearsay evidence and
on statements from unreliable and inaccurate
witnesses. The Duke of Buckingham had the
same opportunity. His motives for murdering
the princes were stronger than Richard's. As
Constable of the Tower, he would find no door
shut to him. He did not go with Richard on
his tour of the country in 1483, but stayed
behind in London for a few days, then he
overtook the king at Gloucester. After he
said farewell to Richard, he rode away into
Wales and began plotting to overthrow him.
The princes were in his way because he wanted
to claim the crown himself, or help Henry
Tudor claim it. By murdering the boys and
then spreading rumours about their death he
could blacken Richard's character. Looking
at the facts, Buckingham appears much more
likely to be their murderer than Richard.
```

Historians use a range of sources when they are investigating an historical problem. Sometimes this leads them to different conclusions.

**Source G:** A portrait of the Duke of Buckingham.

**Source H:** A contemporary portrait of Henry VII.

**Interpretation 2:** From an article written by Philip Lindsay, published in the magazine *Argosy* in 1972.

I do not doubt for one moment that the princes were alive when Henry came to London in August 1485. He issued a proclamation giving out all Richard's supposed crimes and this list does not include the killing of the princes. That to my mind is definite proof that the princes were not even missing. They must still have been in the Tower. Richard had no reason to kill them: Henry had every reason. If they lived, all he had fought for would be useless. Prince Edward had more right to be king than Henry Tudor. Henry was capable of such a crime, so they were quietly but efficiently murdered. Elizabeth Woodville, the boys' mother, was locked into a nunnery. Henry spread the word that Richard had done the killing. Henry Tudor, murderer and liar — it's time the truth was known!

## Your turn!

1 Read Sources E and F.
   a Make a list of the points on which they agree.
   b How likely do you think it is that Elizabeth Woodville would have sent her daughters to court if she believed Richard had murdered her sons?

2 Read Interpretation 1.
   a When does Professor Kendall think the princes were murdered?
   b Why does he blame the Duke of Buckingham for their murders?

3 Read Interpretation 2.
   a When does Philip Lindsay think the princes were murdered?
   b Why does he blame Henry VII for their murders?
   c List the potential murderers of the princes (Richard III, Buckingham and Henry VII) and rate them on a scale of 1–5 (where 1 = 'Least likely' and 5 = 'Most likely') as to whether you think they murdered the princes.
   d Write a paragraph to explain who you think was the likely murderer.

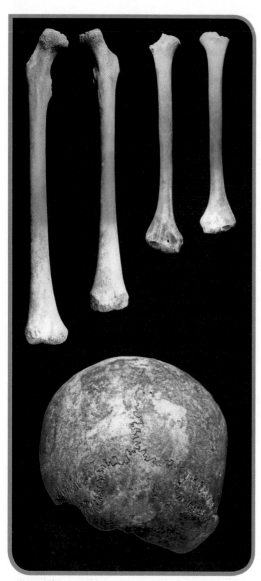

**Source I:** Photographs of the skull of the elder child, and the leg and arm bones of the children, side by side.

# Were the princes murdered at all?

There is no hard evidence that the two princes were murdered. All the written evidence agrees that they disappeared, but the evidence for their murder is based on guesswork. However, children's skeletons have been found, and these might help shed light on the disappearance of the boys.

### Skeletons in the tower

In 1674, some men were working on a stone staircase in the Tower of London. Unexpectedly, about 3 metres underground, they found a wooden box full of children's bones. It was assumed that they were the bones of the lost princes. Charles II, who was king at the time, ordered that the bones had to be put in a special marble urn, and that a funeral service should be held for the two princes. The urn was put in Westminster Abbey, in Henry VII's Chapel, and you can see it there today. But were the bones really those of the two princes?

### Investigation: 1933

In 1933, a surgeon and a dentist, Professor Wright and Dr Northcroft, were asked to examine the contents of the urn to see if they could prove their identity. They decided:

- the bones were of two children: the elder child was between 11 and 13 years old, and the younger child between 9 and 11 years old, when they died

- the children were related

- the skull of the elder child was stained; this could be a blood stain caused by suffocation.

### Investigation: 1955

In 1955, a group of doctors and dentists were asked to examine the report written by Professor Wright and Dr Northcroft. They were not allowed to see the bones, only photographs. Using new knowledge about teeth and bones, they decided:

- the bones could be boys or girls; the bones and teeth of the elder child show that he or she was less than 11 years old, most probably between 9 and 11

- the stain on the skull of the elder child was not caused by blood

- the bones could have been buried long before the time of Richard III.

## Skeletons in St George's Chapel, Windsor

In 1789, men working in St George's Chapel, Windsor, accidentally damaged the tomb of Edward IV and Elizabeth Woodville. They discovered two extra coffins in the tomb, and each contained the remains of an unidentified child. The tomb was resealed without any attempt to identify the children.

In 2013, the skeleton of Richard III was discovered under a car park in Leicester. Scientists now have his DNA and it would be possible to see if this could be linked to that of the children's bones. This would prove whether they were related or not. Despite having been asked many times, Her Majesty the Queen and the Church authorities refuse to allow the tombs in either Windsor or Westminster Abbey to be opened and the children's bones to be tested further.

## Died – but not murdered?

There are two theories about the deaths of the princes that don't involve murder.

- The boys could have died from a fever, possibly an early outbreak of the 'sweating sickness' epidemic that hit England in 1485 and which killed rapidly – usually within hours.

- The room in which the boys slept would have been heated by a fire that burned coal or coke. If the room was poorly ventilated, they could have died from carbon monoxide poisoning.

In both these cases, those looking after the princes would have been horrified and frightened for their lives. They would have done everything possible to hide the boys' bodies and not let it be known that they had died.

## Escape!

In 1490, a young man called Perkin Warbeck appeared and told a fantastic story. He said he was really Richard, Duke of York, the younger of the two princes in the Tower. Edward, he said, had been murdered, but he had been spared because he was so young, and taken to live abroad. Margaret of Burgundy, the aunt of the missing princes, recognised him as her nephew and he had support in Ireland, France and Scotland. Some nobles grew uneasy and made contact with Perkin. Maybe he was their rightful king? Here was trouble indeed for Henry VII. If Perkin really was the younger prince, he had a far better claim to the throne than Henry. Perkin was eventually caught by Henry's forces and confessed to it all being a lie. But was he confessing under torture? Was he really Richard of York? No one will ever know.

### Your turn!

1  Look at the evidence of the bones that were found in the Tower (Source I). How far do they help us understand what happened to the two princes?

2  The Queen and the Church authorities are against opening tombs and testing the skeletons inside. Do you think they are right or wrong? Write a letter either supporting their decision or persuading them to change their minds.

3  How likely do you think it is that the princes were not murdered?

4  You have now answered a lot of small questions about the missing princes, and it is time to put all your thinking together. Write an answer to the question 'What happened to the princes in the Tower?' Remember to back up what you say with evidence.

# Glossary

**Adjuration:** A command ordering sickness or a demon to leave a sufferer.

**Adultery:** Sex between a married person and someone who is not their husband or wife. It was punished with a whipping in a public place.

**Afterlife:** The experience some people believe they will have after death.

**Alms:** A charitable gift to poor people, including money, food or a place to rest.

**Analyse:** Examine something in detail in order to discover more about it.

**Anglo-Saxon:** The name 'Anglo-Saxon' comes from the Angles and the Saxons, two of the north European tribes that invaded and lived in Britain from the fifth century onwards.

**Anglo-Saxon Chronicle:** This book was started by monks towards the end of the ninth century and updated by them until about 1154. It detailed the history of the Anglo-Saxons.

**Anoint:** To give spiritual power to a monarch or priest by rubbing them with holy oil.

**Archaeologist:** A person who studies people in the past, usually by excavating (digging) for the remains they have left behind.

**Astronomy:** The study of the planets and stars. Astronomy was important to Muslims because it helped to work out prayer times and the date of religious holidays.

**Bondage/servitude:** To be an unfree peasant.

**Booty:** The valuable items stolen by the winner after a siege or battle.

**Branded:** A mark (such as 'T' for a thief) was burnt onto the hand with a hot iron.

**Caliph:** The ruler of an Islamic empire.

**Calligraphy:** An artistic form of handwriting.

**Chancellor:** The king's chief servant. The chancellor had many jobs, including writing important documents, managing royal finances and judging some legal cases.

**Chivalry:** The way a knight was supposed to behave. Knights were expected to be strong, brave and skilled in warfare.

**Chronological:** Organised in the order in which they occurred.

**Church of the Holy Sepulchre:** A church built on the site of a cave tomb. Christians believe it is where Jesus Christ rose from the dead. It was built on the orders of the Byzantine emperor Constantine.

**Civil war:** A war between people within the same country.

**Council:** A meeting of important officials. In medieval times, a council might include the king, members of his household, the barons and the bishops.

**Court:** A monarch's household, where all those who meet regularly with the monarch gather.

**Criminous clerk:** Any churchman, including priests and their assistants, who had committed a crime. They could claim the right to be tried in a Church court.

**Crusader:** A person who made a promise to help capture and protect Jerusalem. The first crusaders were a mixed group of people, including knights, peasants, monks, priests and women.

**Crusader states:** The lands taken by the crusaders and ruled by the Christians.

**Danelaw:** The areas of Anglo-Saxon England that were populated by the descendants of Vikings. These areas followed Viking laws and customs.

**Dark Ages:** A term for the period between the Roman withdrawal in AD 410 and the arrival of the Normans in 1066. Not all historians like this term, as it has been used to suggest that there was no culture or civilisation in this period.

**Deadly sin:** The Church organised sins into seven categories: pride, envy, anger, sloth (laziness), greed, gluttony and lust.

**Deposed:** Replaced in their role by someone else.

**Diaspora:** The migration of Jewish people into different countries around the world.

**DNA analysis:** A method used by scientists, which can identify individual people and other organisms such as bacteria.

**Dynasty:** A term for rulers who all come from the same family. The Umayyads set up the first Muslim dynasty and passed on the position of caliph to members of their own family.

**Emir:** A lord in the Islamic world. By 1095, emirs were ruled over by a caliph, the symbolic leader of an empire, and a sultan, who ran the empire. Despite this, emirs still had a lot of power.

**Eulogy:** A piece of writing that praises a person. It is usually written or spoken after their death.

**Excommunication:** When a person in banned from church services and Christian burial. A medieval person believed they were at greater risk of going to hell if they died as an excommunicant.

**Fasting:** A commitment not to eat for either an entire day, part of the day or to avoid eating certain foods like meat.

**Formation:** The way a military force is organised. During Richard's march to Jaffa, he split his army into divisions (sections) and columns (lines) to protect the soldiers carrying supplies.

**Fornicator:** A person who has sex outside of marriage.

**Four Humours:** A theory on the causes of illness first developed by the Greek doctor Hippocrates (460–375 BC) proposed that the body was composed of four 'humours' – phlegm, yellow bile, black bile and blood. The theory argued that people in good health had a balance of all four humours, while ill health was caused by one or more of the humours becoming out of balance.

**Garrison:** The knights who defended a castle. A lord usually expected his knights to do this for a fixed number of days each year.

**Geometry:** A type of mathematics that involves studying lines, shapes and the relationship between points. The Greek mathematician Euclid wrote 13 books about geometry.

**Gluttony:** Eating or drinking too much.

**Great Britain:** By 1801, England, Scotland, Wales and Ireland were united into one country, known as Great Britain, also known as the United Kingdom.

**Great Council:** An assembly of church leaders and wealthy landowners who met with the king from time to time to discuss national affairs.

**Hanged, drawn and quartered:** From 1351, this was a punishment for treason. Victims were hanged until they were almost dead, then they were cut down and cut open while they were still alive. Finally the head was chopped off and the body was cut into pieces and sent to different edges of the kingdom, normally to put on display as a warning to others.

**Heretic:** A person with religious views that disagree with official Church teaching.

**Hide:** The amount needed to support a family.

**Historian:** A person who studies the events of the past, usually by working with written sources, objects and paintings left behind.

**Holy Land:** An area of land in the Middle East that is important to Christians. It includes places like Jerusalem that are linked to the life of Jesus Christ.

**Hunter-gatherers:** People who survive by hunting, fishing and gathering wild food.

**Illegitimate:** A child born to parents who are not legally married.

**Indulgence:** The grant of a reduction in punishment for sins.

**Inference:** Something you can learn from a source, which goes beyond the surface detail of what it says and on to what it suggests.

**Interest:** A fee for lending someone money, usually a percentage of the money lent.

**Jihad:** A holy war fought against Christians and other non-Muslim groups. The term can also mean a personal struggle to improve a believer's faith in Islam.

**Jury:** A group of local men, who were considered respectable and owned land.

**Just war:** A Church theory about what made a war acceptable in the eyes of God. A holy war, or crusade, was also considered just, but it had a religious purpose too.

**Lancing:** Using a sharp tool to 'pop' a boil or bubo.

**Last rites:** A final blessing given by a priest to someone who is about to die, that is thought to prepare their soul for the afterlife.

**Lay brother:** A man who joined a religious order to work on the farm land or make things. They took monastic vows, but did not take part in the same services as the other monks.

**Lay sister:** A woman who took monastic vows, doing jobs for the nuns. The Gilbertines were the first order to have lay sisters, who helped in their hospitals and alms houses.

**Leechbook:** A medical textbook containing natural remedies, magical charms and rituals used by medieval healers, known as leeches.

**Legate:** A representative of the pope, with a lot of power. A legate could remove a bishop from their job an issue sentences of excommunication without asking the pope.

**Leprosy:** A disease affecting the skin and nerves that can cause lumps to appear on the skin and result in the loss of body parts like fingers and toes.

**Low Countries:** Refers to the geographical area including modern-day Belgium and the Netherlands.

**Manorial records:** These are the records compiled within a manor – an area controlled by a lord – during medieval times.

**Martyr:** A person who dies for their faith. A martyr could become a saint if the pope approved and miracles were linked to them.

**Mass:** A Christian religious service performed by a Catholic priest.

**Mercenary:** A soldier who is paid to fight in a foreign army. The Byzantine army contained Germans, Englishmen and Normans amongst others.

**Monastery:** The collection of buildings that monks live in.

**Mosque:** A place of worship for Muslims.

**Old Testament:** The first part of the Bible, believed by both Christians and Jews to be the word of God.

**Ordained:** Clerics who had taken part in a ceremony which allowed them to perform the sacraments.

**Parishioner:** A person who lived in a priest's parish (the area for which he provided services).

**Penance:** A punishment to make up for a bad deed. It might also involve doing good works, like giving to charity.

**Physician:** Another term for a doctor.

**Pilgrim:** A person who is on a religious journey. Muslims are expected to go on a pilgrimage to the holy city of Mecca in modern Saudi Arabia at least once in their lifetime.

**Pillory:** A post to which a criminal was attached by the neck and hands. They were usually put in marketplaces where people could throw things at the criminal.

**Plough team:** A plough team was made up of eight oxen and two men. The oxen pulled the plough. One man guided the plough and the other led the oxen over the fields.

**Posterity:** Future generations of people.

**Poultice:** A mixture designed to heal a wound – for example, butter, onions and garlic – pressed onto a wound with a bandage.

**Protector:** An adult who rules in the name of a young monarch until that monarch is old enough to reign alone.

**Protestants:** Christians who broke away from the Catholic Church to form their own religious groups.

**Purgatory:** A place where medieval Christians believed they would be tortured until they had made up for their bad deeds and thoughts. After this, they would go on to heaven.

**Reformation:** Refers to the rise of Protestantism in the 16th century and the end of the dominance of the Catholic Church in some countries, for example England.

**Religious order:** A group of monks or nuns, who live their life according to a Rule written by their founder.

**Reliquary:** A container in which relics were kept.

**Rent:** Medieval peasants had to pay rent to their lord. As most peasants had no money, this was usually paid in labour and goods – for example, produce from the peasants' land.

**Rustic:** An insulting word for a peasant.

**Sacraments:** The ceremonial actions of a priest or bishop. There are seven sacraments, including baptism and marriage.

**Sanctuary:** A place of safety; a criminal could claim sanctuary in a church for 40 days, protecting them from arrest.

**Secular:** Not related to religious matters.

**Seljuk Turks:** A group of Muslims led by Seljuk, who built up a powerful empire in the 11th century. By 1095, control of the Seljuk lands was divided between different rulers.

**Shield wall:** Barrier created by soldiers standing shoulder to shoulder, holding their shields in front of them so that they formed a wall.

**Shrine:** A place where relics of a saint were kept. Pilgrims would visit shrines, hoping for a miracle or help after death to reach heaven.

**Siege:** An attack on a fortified site, such as a castle or a walled city, cutting it off from supplies to force it to surrender. Sieges could last a long time if the site was well defended.

**Slums:** Poorly built and overcrowded houses, often located in industrial cities.

**Soul:** Christians believe this is a part of a person that can exist after death. The idea exists in some other world religions too.

**Ten Commandments:** A list of rules given to Moses by God, which Jewish and Christian peoples are expected to obey.

**Troubadour:** A poet who writes verse to music.

**Truce:** An agreement to stop fighting for a certain period of time. Richard's truce with Saladin was arranged in 1192.

**Vizier:** A leader who ran an Islamic country on a day-to-day basis. The vizier was chosen by a caliph, but had more power than the caliph.

**West Indians:** People from an area of the Caribbean, including many island nations that were formerly part of the British Empire, such as Jamaica.

# Answers

## Historical anachronisms

**Pages 6–7**

## Chapter 1

**Page 19 Source B**

A cloud.

An onion.

**Page 46**

1   Any two from, for example, woollen industry, silver mining, tin mining, salt production, fishing industry, wheat production. (Figure 1.1 page 19).

2   An assembly of wise men – usually the most powerful nobles in the country.

3   Any two from, for example, keep law and order, defend the country, successfully lead the army, work with the church, marry and have healthy sons, gain the respect of the people, spend taxes wisely, take nobles' advice, have a claim to the throne that people respect. (Figure 1.3 page 22).

4   Harald Hardrada.

5   William I was crowned king of England.

6   1069.

7   Any two from:
   • the landscape: castles appeared, land in the north burned
   • land ownership: Normans replaced Saxons
   • the Church: Norman bishops replaced Saxon ones
   • language: new words appeared
   • new laws: Forest laws and Murdrum fine.

8   Any two from: farming the land, working for a lord, being protected by a lord, trade and towns, going to church.

9   The king.

10  a  Peasants had to spend part of their time working for their lord/give him some of their crops/obey him.
    b  Their lord had to protect them.

11  Any two from: to remind the English that the Normans were in control, keep Normans safe in hostile areas, provide a base from which Normans could launch attacks, control the surrounding countryside.

12  • Either: The Domesday Book provided information so that the king could tax the people fairly.
    • Or: It showed the people that William was following what was customary in Edward the Confessor's time.

## Chapter 2

**Page 74**

1   Heaven, hell or purgatory.

2   Priest, monk or nun.

3   A relic.

4   Criminous clerks.

5   1170.

6   Pride, envy, anger, sloth, greed, gluttony or lust.

## Chapter 3

**Page 102**

1   House of Wisdom.

2   Seljuk Turks.

3   Indulgence.

4   Templars, Hospitallers or Crusaders.

5   Jerusalem.

6   Richard I.

## Chapter 4

**Page 134**

1   That they would support his daughter Matilda as queen after his death.

2   That Matilda's son Henry would become king when Stephen died.

3   1154–89.

4   Any two from Figure 4.9 on page 120.

5   Four castles built by Edward I to subdue the Welsh: Conwy, Harlech, Caernarfon and Beaumaris.

6   1314; between Edward II of England and Robert the Bruce of Scotland.

## Chapter 5

**Page 160**

1   Buboes, fever, coughing and sneezing.

2   Bleeding, purging, lancing buboes, using herbs to drive away bad smells, praying, going on a pilgrimage, whipping themselves, running away.

3   Family members had died, prices rose, more and better farms were available to rent, peasants were able to ask for better conditions as there were fewer of them.

4   The Statute of Labourers and the Poll Tax.

5   Wat Tyler and John Ball. Wat Tyler was killed during a meeting with the king at Mile End on 15 June 1381. John Ball was hanged, drawn and quartered for his role in the rebellion.

6   Feudalism was eventually ended and the lives of peasants continued to improve.

7   The rebellion was crushed and ordinary people still had very little power for hundreds of years after the revolt.

## Chapter 6

**Page 193**

1   The Romans.

2   The Anglo-Saxons.

3   Jews.

4   To escape religious persecution, especially after the St. Bartholomew's Day massacre.

5   The Great Famine (or Potato Famine).

6   It was a ship that brought immigrants to Britain from the West Indies in 1948. It is seen as being the start of mass immigration after the Second World War.

# Index

# Acknowledgements

The author and publisher would like to thank the following individuals and organisations for their kind permission to reproduce copyright material.

**Photographs**

(Key: b-bottom; c-centre; l-le ; r-right; t-top)

**akg-images Ltd**: Jean-Louis Nou 77tr, Pictures from History 97b; **Alamy Stock Photo**: AF archive 115, Alison Thompson 180, ART Collection 108, Art Collection 3 119, Best View Stock 8 (b), ClassicStock 183, David Ball 129, David Lyon 92, Elitsa Lambova 8 (a), EXJRA2 8 (g), Eye Ubiquitous 97t, FLPA 159, Granger Historical Picture Archive 73, 123, Heritage Image Partnership Ltd 166, Ian Dagnall 106, Ian G Dagnall 197, Image Source 11r, INTERFOTO 107, Ionut David 190r, J Richards 8 (f), John Gaffen 190l, Josse Christophel 8 (e), Les Ladbury 13bl, Martyn Williams 59, Mary Evans Picture Library 24bl, National Geographic Creative 10tr, Niday Picture Library 182, Paul Fearn 171, Simon Jeacle 11tl, Steve Speller 120, Timewatch Images 114, Tomas Burian 172, World History Archive 16bl, 22; **Arturas Slapšys**: 24br; **Bridgeman Art Library Ltd**: 1390s (oil on panel), English School, (14th century) / Westminster Abbey, London, UK 158, 1411, German School, (15th century) / Kupferstichkabinett, Berlin, Germany / Pictures from History 141, Al-Idrisi or Edrisi, Abu Muhammad (c.1100-64) (after) / Bibliotheque Nationale, Paris, France 78b, Battle of Hastings (engraving), Neuville, Alphonse Marie de (1835-85) / Private Collection / © Look and Learn 33, Bayeux Tapestry 1067: Harold Godwinson, Earl of Wessex (Harold II) swearing oath of fealty to William of Normandy (William I, the Conqueror) on holy relics, 1064. William used this oath to boost his claim to English throne. Textile / Universal History Archive / UIG 5, 25, Bishop Odo, holding a club, urges on the young soldiers, detail from the Bayeux Tapestry, before 1082 (wool embroidery on linen) / Musée de la Tapisserie, Bayeux, France 30, British Library, London, UK / © British Library Board. All Rights Reserved 18t, 20, By Hunayn ibn Ishaq (809-873), 12th century CE manuscript / Pictures from History 78t, Byzantine, (10th century) / Hagia Sophia, Istanbul, Turkey / De Agostini Picture Library / C. Sappa 81, c.1220-40 (vellum), English School, (13th century) / Private Collection 65b, Cantigas de Santa Maria (Canticles of Holy Mary). Reign of Alfonso X of Castile, 'the Wise' (1221-1284). Jewish bankers. / Photo © Tarker 181, Cask containing the remains of Thomas à Becket (c.1118-70), c.1190 (gold, lapis lazuli and semi-precious stones) / Private Collection 63, CLAUDIUS I (10 B.C.-54 A.D.) Roman emperor, 41-54 A.D. Roman bronze head. / Photo © Granger 168t, Death of Thomas Becket / British Library, London, UK / © British Library Board 67, Evans, Chris (20th Century) / Private Collection / © Historic England 21, Four Kings of England: William I, William II, Henry I and Stephen, from the 'Historia Anglorum', 1250 (vellum), Paris, Matthew (c.1200-59) / British Library, London, UK 111, from 'British Battles on Land and Sea' edited by Sir Evelyn Wood (1838-1919) first published 1915 (colour litho), Wollen, William Barnes (1857-1936) (after) / Private Collection 122, illustration from 'Chroniques de France et d'Angleterre', by Jean Froissart, c.1460-80 (vellum), Netherlandish School, (15th century) / British Library, London, UK / © British Library Board 155, illustration from 'The History of the Nation' (litho), Payne, Henry A. (Harry) (1868-1940) / Private Collection / The Stapleton Collection 168b, illustration from the 'Chronicle of England', c.1307-27 (vellum), English School, (14th century) / British Library, London, U 68, illustration from the 'Golden Book of St Albans', 1380 (vellum), Strayler, Alan (fl.1380) / British Library, London, UK / © British Library Board. All Rights Reserved 12br, 109, Many fall in battle and King Harold is killed, detail from the Bayeux Tapestry, before 1082 (wool embroidery on linen) / Musée de la Tapisserie, Bayeux 12bl, 32, Market Court, London, 1868 (b / w photo), English Photographer, (19th century) / London Metropolitan Archives, City of London 185, Photo © Tallandier 196, Reliquary statue of St. Foy, c.980 (gold, silver, wood, precious and semi-precious stones) (see 69382 and 162668), French School, (10th century) / Church of St. Foy, Conques, France 51,

## Acknowledgements

Royal 18 E.1, F.175 The death of Wat Tyler at Smithfield, London, in 1381 during the Peasants' Revolt, illustration from 'Chroniques de France et d'Angleterre', by Jean Froissart, c.1460-80 (vellum), Netherlandish School, (15th century) / British Library, London, UK / © British Library Board. All Rights Reserved 157, Shepherds and flock / British Library, London, UK / © British Library Board. All Rights Reserved 18b, Society of Antiquaries of London, UK 194, Spanish Cordoba, 968 CE / Pictures from History 77tl, St Patrick surrounded by demons / British Library, London, UK / © British Library Board. All Rights Reserved 50, Textile Linen / Universal History Archive / UIG 39, The Alfred Jewel (gold, rock crystal and enamel) (for reverse see 100549), Anglo-Saxon (9th century) / Ashmolean Museum, University of Oxford, UK 17, The Flagellants at Doornik in 1349, copy of a miniature from the Chronicle of Aegidius Li Muisis / Private Collection 143, The Princes Edward and Richard in the Tower, 1878 (oil on canvas), Millais, John Everett (1829-96) / Royal Holloway, University of London 13br; **Colin Smith**: 130; **Copyright: Dean and Chapter of Westminster**: 198tl, 198tr, 198b; **Crown copyright (2017) Cadw, Welsh Government**: 127, Illustration by Terry Ball, 126; **digital artwork by Benjamin Slade**: combining British Library MS Cotton Vitellius A.xv, fol.129r with an 173; **Getty Images**: BSIP 83, Heritage Images 93, Hulton / Heritage Images / Contributor 13bc, Keystone / Stringer 186t, MOLA / Contributor 146tl, Photo12 100, Universal History Archive 15; **Historic England**: 147, Jason Askew 34; **Mary Evans Picture Library**: Illustrated London News Ltd 184; **University of Sheffield**: 11bl, 146br; **Shutterstock.com**: Bill Orchard / REX 186b, Icon / Ladd Co / Paramount / REX 131; **Sue Walker White 2002**: 40; **Daily Express/N&S Syndication**: 191; © **The Trustees of The British Museum. All rights reserved.**: 16br; **TopFoto**: 16tl, Granger NYC 55, The Print Collector / HIP 24tr; **Women Warlords by Tim Newark**: 112, 117

All other images © Pearson Education

### Text

**Page 51 Source C:** From '2. John of Gaddesden's Rosa medicinae (c. 1305–17)', page 318, translated into English by John R. Shinners from Tony Hunt, *Popular Medicine in Thirteenth-Century England: Introduction and Texts* (Cambridge: D.S. Brewer, 1990), pp. 27–28. Reprinted with permission of University of Toronto Press.

**Page 52 Source A:** From *Medieval Popular Religion, 1000–1500: A Reader* by John R. Shinners. © 2006 University of Toronto Press.

**Page 63 Source B and page 66 Source A:** From *The Lives of Thomas Becket* by Michael Staunton. © 2001 Manchester University Press.

**Page 105 Table 4.1:** From *Medieval Minds 1066–1500* by Jamie Byrom, Christine Counsell and Michael Riley. ©1997 Pearson Education, Inc.

**Page 144 Table 5.1:** From *British Economic Growth, 1270–1870* by Stephen Broadberry, Bruce M.S. Campbell, Alexander Klein, Mark Overton and Bas van Leeuwen, table 1.06, p.20. © 2015 Cambridge University Press.

**Page 192 Interpretation 1:** From A summary history of immigration to Britain'. Migrationwatchuk. (https://www.migrationwatchuk.org/briefing-paper/48) Last updated 2012.

**Page 192 Interpretation 2:** From 'Ten things that immigration has done for Britain' by Sean O'Grady. © 2014 *Independent*.